The Irish Famine – A Documentary History

Please remember that this is a library book,
and that it belongs only temporarily to each
person who uses it. Be considerate. Do
not write in this, or any, library book.

Noel Kissane

The Irish Famine

A DOCUMENTARY HISTORY

SYRACUSE UNIVERSITY PRESS

First published 1995

National Library of Ireland
Kildare Street
Dublin 2, Ireland

Tel: +353 1 661 8811
Fax: +353 1 676 6690

ISBN 0-907328-24-5 (paper)
ISBN 0-907328-25-3 (cloth)

Index compiled by Helen Litton
Designed by Bill Bolger
Photography by Eugene Hogan
Typesetting and origination by Typeform Repro

CONTENTS

ACKNOWLEDGEMENTS

We are grateful to the following individuals and institutions for kindly permitting the reproduction of documents in their custody or for other assistance:

H.E. President Mary Robinson; 3M, Saint Paul Minnesota, and Charles Helsell, Art Curator; Allen & Unwin; Mark Bence-Jones; Birmingham Library Services, and Robert Ryland, Local Services Librarian; the British Library and staff, especially Paul Goldman, Alan Marshall and Chris Payne; the Brother Allen Library, Brother Thomas Connolly and Pat Hawes; Davis Coakley; Fergus Corcoran; Con Costello; Mary Daly; James S. Donnelly; Pauline Doran; Dublin Diocesan Archives, Most Rev. Dr Desmond Connell, D.D., Archbishop of Dublin, and David Sheehy, Archivist; Davison & Associates; the Department of Irish Folklore, University College Dublin and staff, especially Bo Almqvist, Bairbre Ó Floinn, Ríonach Uí Ógáin and Micheál Ó Curraoin; Paul Ferguson; Rosemary ffolliott; Very Rev. Anthony J. Gaughan; Gill & Macmillan; Elizabeth Hawes; Hulton-Deutsch Collection Limited; the Irish-American Heritage Museum, Albany, New York, and Joseph Dolan, Chairman of the Board; *The Irish Times*, and Rachel Burrowes; Albert Kennedy; Michael Kenny; John Killen; Christine Kinealy; the Knight of Glin; Helen Litton for indexing and proof-reading; Peter McDonagh; Brian MacDonald for cartography; the McKinney Library, Albany Institute of History and Art, and Wesley Balla, Curator; Edward McParland; Louis Marcus; Marsh's Library, the Delmas Bindery, Muriel McCarthy and Sara McCartan; Catherine Marshall; Joel Mokyr; Robert Monks; Dymphna Moore; the National Archives and staff, especially David Craig, Director, Ken Hannigan, Aideen Ireland, Marian Cosgrove and Rena Lohan; the National Archives of Canada; the National Botanic Gardens, and Charles Nelson, Curator; the National College of Art and Design, especially Bill Bolger, Head of the Department of Visual Communication, for designing the book and exhibition poster; the National Library of Scotland and staff, including Kenneth Gibson, Susan Kumi and Janice McFarlane; Eva Ó Cathaoir; Cormac Ó Gráda; Timothy P. O'Neill; Pádraig Ó Snodaigh; Peter Pearson; the Public Record Office of Northern Ireland, and Anthony Malcomson, Director; the Religious Society of Friends, Swanbrook House; the Religious Society of Friends in Britain; John Roe; Sean Sexton; St Columb's College, Derry, and Rev. John R. Walsh, President; Typeform Repro, especially Mark Mulholland, Roy Thewlis, Seán McGill and Pat Conneely; the Ulster Folk and Transport Museum, and Roger Dixon; the Ulster Museum, and Vivienne Pollock; Bill Vaughan.

Our special thanks to seven graduate trainees involved in a National Library of Ireland / FÁS Training Programme for Librarians / Archivists in 1994-95, who carried out initial research for the book and an associated exhibition: Sarah Ball, Joanna Finegan, Louise Kavanagh, Niamh Maguire, Máire Ní Chonalláin, Emma O'Donoghue, Aoife O'Shea. Our thanks also to FÁS, and the co-ordinator, David English.

The National Library is fortunate in that two former members of staff who are distinguished authorities on the Famine have made special contributions – Thomas P. O'Neill and Kevin Whelan, both of whom read the text, made many helpful suggestions, and drew attention to a number of important sources; to both we acknowledge our gratitude.

The material in this book is drawn from all departments of the National Library, and all members of staff contributed directly or indirectly and are gratefully acknowledged:

Bernard Barry, Donal F. Begley, Teresa Biggins, Noel Brady, John Brazil, Rose Breslin, Christopher Briody, William Buckley, Patricia Butler, Matthew Cains, Kieran Carey, Francis Carroll, Adrienne Darcy, Lucy de Courcey, Thomas Desmond, Bernard Devaney, Margaret Doolan, Michael Drew, Deirdre Duffy, Fintan Dunne, Glenn Dunne, James Dunne, Mary Dunne, Catherine Fahy, James Fleming, Inez Fletcher, Fergus Gillespie, Leslie Guider, Mark Hardy, Anne Harte, James Harte, Paul Jones, Anita Joyce, Gerard Kavanagh, Peter Kenny, Elizabeth Kirwan, Gerard Long, Sinéad Looby, Sister Frances Lowe, Sylvia Lynam, Gerard Lyne, John Lyons, Philip McCann, Irene McCormack, Sandra McDermott, Anita McGlynn, Brian McKenna, Gráinne MacLochlainn, David McLoughlin, Denis McQuaid, Declan Maxwell, Irene Meehan, Michael Moran, Marie Moylan, Liam Murphy, Olive Murphy, Eilís Ní Dhuibhne, Sophia O'Brien, Colette O'Daly, Colette O'Flaherty, Marie O'Gallagher, John O'Leary, Dónall Ó Luanaigh, James O'Shea, John O'Sullivan, Margaret Reilly, Noel Stapleton, Patrick Sweeney, Patrick Thompson, Margaret Trimble, Raymond Weafer.

In addition, five members of staff had a special involvement with the book and exhibition: Eugene Hogan, Photographer; John Farrell, Preservation Officer, who mounted the exhibition; Kathleen Roche, who provided typing and secretarial services; Kevin Browne, Library Administration Officer; and Mary Hurley, Development Officer.

FOREWORD

The accounts and extracts gathered here under the title, *The Famine – A Documentary History*, are like a chorus of voices from the past sounding their lamentation over the dividing years. There are eye-witness accounts of the horror and devastation endured by our forebears as they witnessed the reality of the Great Hunger. Each writer tells the story from his or her perspective, as traveller, parliamentarian, civil servant, botanist, professional reporter or bystander. Each writer brings an awareness and immediacy which comes from the ability to state 'I was there'. This immediacy has the freshness and rawness of the incomplete. It is history as yet unwritten, with no explanation, no interpretation, no hindsight; simply the power of the real and actual. The cumulative effect of these accounts is, I believe, a compelling, harrowing but ultimately moving experience. Many of the extracts can be dated accurately to a time and day, and we the readers become helpless bystanders watching events unfold.

The immediate aftershocks of the potato blight on the population are also documented through the reports on the relief works, the workhouses, and that most enduring of effects, emigration. Though Europe as a whole was to experience an unprecedented wave of mass emigration in this period, Ireland lost a greater percentage of its population and suffered more deeply its loss. The very people who grieved over the loss of loved ones, friends and neighbours brought down by disease and starvation survived to mourn the departure of their young people to another world, another life.

In today's world of mass communication and ease of travel, it is difficult to contemplate or comprehend the enormity of the losses suffered by Irish people a mere century and a half ago. We too need the jolt of the ancient, the voice of the eye-witness. Hence, this volume ends with a lone twentieth-century voice in the only modern document in the book, an extract from the keynote address by President Mary Robinson at the International Conference on Hunger held in May of this year at Glucksman Ireland House, New York University. More than any other citizen this century, it is Mary Robinson who in her own special way recalls, remembers and is witness to, on the one hand, the continuing obscenity of famine in the world, and on the other, the presence and pulse of the Irish diaspora. Reading her speech, we catch an echo of an earlier author, Hugh Dorian, who in 1896 said:

'The satiated never understand the emaciated'.

Dr Pat Donlon,
Director,
National Library of Ireland.

CHRONOLOGY

1845
Aug. 20	First report of potato blight in Ireland.
Oct.	One-third of crop lost.
Nov. 9–10	Peel orders purchase of Indian corn in U.S.A.
Nov. 18	Relief Commission established.

1846
Mar. 5	Public works act, to provide employment.
Mar. 28	Sale of cheap Indian corn begins.
June 26	Peel virtually eliminates duties on corn.
June 30	Russell replaces Peel as Prime Minister.
July	Blight reappears; three-quarters of crop lost. Emigration escalates.
Aug. 28	Poor Employment Act (new round of public works).
Nov.	Abnormally severe winter sets in. Fever and dysentery epidemics begin. Mortality soars.
Nov. 13	Relief Committee of Society of Friends formed.

1847
Jan. 1	British Relief Association formed.
March	Peak of 714,000 on relief works. Soup kitchens replacing relief works.
April 27	Fever act to cope with epidemic.
June 8	Poor Relief Act providing for outdoor relief for most vulnerable categories.
July	Blight is slight but potato harvest is only a quarter of normal. Three million people in receipt of soup.
July 22	Separate Poor Law Commission created for Ireland to oversee Poor Law unions.
Oct.	Soup kitchens close; relief to be provided by Poor Law unions and workhouses. An estimated 220,000 emigrated in 1847.

1848
July	General failure of potato crop; only one-third of usual crop saved.
July 29	Young Ireland Rising, Ballingarry, Co. Tipperary.
Aug. 14	Encumbered Estates Act (amended July 1849).
Nov.	Cholera epidemic begins. Rural evictions increased from 1847 level. An estimated 180,000 emigrated in 1848.

1849
May	Potato blight confined to west and south.
June	Peak of 800,000 on outdoor relief. Rate-in-aid, to levy rates fairly over all Poor Law unions.
Aug. 3–12	Visit of Queen Victoria and Prince Albert.
Dec.	Workhouse accommodation available for 250,000, most of it occupied. Evicted families total 16,686 in 1849. An estimated 220,000 emigrated.

1850
Evicted families total 19,949.
An estimated 210,000 emigrated.

1851
Evicted families total 13,197.
An estimated 250,000 emigrated.
Census gives population as 6,552,385
(1841 census: 8,175,125).

1852
Evicted families total 8,591.
An estimated 250,000 emigrated.
Outdoor relief virtually phased out.

EDITORIAL NOTE

These contemporary documents provide evidence on aspects of the Famine as perceived at the time. They represent the state of knowledge and also the perspectives, the attitudes and the prejudices of those involved. Some guidance is provided, but the reader should exercise discrimination, and arrive at independent conclusions.

Spelling and punctuation are standardised, except in the case of placenames, or where the spelling indicates archaic usage, regional pronunciation, or the standard of literacy.

The documents and illustrations are from the National Library of Ireland unless otherwise stated.

ABBREVIATIONS

BL	British Library
NLI	National Library of Ireland
NLS	National Library of Scotland

I

BEFORE THE FAMINE

In the early 1840s, a large percentage of the eight million then living in Ireland were, in economic terms, in a precarious and highly vulnerable position. Irish society was then predominantly rural and the economy was mainly based on agriculture; around seven of the eight million inhabitants lived in the countryside and made their living from the land. While this way of life was then common throughout Europe, the density of population in rural Ireland was exceptional. Moreover, the system under which the land was owned and managed was also unusual and potentially disastrous.

By the nineteenth century, the native Gaelic property tradition under which land was held in common had long since disappeared. In its place was the landlord system which had been imposed over the centuries under an English policy of conquest, confiscation and plantation. The Irish landlords were an hereditary ruling elite whose wealth and political power were based on the land. While the majority were descended from families which had lived in Ireland for generations, most considered themselves as essentially British; some lived in Britain and managed their Irish estates as absentee landlords.

Whether resident or absentee, many landlords administered their estates in an extremely short-sighted fashion; their priority was to extort the highest possible rents, and only a minority were 'improving' landlords who re-invested in their estates. The result was that the land was not exploited to its full potential, with a proportionate loss to those involved at the various levels, that is the landlords themselves, the tenant farmers and the farm labourers.

While the landlords owned the land, their welfare ultimately depended on their tenant farmers, the class which encompassed perhaps a third of the population. But this bedrock class was itself in a precarious situation; while a small proportion made a modest living on farms of twenty acres and upwards, the majority had holdings of less than ten acres and

eked out an existence at subsistence level. In good years, when the crops yielded a fair harvest and the stock thrived, it was possible to grow enough food for the family, remit the rent to the landlord, and pay cess or tax for the upkeep of the county and Poor Law rates to maintain the local workhouse.

The third class which depended on the land consisted of the farm labourers. Most had the use of a plot of ground on which to grow potatoes; it was usually rented from a farmer and paid for by so many days' labour. Both the labourers and the smaller farmers existed at subsistence level; in good times, they got by mainly because they had a source of cheap food readily available in the potato. An acre of ground provided a family of four with enough food for most of the year, and the ubiquitous potato helped to support a phenomenal growth in population since the mid-eighteenth century. While the country as a whole was not overpopulated relative to overall resources, three million people of the small-farmer and labouring classes lived at subsistence level. These were the 'potato people' who each year depended on a bountiful crop of potatoes for their very lives; if the crop were to fail completely, they would have no other resource and their ruin would ultimately impinge on the large farmers, the landlords and the country as a whole.

The social and economic situation was complicated by the fact that since the Act of Union of 1800 Ireland no longer had its own parliament, but was subject to the parliament of the United Kingdom of Great Britain and Ireland. In effect, Ireland was governed from London by Ministers and administrators who, for the most part, had no real understanding of, or sympathy with, the Irish and Irish problems. In normal times, this gulf between government and governed was counter-productive; in the crisis which developed in the autumn of 1845 it was disastrous.

1. *Landlords, middlemen and absentees*

A major problem with the Irish land system was that many landlords did not own their estates but leased them from other landlords; in many cases there were two or more intermediaries or middlemen interposed between the tenant and the head landlord. This multiplicity of interests in the one parcel of land was detrimental to all involved. A good outline of the land system is provided by Mr and Mrs Samuel Carter Hall. The Halls were an Irish-born couple living in England who toured this country extensively; their three-volume book is a relatively sympathetic source on social conditions in Ireland before the Famine. The extracts given here portray the estate of an improving landlord, and illustrate some of the difficulties arising from the middleman system.

An account of the estate of an improving landlord.

Happily, Wexford is, in one respect, highly privileged – few of its landed proprietors are absentees. There are no huge estates over which several agents must, of necessity, be placed; and as very few of its gentry have involved [encumbered] properties, it follows as a matter of course that the tenants are in easy circumstances, and are neither rack-rented nor pressed for sudden payments. Unfortunately, few of the Irish counties are so auspiciously circumstanced; in many instances a nominal rent-roll misleads the owner into an expenditure far beyond his actual income; the consequence naturally is that the landlord and the tenant are mutually embarrassed, that an air of poverty equally pervades the mansion and the cottage, and that prosperity to either is totally out of the question.

The estate of Mr Morgan is as beautiful a picture of healthful improvement and happy independence as the country can supply. Possessed of a very large fortune, and resident in one of the most fertile tracts of the kingdom, his efforts, seconded by those of his most estimable lady, have been devoted to bettering the condition of their tenantry, and they have been eminently successful. The visitor sees no miserable hovel in this neighbourhood; no sickly, or squalid, or sturdy mendicant; no ill-clad workmen;

nothing, in short, which indicates that hard-handed labour is barely sufficient to keep the wolf – hunger – from the door... And how has this glorious object been attained? The secret is told in a sentence: by letting the land upon terms so just and equitable – and, we may add, wise – that every industrious renter of it is assured a profit sufficient, not alone to supply his wants, but to surround himself with the comforts which invariably elevate the mind and convert the thin and decaying tie which too frequently connects landlord and tenant into an enduring link that cannot be broken.

(Mr and Mrs S.C. Hall, *Ireland: its scenery and character, &c.*, London, 1841-3, vol.II, p.167-9.)

Johnstown Castle, Co. Wexford,
seat of Hamilton Knox Grogan Morgan.
(Hall, *Ireland*, II, 167.)

Description of the middleman system.

A middleman was usually, in his origin, 'one of the people', who, having made money, took a farm or an estate, rented a hundred, or, as was often the case, a thousand acres; the landlord-in-chief, generally an absentee, looked to him alone for the payment of his half-yearly rent, and knew nothing whatever of the condition of the cottiers who dwelt upon his estate; if we add that he cared nothing as well as knew nothing, we shall not be far from the truth; for, while pursuing a course of pleasure in the metropolis, in Dublin sometimes but in London more frequently, he was far away from the sight of their sufferings.

The peasantry, badly housed, badly clothed, badly fed, were in no way necessary either to his luxuries or his necessities; the middleman was always a punctual paymaster, and he was the only person upon his estate with whom the landlord was brought into contact or called upon to correspond. This middleman had to transmit to his employer perhaps three or four thousand pounds, often more, every year. And how was he to procure it? First, his system was to parcel out the estate into small bits, seldom more than two or three acres to each but generally averaging an acre. These 'bits' were invariably let annually, and never on lease; the occupier, therefore, had no temptation to cultivate the land. His slip of ground seldom bore any other produce than potatoes; these were designed solely for the consumption of his own household and the support of a pig, which, if it lived and no unusual misfortune attended the family, was to pay the rent. Of course, the land was let at the highest possible rate, and to the highest or most thoughtless bidder; the middleman had to pay the landlord, and to grow rich himself; as the tenant was invariably in arrear, he was at all times in the power of the middleman; and the putting on a new coat, the addition of a trifling article of furniture, or the appearance of anything like comfort in or around his dwelling was a sure and certain notice that the bailiff would be 'down upon him' ere the sun had set.

The general want of employment, and the consequent anxiety of obtaining for their families the means of even temporary subsistence, produced such an eagerness on the part of the peasantry to get possession of land, as to induce them to engage for the payment of a rent, which the crops, even under the most favourable circumstances, must have failed to yield. This circumstance was too frequently taken advantage of; and the ultimate ruin of the mis-calculating tenant was the invariable result.

(Hall, *Ireland,* II, 123-4.)

'The Absentee. Scene Naples – Enter the ghosts of the starv'd Irish peasentry' [*sic*]; by Robert Seymour. Generally, the estates of absentees were not managed as well as those of resident landlords, and the tenants were more vulnerable in time of distress. (*The Looking Glass,* 1 August 1830.)

2. Farms and farmers

A notable feature of the land system was the large number of small and uneconomic holdings. This was due to a process of subdivision over the previous century. Small farmers tended to subdivide their farms between their children as they had nothing else to give them when they married. A realistic account of the economy of a ten-acre farm is provided by Thomas Campbell Foster. His book, based on a series of articles for The Times, *is a valuable source for the state of the country in 1845. Regarding the table of farm sizes, it is worth remembering that many farms supported an extended family of eight people or more.*

Outline of the economy of a small farm.

The common size of farms in this country is five or six acres; ten acres is thought to be a good farm. I have ascertained that in this part of the county of Donegal, where rents are reasonable and the landlords fair, the following is the produce and cost of cultivation of a ten-acre farm at the fair rent of £1 an acre. Two-thirds of such a farm will be under cultivation, the rest fallow or grazing, as it is here called. The whole produce of such a farm has been estimated to me by an experienced agent and practical farmer at £30. The rent is therefore fair. The farm, however, is so small that the farmer is but a superior kind of labourer, rather better paid:

	£	s	d
The seed will cost, at least	4	0	0
County cess, at 5s an acre	2	10	0
Poor-rates, at 1s an acre	0	10	0
No tithe here	0	0	0
The farmer labours himself, and estimating his labour at the usual wages of a labourer	10	0	0
Tenant-right of ten acres at £4, £40; interest of £40 at 5%	2	0	0
Rent of the land	10	0	0
Profit of the farmer for his care, skill, and diligence	1	0	0
	£30	0	0

'The house of Pat Brennan', a small farmer on Daniel O'Connell's estate at Derrynane, Co. Kerry. Potatoes are stored in a loft near the fireplace. (*The Pictorial Times,* 7 Feb. 1846; courtesy of NLS.)

This farmer, therefore, holding an average-sized farm, is merely a labourer paid at the rate of £1 a year higher wages than a common labourer. Still, he has a house to live in and potatoes for his family the year round, and is therefore tolerably comfortable, though his positive remuneration is only some 5d a week more than a labourer receives.

(Thomas Campbell Foster, *Letters on the condition of the people of Ireland*, London, 1846, p. 73-4.)

		LAND HOLDINGS IN ACRES				ACRES	
		From 1 to 5	From 5 to 15	From 15 to 30	Above 30	Arable and Pasture	Uncultivated
Ulster	Antrim	6,991	10,766	4,314	1,922	515,771	180,423
	Armagh	11,632	9,428	2,072	666	265,243	35,117
	Cavan	10,807	12,208	1,958	668	375,473	71,918
	Donegal	15,567	12,931	3,527	1,699	393,191	769,587
	Down	13,753	11,991	3,865	1,508	514,180	78,317
	Fermanagh	7,371	8,540	1,696	529	289,228	114,847
	Londonderry	7,866	8,755	2,675	1,143	318,282	180,709
	Monaghan	12,275	9,702	1,216	317	285,885	21,585
	Tyrone	14,555	14,671	3,776	1,139	450,286	311,867
Munster	Clare	11,593	12,049	2,234	1,052	455,009	296,033
	Cork	13,683	15,790	10,362	5,691	1,308,882	465,889
	Kerry	8,689	10,830	4,068	2,172	414,614	726,775
	Limerick	6,841	6,840	3,700	2,346	526,876	121,101
	Tipperary	13,032	12,787	4,938	2,960	843,887	178,183
	Waterford	3,190	3,024	2,179	2,336	325,345	105,496
Leinster	Carlow	1,933	2,357	1,056	950	184,059	31,249
	Dublin	1,866	1,285	749	1,102	196,063	19,312
	Kildare	3,104	2,123	991	1,845	356,787	51,854
	Kilkenny	5,131	5,752	3,601	2,006	470,102	21,126
	King's [Offaly]	5,657	4,502	1,374	1,213	337,256	145,836
	Longford	4,396	4,880	1,045	411	191,823	58,937
	Louth	3,992	2,589	628	632	178,972	15,603
	Meath	5,339	3,971	1,637	2,554	547,391	16,033
	Queen's [Laois]	5,629	4,825	1,813	1,334	342,422	69,289
	Westmeath	4,266	4,076	1,648	1,385	365,218	56,392
	Wexford	5,219	6,313	4,151	2,457	510,702	45,501
	Wicklow	2,620	2,922	1,891	2,000	280,393	200,754
Connaught	Galway	27,992	12,663	2,030	1,645	742,805	708,000
	Leitrim	9,373	7,971	877	202	249,350	115,869
	Mayo	33,790	10,331	1,265	1,135	497,587	800,111
	Roscommon	17,472	8,066	913	895	440,522	130,299
	Sligo	11,291	6,190	705	398	290,696	151,723
	Gross Total	306,915	251,128	78,954	48,312	13,464,300	6,295,735

Return taken from the census of Ireland for 1841, showing the size of farms.

(*Correspondence from July 1846 to Jan. 1847 relating to the measures adopted for the relief of the distress in Ireland*, p. 27; P.P. 1847 (761) LI.)

Note: This table is useful as a general indication but is misleading in two respects:

1. The returns were mostly given in Irish acres (1.62 statute acres); 2. In the computation of farm size, waste land was excluded.

3. The farm labourers

A letter of Richard Griffith to Lord Lincoln, Commissioner of the Office of Woods and Forests, summarises the situation of farm labourers. Griffith, a geologist and civil engineer, was involved in a number of major schemes and surveys and had an intimate knowledge of rural society. From September 1846, he was employed on Famine relief schemes as a special commissioner of the Board of Works. Among the most comprehensive sources of information on farm labourers in the decade before the Famine are the reports of the Commissioners for Inquiring into the State of the Poorer Classes in Ireland. In 1834-35, the Commissioners took evidence from a wide range of witnesses, an extract from which is given here.

Letter of Richard Griffith to the Earl of Lincoln.

Limerick, 18 April 1846.

One-fourth, and in many cases upwards of one-third, of the rural population have no land, or at least less than half an acre which is usually held under a farmer or middleman. These people live chiefly by barter. They rarely have any money transactions, except, perhaps, from the sale of a pig. They are usually employed part of the year by the farmers or neighbouring gentlemen. They take from the farmer, on the conacre system, a sufficient quantity of land on which they plant potatoes for their support. If the farmer manures it, the amount charged varies from £5 to £8 per acre; but if the cottier has manure of his own, derived from the pig, scraping the road, etc., he is rarely charged any rent for the part so manured. The cottier plants his crop, and works out the rent with the farmer. When unemployed, he has his potatoes to live on, and with the small potatoes he rears and fattens a pig, from the produce of which the family are clothed. Such is the state of dependence of at least one-fourth, or probably one-third, of the Irish people.

(*Correspondence explanatory of the measures adopted by H.M. government for the relief of distress ... p. 109; P.P. 1846 (735) XXXVII.*)

'Peasantry on the O'Connell farms', at Derrynane, Co. Kerry. (*The Pictorial Times*, 31 Jan. 1846; courtesy of NLS.)

Extract from evidence taken by the Commissioners on the State of the Poorer Classes, 1834-35.

County Longford, Parish of Abbeyshrule, including Town of Ballymahon. Examinations taken by John Spencer, Esq., Wilson Gray, Esq.

Persons who attended the examination: John Casey, cottier; Hugh Doogan, small farmer (10 acres); Captain Graham, magistrate; Mr Johnston, an extensive farmer; Rev. Mr McCann, parish priest; Rev. Mr Maguire, rector; Rev. Mr Moffet, Protestant curate of an adjoining parish and a magistrate residing in the town of Ballymahon; Mr. Edward Rooney, a general merchant; Michael Rooney, a general merchant; Michael Rourke, labourer.

According to the evidence given by the Rev. Mr McCann, Captain Graham and Mr Rooney, there is not employment for a fourth part of the labourers belonging to the parish between the months of September and March, and again during the interval between the 1st of June and the middle or latter end of August. Michael Rourke details as follows the circumstances of his own mode of life, as well as of the greater number of his fellow labourers: 'In winter, we have a stock of conacre potatoes, the rent of which we are enabled to pay by the sale of our pig at Christmas. Some labourers belonging to the town endeavour to help out their stock by bartering herrings for potatoes throughout the country. In spring, the conacre potatoes begin to run out, and though there is then a demand for labour, the working man must in general pay away his wages for food just as quick as he gets them. By the time the summer comes, the conacre potatoes are usually exhausted, and at the same time there is no employment to be had. Some few who are known to be honest men and good labourers, by getting another person to join them in a promissory note, obtain meal on credit at an interest of from 30 to 40 per cent, to be paid for by their harvest wages. It depends entirely on the heart of the man that sells it whether he contents himself with a certain advance on the price, or whether he also stipulates for the advantage of any rise that may take place in the article before the time for paying for it. I have known the price to have doubled between the day on which the meal was delivered and that on which it was paid for, and the labourer had to pay the double price in consequence of such stipulation'.

Upon this statement being made by Rourke, James Magrath, a labourer who was standing by listening, observed, 'I got meal on credit last July, when it was selling at 10s the hundredweight. My bargain was to pay 16s 6d at Christmas, without any regard to a rise or fall in prices. I have no blame to the person selling it at so exorbitant a profit; if he gains largely by one, he loses by another'. Magrath was asked whether, with the aid of such credit, a labourer could afford himself a sufficiency of food. His answer was, 'You know we will not eat plenty, not half plenty, when we are paying such prices; and, moreover, he is a favoured man that can get credit; not one-fourth of the labourers can obtain it; so that we are often obliged to dig our potatoes long before they are half-grown'.

(Appendix to first report of the Commissioners for Inquiring into the State of the Poorer Classes in Ireland, p.402; P.P. 1835 (369) XXXII(I).)

'Ardcara – cabin of J. Donoghue', on the O'Connell estate. (*The Pictorial Times*, 7 Feb. 1846; courtesy of NLS.)

4. *Housing and accommodation*

In the 1840s, there was an extreme disparity in housing and accommodation, which ranged from the mansions of the gentry to the mud-walled and clay-floored cabins of the small farmers, the labourers and the destitute. Cabins were often erected in a day by the friends and neighbours of a young couple about to marry. They were generally thatched, and consisted of one room with a fireplace and chimney but without sanitation. In the congested rural areas, the houses tended to be clustered in clacháns *or villages. The map from the 1841 census gives a reliable indication of housing and accommodation on the eve of the Famine.*

Extract from the report of the Census Commissioners, 1841.

The necessity of some classification is so obvious, and the want of it so serious, that we proceed at once to describe the mode we adopted, without going farther into the reasons which led us to the attempt. The value or condition of a house, as to the accommodation it affords, may be considered to depend mainly on, 1st, its extent, as shown by the number of rooms; 2nd, its quality, as shown by the number of its windows; and 3rd, its solidity or durability, as shown by the material of its walls and roof. If numbers be adopted to express the position of every house in a scale of each of these elements, and if the numbers thus obtained for every house be added together, we shall have a new series of numbers, giving the position of the house in a scale compounded of all the elements, i.e. their actual state. We adopted four classes, and the result was that in the lowest, or fourth class, were comprised all mud cabins having only one room; in the third, a better

description of cottage, still built of mud, but varying from two to four rooms and windows; in the second, a good farmhouse, or in towns, a house in a small street having from five to nine rooms and windows; and in the first, all houses of a better description than the preceding classes.

We tested the rule practically on several houses in different localities, both town and country, and found the result sufficiently satisfactory. We, at first, intended to have thrown the third and fourth classes together, and it is to be hoped that hereafter they may be consolidated. But we thought it desirable to retain at present a separate column for the mere hut, still too common throughout the country. The floor of a cabin is a very essential criterion of its quality, which perhaps, we might, with advantage, have also inquired into and used as an element of classification for houses of the third and fourth classes.

(*Census of Ireland for the year 1841*, vol. I, p. xiv; P.P. 1843 (504) XXIV.)

Keel, Achill Island, Co. Mayo. (Hall, *Ireland*, 1841-3, III, p. 404.)

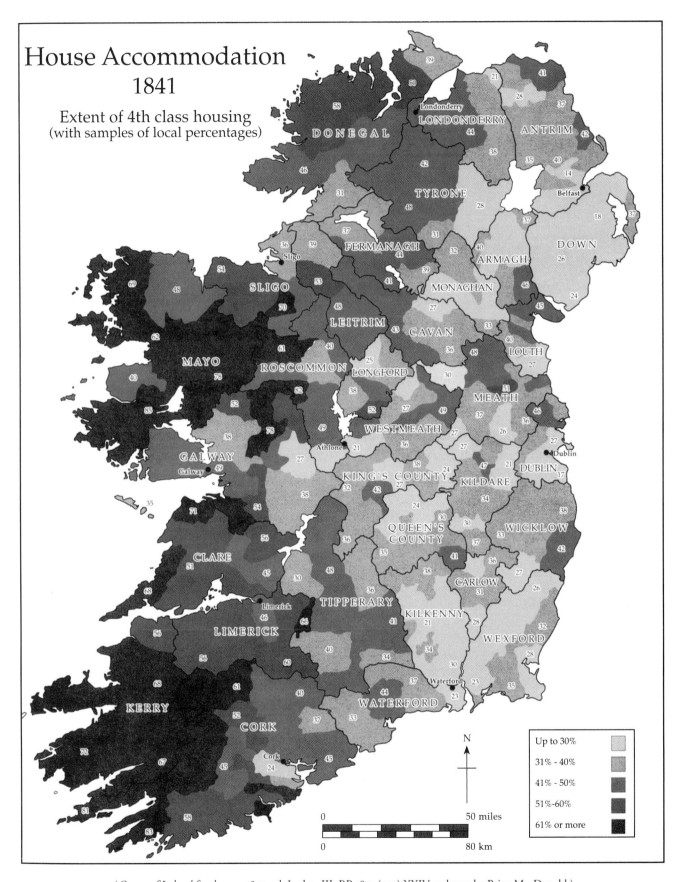

House Accommodation
1841

Extent of 4th class housing
(with samples of local percentages)

DONEGAL

Londonderry

LONDONDERRY

ANTRIM

Belfast

TYRONE

FERMANAGH

Sligo

DOWN

ARMAGH

SLIGO

MONAGHAN

LEITRIM

CAVAN

MAYO

ROSCOMMON

LONGFORD

LOUTH

MEATH

WESTMEATH

Athlone

GALWAY

Galway

KING'S COUNTY

KILDARE

DUBLIN

Dublin

QUEEN'S
COUNTY

WICKLOW

CLARE

Limerick

TIPPERARY

CARLOW

KILKENNY

LIMERICK

WEXFORD

KERRY

WATERFORD

Waterford

CORK

Cork

N

Up to 30%	
31% - 40%	
41% - 50%	
51%-60%	
61% or more	

0   50 miles

0   80 km

(*Census of Ireland for the year 1841*, vol. I, plate III; P.P. 1843 (504) XXIV; redrawn by Brian MacDonald.)

5. The political situation

For centuries prior to the Act of Union in 1800, Ireland was subject to Britain, but had its own parliament in Dublin. The Irish parliament had considerable autonomy but membership was restricted to Protestants. Under the Union, while Ireland was represented in the parliament of the United Kingdom at Westminster, its interests were generally subordinated to those of Britain. The following extract from a speech by Earl Grey, in the early days of the Famine, expresses the views of an influential member of the British establishment on Ireland's situation under the Union. Grey, the son of a former Prime Minister, was then a member of the Liberal opposition party; following the change of government later that year he held office as Colonial Secretary.

Extract from a speech by Earl Grey in the House of Lords.

The state of Ireland is one which is notorious. We know the ordinary condition of that country to be one both of lawlessness and wretchedness. It is so described by every competent authority. There is not an intelligent foreigner coming to our shores, who turns his attention to the state of Ireland, but who bears back with him such a description. Ireland is the one weak place in the solid fabric of British power; Ireland is the one deep (I had almost said ineffaceable) blot upon the brightness of British honour. Ireland is our disgrace. It is the reproach, the standing disgrace, of this country that Ireland remains in the condition she is. It is so regarded throughout the whole civilized world. To ourselves we may palliate it if we will, and disguise the truth; but we cannot conceal it from others. There is not, as I have said, a foreigner – no matter whence he comes, be it from France, Russia, Germany, or America – there is no native of any foreign country, different as their forms of government may be, who visits Ireland, and who on his return does not congratulate himself that he sees nothing comparable with the condition of that country at home.

If such be the state of things, how then does it arise, and what is its cause? My Lords, it is only by misgovernment that such evils could have been produced; the mere fact that Ireland is in so deplorable and wretched a condition saves whole volumes of argument, and is of itself a complete and irrefutable proof of the misgovernment to which she has been subjected. Nor can we lay to our souls the 'flattering unction' that this misgovernment was only

of ancient date, and has not been our doing. It is not enough in our own excuse to say, 'No wonder this state of things exists; the government of Ireland before the Union was the most ingeniously bad that was ever contrived in the face of the world; it was the government of a corrupt minority, sustained by the superior power of this great country in oppressing and tyrannizing over the great body of the nation; such a system of government could not fail to leave behind it a train of fearful evils from which we are still suffering at the present day'.

To a certain extent, no doubt, this is true. No man has a stronger opinion than I regarding the iniquitous system of misgovernment in Ireland prior to the Union. But the Union is not an event of yesterday. It is nearly half a century since that measure passed. For nearly fifty years, now, Ireland has been under the immediate control of the Imperial Parliament. Since it has been so, a whole generation has grown up, and is now passing away to be replaced by another; and in that time, I ask you, what impression has been made upon the evils of Ireland? It is true some good has been done. I gladly acknowledge that many useful measures have been adopted, which have, I hope, contributed in some respects to the improvement of Ireland; but none of these measures have gone to the root of the social disease to which Ireland is a prey, in the worst symptoms of which no amelioration whatever can be observed: the wretchedness and misery of the population have experienced no abatement. Upon that point I can quote high authority. I find that the Commission presided over by a noble earl, whom I do not now see in his place [the Earl of Devon], reported the year before last, that 'improvement was indeed beginning to take place in agriculture, but there had been no corresponding advance in the condition and comforts of the labouring classes'. By the report of that Commission we are informed that the agricultural labourers are still suffering the greatest privations and hardships, and still depend upon casual and precarious employment for their subsistence; that they are badly fed, badly clothed, badly housed, and badly paid for their labour; and the Commissioners conclude this part of their report by saying:

'We cannot forbear expressing our strong sense of the patient endurance which the labouring classes have generally exhibited under sufferings greater, we believe, than the people of any other country have ever endured'.

But there is another symptom of the condition of Ireland, which seems to me even more alarming than the prevalence of distress – I mean the general alienation of the whole mass of the nation from the institutions under which they live, and the existence in their minds of a strong deep feeling of hostility to the form of government under which they are placed. This feeling, which is the worst feature in the case, seems to be rather gaining strength than to be diminishing. I am led to that opinion by what I heard two years ago fall from the Secretary of State for the Home Department [Sir James Graham] in the House of Commons. I heard that right hon. gentleman – and it was a statement which made a deep impression upon me – I heard the right hon. gentleman, in answer to a speech made by a noble friend of mine, distinctly admit that we had military occupation of Ireland, but that in no other sense could it be said to be governed; that it was occupied by troops, not governed like England. Such was the admission of the Secretary of State for the Home Department.

(*Hansard*, House of Lords, 23 March 1846, 1345-7.)

The House of Lords. (L. Galibert et C. Pellé, *Angleterre, Écosse et Irlande,* Paris, 1844.)

II

THE POTATO

The potato is not an indigenous Irish plant but was introduced, allegedly by Sir Walter Raleigh, in the reign of Queen Elizabeth I. It thrived in the mild and damp Irish climate, and produced a good yield even on marginal land. An easy crop to grow, it was palatable and nutritious for man and beast, and gradually replaced grain as the staple diet of the poor, especially in Munster and Connacht.

In the sixty years before the Famine, the population doubled from four million to eight million, and this expansion was made possible by the potato. An acre of ground could produce enough potatoes for a family for most of the year; a young man considering marriage knew that all he needed to support a wife and start a family was a plot of rented land for which he could pay by casual labour. With an expanding population, there was great demand for land, which resulted in a gradual move onto the more marginal areas, such as reclaimed bog and the slopes of hills and mountains. When worked with the spade and well manured, these terrains produced good yields of potatoes. By the 1840s, many of the reclaimed areas supported large populations living at subsistence level. The paradox of Irish rural population was that the heaviest densities were on the poorest land.

As the poor had only small plots of land, they needed varieties of potatoes that gave good yields. Under this pressure, they gradually abandoned the red varieties in favour of white, especially the Lumper, known as the horse potato, which was coarse and of inferior quality but high-yielding. Unfortunately, it was less immune to disease, a very serious defect when the potato was practically the only source of food for over a third of the population.

Normally the crop lasted nine or ten months, that is, from the early crop at the end of August until the following June. The summer months were hungry times for many, but the smallholders sometimes had a little money in hand from cash crops or the sale of stock, and many of the labourers got support from the farmers for whom they worked at planting and harvesting. In the hungry summer months, meal, made from Indian corn (maize), was used by the poorer classes as a cheap substitute for potatoes.

Periodically, there were partial failures of the potato crop due to bad weather or disease. These caused hunger and hardship, and deaths from virtual starvation or its attendant diseases were common. But failures were always only partial and generally only occurred for the one season. In 1845, however, a new disease appeared, which was devastating in its effect and, moreover, had come to stay. The disease, commonly called potato blight, is caused by a fungus, *phytophthora infestans*. It was introduced to Europe from the American continent, possibly in diseased potatoes in cargoes of guano (bird manure) imported from South America. It affected the stalks and the tubers, that is the actual potatoes, though sometimes it did not become obvious in the tubers until after they were dug and stored. The fungus which causes the disease thrives in humid conditions and is disseminated by spores transported in the air.

In 1845, the blight caused a loss of one-third of the crop. In the following years, the situation was aggravated by disruption in planting and shortage of seed; only a quarter of the usual crop was harvested in 1846 or 1847, and one-third in 1848. These losses were extremely serious for the small farmers, the labourers and, especially, for the very poor. But potatoes were an important part of the diet of all classes, so everybody was affected to some extent; in addition, the loss of the potato meant that smallholders unable to afford alternative feed could no longer keep pigs.

Since 1845, the potato blight has been endemic in Ireland, and when conditions are right it attacks unprotected crops. Since the 1880s, however, growers have had an effective deterrent; a solution containing copper sulphate sprayed onto the stalks prevents invasion by the fungal spores.

1. *Planting potatoes*

The smallholders planted potatoes with the spade and used farmyard manure or seaweed for fertiliser. The potatoes were sown in ridges known as lazy-beds. The large farmers generally planted a greater acreage and used horse-drawn ploughs and harrows to prepare the ground. Many of them could also afford guano and lime in addition to farmyard manure or seaweed. A good account of a progressive method of planting potatoes and using them to reclaim poor ground is given by William Steuart Trench, who acted as land agent for a number of the great landlords of the period. At the outbreak of the Famine, he had a large farm in Queen's County (Co. Laois) which he worked according to contemporary scientific principles.

William Steuart Trench's method of planting.

On leaving Carrickmacross I went to reside at Cardtown, my place in the Queen's County. It adjoins an extensive mountain tract of land which I had purchased and which I had for some years previously been engaged in reclaiming. Having resigned Mr Shirley's agency, I was able to devote my time and energies more exclusively to this work, and the mode of reclaiming being chiefly through the means of the potato, as the only green crop which grows luxuriantly in rough ground with previously imperfect tilth, I planted each year larger and larger quantities of that root. Guano, having been at that time (1845) recently brought into use as a manure, was found to be particularly suited to the production of the potato; I accordingly applied a liberal quantity to the crop, which was most luxuriant, and well repaid the labour, money and attention necessarily bestowed upon it.

My plan of reclaiming was very simple. The land to be acted on consisted generally of rough mountain pasture covered with heather. There were no stones,

Potatoes growing on lazy-beds on a hillside. (Arthur Young, *A Tour in Ireland,* London, 1780.)

or few of sufficient size to impede the course of the plough. The land was first limed with eighty barrels (thirty-two gallons per barrel) of lime to the Irish acre (about fifty to the statute acre), spread broadcast upon the surface. The land was then ploughed down into what were termed lazy-beds, that is, narrow ridges about five feet in width, with a furrow between each ridge. Into these ridges the seed of the potato was put by merely sticking the spade into the rough ground and dropping in the seed or 'set' at the back of the spade; the spade being then withdrawn, the seed remained two or three inches under the surface. Guano, six hundredweight to the acre, was then scattered over the ridges, care being taken that the guano should not come into immediate contact either with the seed or with the lime. And this being done, the furrows were dug, the clay shovelled over the ridges, and the whole made up into lazy-beds – rough underneath where heather and sods lay rudely massed together, but when covered up with the fresh-dug soil from the furrows, presenting a neat and finished appearance above. The potato grew to perfection in this rude description of tillage; and whilst it was growing, the heather rotted under the influence of the lime, and, together with the other superabundant vegetable matter, was turned by the action of the lime into a most valuable manure. The guano stimulated an enormous and luxuriant growth, and when the potatoes were in course of being dug out, the act of digging mixed the lime, manure, and the several soils together into an even texture, leaving the land, which had hitherto been scarcely worth one shilling per acre, in excellent order for sowing corn crops or grass seeds, and permanently worth at least one pound per acre.

(William Steuart Trench, *Realities of Irish life*, London, 1868, p. 97-8.)

The village of Doogort, Achill Island, Co. Mayo, with lazy-beds in the foreground. (John Eliot Howard, *The island of saints, or Ireland in 1855*, London, 1855.)

2. Food and diet

The potato is an extremely nutritious food and contains traces of most of the elements necessary for a healthy diet. It is possible to live almost exclusively on a diet of potatoes, and in the early 1840s about three million people did so because they could afford nothing else. Important contemporary sources on the way of life of the poorer classes are the annual reports of the Poor Law Commissioners; following the 1838 Irish Poor Law Act, the Commissioners' responsibilities extended to Ireland.

Description of a potato diet.

It is universally admitted that a finer or hardier race of peasantry cannot be found in the world; and although it is considered that their strength fails them at a comparatively early age, it is impossible to deny the nutritive qualities of a food upon which so many millions have thriven and increased. But there can be as little doubt that the ease with which the means of existence are procured has been the cause of evil. A very limited portion of land, a few days of labour, and a small amount of manure, will create a stock upon which a family may exist for twelve month; too generally, indeed, the periods between exhausting the old stock and digging the new are seasons of great want, if not of absolute famine; but if the season is propitious, the peasant digs day after day the produce of his plot of ground, and before the winter sets in, places the residue in a pit to which he has access when his wants demand a supply. Nearly every soil will produce potatoes; they may be seen growing almost from a barren rock, on the side of a mountain, and in the bog, where the foot would sink many inches in the soil. Every cottage has its garden – its acre or half acre of land, attached; and as the culture requires but a very small portion of the peasant's time and still less of his attention, his labour is to be disposed of, or his time may be squandered, in idleness. He can live, at all events – if his crop does not fail; and he can pay his rent, if his pig, fed like himself out of his garden, does not die.

We refer, in a great degree, to our recollections, when we describe the lower classes of the Irish as existing, almost universally, on the potato; we

have known many families who very rarely tasted flesh or fish, and whose only luxury was 'a grain of salt' with their daily meals; we do not speak of families in poverty, but of those who laboured hard and continually – the produce of whose labour barely sufficed to preserve them from utter want. Generally, however, they contrived to have a salt herring with their dinners; this was placed in a bowl or dish, water was poured upon it, and the potato, dipped into it, obtained a relish. We  shall have other occasions for describing the economy of the Irish cottage; at present, we confine ourselves to illustrate this branch of it. The peasant usually has three meals – one at eight in the morning; at noon; and at seven or eight in the evening, when his work is done. The potatoes are boiled in an iron pot – such as that represented in the print; they are strained in 'the basket' – pictured also; from which they are thrown upon the table, seldom without a cloth, and around it the family sit on stools and bosses (the boss is a low seat made of straw); the usual drink is buttermilk, when it can be had: which drink goes round in a small 'piggin' [*pigín*], a sort of miniature of the English pail. This, the three-legged stool and the 'borrane' [*bodhrán*] are delineated in the annexed engraving. The borrane is formed of a scraped sheepskin, drawn round a hoop; and is used instead of a sieve for winnowing corn, filling sacks with grain, holding wool when carded and ready for the spinning-wheel, or the feathers, plucked three times in the year from an unfortunate gander and his wives, and sometimes as a lordly dish – though of inexpensive workmanship – to hold the potatoes which constitute the family fare.

(Hall, *Ireland,* 1841-3, I, 82-4.)

The quantity of food consumed by the labouring poor in the undermentioned Poor Law unions.

Union		Breakfast	Dinner	Supper
Limerick	Men	4½lbs potatoes, 1 pint skimmed milk.	The same, and in winter herrings and water instead of milk.	This meal is occasionally omitted in the city of Limerick, particularly during the short days, and chiefly by labourers employed in stores, etc.
	Women	The same.	The same.	
Kilmallock	Men	4½lbs potatoes, 1 quart skimmed milk.	The same, with herrings and dripping when milk is scarce.	The same, but supper is not always eaten.
	Women	3½lbs potatoes, from 2½ pints to a quart of milk [*sic*].	The same.	The same.
Thurles	Men	3 to 5lbs potatoes, from 1 to 2 pints of skimmed milk.	The same; but a herring, weighing 4oz, is sometimes used instead, and occasionally eggs and butter.	Supper is only eaten at plentiful seasons of the year.
	Women	3 to 3½lbs potatoes, 1 pint skimmed milk.	The same.	
Nenagh	Men	4½lbs potatoes, 1 pint milk.	The same, and herrings when milk cannot be obtained.	The same.
	Women	3lbs potatoes, ¾ pint milk.	The same.	The same.
Ennistymon	Men	5lbs potatoes, 1 pint of milk.	The same.	The same, but supper is not always eaten.
	Women	The same, when at work.	The same.	The same.

(*Sixth annual report of Poor Law Commissioners for England and Wales,* appendix D, p.244; P.P. 1840 (245) XVII.)

'A potato dinner', at Cahirciveen, Co. Kerry. (*The Pictorial Times,* 28 Feb. 1846; courtesy of NLS.)

3. The risks inherent in a potato economy

The civil servant who was mainly responsible for relief measures during the Famine was Charles Edward Trevelyan, Assistant Secretary to the Treasury. He was a most conscientious public servant, but his handling of the situation was undermined by his negative opinion of the Irish. Moreover, he believed that the Famine was an ecological mechanism or an act of divine providence designed to reduce the population to realistic levels. The potato had failed the people on a number of occasions in the past; this extract from a book by Trevelyan recalls the famine of a century earlier; relative to the population of the time, it was equally disastrous. Many of the relief measures employed then were adopted by Trevelyan to deal with the Irish crisis of his day.

Trevelyan's views on the potato economy.

A population, whose ordinary food is wheat and beef, and whose ordinary drink is porter and ale, can retrench in periods of scarcity, and resort to cheaper kinds of food, such as barley, oats, rice, and potatoes. But those who are habitually and entirely fed on potatoes live upon the extreme verge of human subsistence, and when they are deprived of their accustomed food, there is nothing cheaper to which they can resort. They have already reached the lowest point in the descending scale, and there is nothing beyond but starvation or beggary. Several circumstances aggravate the hazard of this position. The produce of the potato is more precarious than that of wheat or any other grain. Besides many other proofs of the uncertainty of this crop, there is no instance on record of any such failure of the crops of corn, as occurred in the case of potatoes in 1821, 1845, 1846, and 1847, showing that this root can no longer be depended upon as a staple article of human food.

The potato cannot be stored so that the scarcity of one year may be alleviated by bringing forward the reserves of former years, as is always done in corn-feeding countries. Every year is thus left to provide subsistence for itself. When the crop is luxuriant, the surplus must be given to the pigs; and when it is deficient, famine and disease necessarily prevail. Lastly, the bulk of potatoes is such, that they can with difficulty be conveyed from place to place to supply local deficiencies, and it has often happened that severe scarcity has prevailed in districts within fifty miles of which potatoes were to be had in abundance. If a man use two pounds of meal a day (which is twice the amount of the ration found to be sufficient during the late relief operations), a hundredweight of meal will last him for fifty-six days; whereas a hundredweight of potatoes will not last more than eight days; and when it was proposed to provide seed potatoes for those who had lost their stock in the failure of 1845-46, the plan was found impracticable, because nearly a ton an acre would have been required for the purpose.

Potatoes on sale at Youghal, Co. Cork, 1831; from a sketch-book by Sampson Towgood Roch. (Private collection.)

Sir Charles Edward Trevelyan (1807-86).
(Hulton-Deutsch Collection.)

The potato does not, in fact, last even a single year. The old crop becomes unfit for use in July, and the new crop, as raised by the inferior husbandry of the poor, does not come into consumption until September; hence, July and August are called the 'meal months', from the necessity the people are under of living upon meal at that period. This is always a season of great distress and trial for the poorer peasants; and in the districts in which the potato system has been carried to the greatest extent, as, for instance, in the barony of Erris in the county of Mayo, there has been an annual dearth in the summer months for many years past. Every now and then a 'meal year' occurs, and then masses of the population become a prey to famine and fever, except so far as they may be relieved by charity.

In 1739, an early and severe frost destroyed the potatoes in the ground, and the helplessness and despair of the people having led to a great falling off of tillage in 1740, the calamity was prolonged to the ensuing year, 1741, which was long known as the

bliadhain an áir, or year of slaughter. The ordinary burial-grounds were not large enough to contain those who died by the roadside, or who were taken from the deserted cabins. The 'bloody flux' [bacillary dysentery] and 'malignant fever', having begun among the poor, spread to the rich, and numerous individuals occupying prominent positions in society, including one of the judges, Mr Baron Wainwright, and the Mayor of Limerick, Joseph Roche, Esq., and many others of the corporation, fell victims. Measures were adopted at Dublin on the principle of the English Poor Law, some of the most essential provisions of which appear to have been well understood in the great towns of Ireland in that day; and it was 'hoped, since such provision is made for the poor, the inhabitants of the city will discourage all vagrant beggars, and give their assistance that they may be sent to bridewell to hard labour, and thereby free themselves from a set of idlers who are a scandal and a reproach to the nation'. Soup kitchens and other modes of relief were established in different parts of the country, in which Primate Boulter and the Society of Friends took the lead; and numerous cargoes of corn were procured on mercantile account from the North American Colonies, the arrival of which was looked for with great anxiety. In only one point is there any decided difference between what then took place in Ireland and the painful events which have just occurred, after the lapse of upwards of a century. The famine of 1741 was not regarded with any active interest either in England or in any foreign country, and the subject is scarcely alluded to in the literature of the day. No measures were adopted either by the executive or the legislature for the purpose of relieving the distress caused by this famine. There is no mention of grants or loans; but an act was passed by the Irish parliament in 1741 (15 George II, chapter 8), 'For the more effectual securing the payment of rents, and preventing frauds by tenants'.

(C.E. Trevelyan, *The Irish crisis,* 1848, p. 9-13. He attributes the details of the 1740-41 famine to 'Mr McCullagh, who has lately collected the contemporary accounts of this famine', i.e. William Torrens McCullagh, Private Secretary to the Chief Secretary, and later a distinguished historian and politician.)

4. *The coming of the potato blight*

*I*n *June 1845, a new potato disease was observed in Belgium. By mid-August it was in the Isle of Wight, and within days there were sightings in southern England. David Moore, curator of the Royal Dublin Society's Botanic Gardens at Glasnevin, was alerted by the reports, and noted the first symptoms of the disease at Glasnevin on 20 August. By the beginning of September, the newspapers were reporting outbreaks in various parts of the country. The English horticultural magazine,* The Gardeners' Chronicle, *which reported the progress of the disease over the summer, was concerned at the implications for Ireland, with its three million people dependent on potatoes. On 13 September, it interrupted the presses to include the announcement that the disease had reached Ireland.*

Extract from a report by Moore to the Royal Dublin Society.

Being aware of the intense anxiety felt by you, in common with a large portion of inhabitants of the British Islands, at the consequences likely to result from the destruction of so great a portion of the potato crop, and observing the steady onward movement the epidemic is still making, I consider it my duty at once to communicate to you the results of my experience in the matter; trusting that you will deem any ascertained practical facts of importance at the present moment when the cause and nature of the malady are so little understood. From the first intimation given by Dr Lindley of the potato crop in England being attacked, my attention was turned to the subject, as I fully expected it would reach this country, judging from the progress it had made from the Continent to the Channel Islands, thence to the southern counties; and considering it, as I still do,

epidemic, I was consequently watching the appearance of the potato fields here, and observed the first symptoms on the 20th of August. On the first week in September, I accompanied a gentleman to see a field on the Earl of Charlemont's demesne, which was then a good deal affected, and at the same time received communications on the subject and samples of diseased potatoes from several persons in this neighbourhood, affording proofs that the disease was beginning to be general about Dublin at that period, as I stated in a letter published in the *Irish Farmers' Journal* on the 10th September, and also my opinion of the nature of the disease, which subsequent events have, to a great extent, corroborated to have been correct.

(*Irish Farmers' Journal,* 5 Nov. 1845.)

David Moore (1807-79).

References to potato blight in Ireland.

In the part of *The Evening Post* dedicated to the interests of the farming world, we have made rather an ample report of a matter of great importance indeed, namely, the failure of the potato crop – very extensively in the United States, to a great extent in Flanders and France, and to an appreciable amount in England. We have heard something of the kind in our own country – especially along the coast – but we believe that no apprehension whatever is entertained even of a partial failure of the potato crop in Ireland.

Nevertheless, it is impossible that the subject can be otherwise in Ireland than one of the deepest interest, and it, therefore, became an imperative duty on our parts to collect all the information we could accumulate on the matter. The result will be found in the place we have indicated, and we should suppose that there is hardly one of our readers who will not peruse the different statements with interest...

The human, the brute, and the vegetable creations, we know from experience, are subjected to periodical checks. Plague and cholera are sufficient examples in the first case; the distemper amongst cattle in the second; and the great mortality of the eel in the Boyne, and, perhaps, in other streams, if the matter was investigated, in the third. With regard to the vegetable world, it is well known to the husbandman, that you must not continue, for more than two seasons or three, the same sort of crop on the same ground. It deteriorates – it becomes non-productive. But none of the reasons which supply an explanation to these phenomena can account for the general and apparently simultaneous failure of the potato in the United States and in several parts of Europe...

But, the general failures of which we read, are producing serious apprehensions. Yet, surely the United States have little real cause to fear. If the potato were entirely extirpated, the people would enjoy an ample sufficiency of food. It is in the densely packed communities of Europe that the failure would be alarming, and in no country more, or so much, than in our own.

But, happily, there is no ground for any apprehensions of the kind in Ireland. There may have been partial failures in some localities; but, we believe that there was never a more abundant potato crop in Ireland than there is at present.

(*The Dublin Evening Post,* 9 Sept. 1845.)

The Gardeners' Chronicle.

SATURDAY, SEPTEMBER 13, 1845.

MEETINGS FOR THE TWO FOLLOWING WEEKS.
WEDNESDAY, Sept. 17—South London Floricultural . 1 P.M.

COUNTRY SHOWS.
WEDNESDAY, Sept. 17—Hexham Floral and Horticultural.
FRIDAY, Sept. 19—Devon and Exeter Botanical and Hort.
THURSDAY, Sept. 25—Surrey Horticultural and Floral.

WE stop the Press, with very great regret, to announce that the POTATO MURRAIN has unequivocally declared itself in Ireland. The crops about Dublin are suddenly perishing. The conversion of Potatoes into flour, by the processes described by Mr. BABINGTON and others in to-day's Paper, becomes then a process of the first national importance; for where will Ireland be, in the event of a universal Potato rot?

5. The nature of the disease

Botanists and horticulturalists did not understand the nature of the potato blight. The general consensus was that the decay was caused by excessive humidity that summer, and that a fungus which was discernible on the stalks was the result of the decay and was a symptom of the disease rather than the source. The Rev. Miles Berkeley, an English clergyman, identified the fungus as the cause, but his suggestion was scotched by the editor of The Gardeners' Chronicle, Dr John Lindley, and other eminent authorities. David Moore was initially inclined to attribute the disease to climatic factors. However, on the basis of a series of experiments carried out at Glasnevin over the next year, he concluded that Berkeley was correct and that the fungus was indeed responsible.

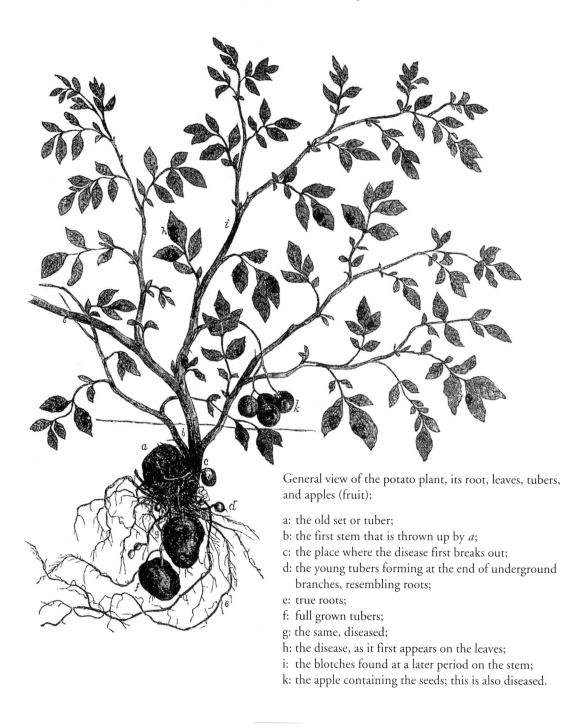

General view of the potato plant, its root, leaves, tubers, and apples (fruit);

a: the old set or tuber;

b: the first stem that is thrown up by *a*;

c: the place where the disease first breaks out;

d: the young tubers forming at the end of underground branches, resembling roots;

e: true roots;

f: full grown tubers;

g: the same, diseased;

h: the disease, as it first appears on the leaves;

i: the blotches found at a later period on the stem;

k: the apple containing the seeds; this is also diseased.

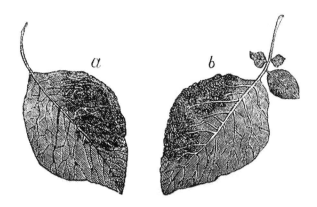

Above. The blotches on the potato leaf; *a* shows the upper side, on which there is no mouldiness; *b* presents the under side, with white spots which indicate the presence of the mould.

Right. A diseased stem with the lower leaves dead, and the upper attacked by the disease. Here, the blotches on the stem are running into the state of gangrene.

(*The Illustrated London News,* 29 Aug. 1846.)

'Destitution in Ireland – failure of the potato crop'. (*The Pictorial Times,* 22 Aug. 1846.)

6. Attempts at preserving potatoes

Potato blight can be prevented but not cured. Once a crop is infected and the fungus reaches the tubers, there are no effective remedial measures. Even cutting down the stalks is rarely of much use, as the disease has already invaded the tubers by the time it becomes evident on the leaves. Various remedies were suggested and tried; they included running ventilation shafts through the pits, storing the potatoes in lime, and cutting off the uninfected parts. By April 1846, Moore's experiments had shown that diseased tubers decayed no matter how they were stored, that infected seed propagated the disease and, more ominously, that the new season's crop already showed signs of blight.

Paiṁt don' liṫip fip Seaȝaiṗe 'ran Iaṗċap.

Ċum cunȝṅaṁ a ṫaḃaipṫ dona ḣuiliḃ a mḃeiȝ ciocṗaċ cum na llaṁ a ċuip aip an oḃaip, ṫaipḃeanḟeaḋ me foipṁ na ḃpoll map d'opduiȝeap a mḃeiṫ deanṫa; ⁊ b-feidip ȝo mḃeiċ an pic-ṫúippe ṗíop upaideaċ dóiḃ:—

() Poll-ȝaoiṫe.

Toȝ ionad ṫipim ṫpeanuiṁil don ḃpoll. An pin dean poll-ȝaoiṫe leaṫan ȝo leoip, aip ḃappa na ṫalṁan, a ḃfoipṁ ṫipipe opȝuilṫe no aḃfoipṁ lipṫeipe, le ȝeapaḋ ṫipipe naoi noipluiȝe no ṫpoiȝ aip leaṫaḋ ⁊ aip doiṁneaċd, ⁊ le cuip mion cloċ aip a dṫpeapna aip. Tappaiȝ an ṫipipe no an lipṫeipe aip fad an ṗoill ⁊ faȝ opȝuilṫe 'na da ċeann e, ioṅup ȝo nȝeaḃaċ an ȝaoċ ṫpid ȝo ċaopȝa. Ċum na ȝaoiṫe a ȝaḃail ṅíop feap (an ṅíd ip ṅíop ṅioċdanaiċe,) dean poill-ȝaoiṫe a dṫaoḃaiḃ an ṗoill a m-ballaiḃ ȝo ṅeapanṫa a b-fad o ċeile. Aip uplaip an ṫipipe pe dȝnṫaip an poll, aȝ ṫaḃaipṫ aipe aip poill-ȝaoiṫe d'faȝail aȝ an ḃappa, ċum an ȝal a leiȝinȝ amaċ. Ip upaipd e po a deanaṁ le fóid a ċapaḋ ṫiomċuil feaċ ṗáine.

An aon focal ȝaḃaċ an ȝaoċ ȝan ċopȝ faoi an b-poll, ⁊ bioċ pliȝe ealuiȝṫe aice ap a ḃappa. Aip a pliȝe po coiṁeadṫeap an poll an b-fuap, coipȝpuiȝeap ȝo ċiomlan o ċeiṁ e, ⁊ ṫabalpuip na poṫaṫaoi aip a fon ȝo ṅabaḃap ȝaiṅaiċe, ⁊ aiciḃeaċ. Do fuapap map pin e le mo ṗollaiḃ fein. An meid, do cuippeaḋ 'ra poll aiciḃeaċ ⁊ boȝ ṫanȝaḃap ap ċpuaiȝ ṫippim, ⁊ do ċuiṫ an ċuid diomḃalaċ díoḃ map ȝaṅb ṫippim le pȝpioḃ na ċuinȝṅe, a ḃfaȝailṫ na díaiȝ na poṫaṫaoi ṫippim ⁊ plán.

Extract from the Letter of a "Western Rector."

To assist all who may be desirous to lay their hands to the work, I shall describe the pits as I have directed them to be formed; and perhaps the subjoined diagram may aid them:—

() Air Pipe.

Let a dry and airy site be chosen for the pit; then let an air-pipe or funnel be made, of tolerable width, either on the surface of the ground, in form of a French drain, or in that of a lintern, by cutting a trench nine inches or a foot in depth and breadth, and laying stones loosely across it; and let this funnel be carried the whole intended length of the pit, and left open at both ends, freely to admit the air. To render the ventilation—and ventilation is the great desideratum—still more complete, let air-holes be made in the sides of the pit, at moderate distances.

Over this frame-work let the pit be constructed, care being taken to leave valves or air-holes at the top, which may be done by the simple process of a sod turned round the handle of a spade, to permit the escape of the heated air. In a word, *let the air pass freely underneath the pit, and allow it an easy escape above.* Thus will the pit be kept cool—the progress of fermentation effectually checked—and the Potato, even though diseased, preserved. I found it so with my own pits. The Potato, which was put in diseased and soft, came out dry and hard, and the affected part came off by a touch of the nail like a dry scab, leaving the Potato dry and healed beneath it.

(National Archives, Relief Commission Papers, 1/2 Z 17206.)

SUGGESTIONS
TO
COTTAGERS
In COOKING their
POTATOES.

Commence with YOUR DISEASED POTATOES, by washing them well, then peel or scrape off the skins, carefully cutting out such parts as are discoloured; cut the large Potatoes to the size of the smaller ones, and steep them for a short time in salt and water.

Provide a few cabbage leaves (the white kind is the most suitable;) steep them in cold water, then line the bottom and sides of a common metal or oven pot, with the wet leaves; pack in it, the peeled Potatoes in layers, shaking salt and pepper over each layer until the vessel is nearly full; spread more wet cabbage leaves over them, cover all close down with a lid, and set them on a hot-hearth, or a moderate fire, as too hot a fire might be attended with risk.

The object of the above-mentioned method is, that the Potatoes should be cooked through the medium of their own moisture, instead of the usual mode of steaming or boiling them in water.

The following additions may be made by those who can afford to improve upon the above, by introducing sliced Onions, salt Herring, salt Butter, salt Pork, Lard or Bacon cut in slices, or small pieces, or Rice, previously boiled.

It would be found more economical, instead of peeling, to scrape off the skins of such Potatoes as are only slightly discoloured, or altogether free from taint.

Those who have a Cow or Pigs to feed should collect the peelings and rejected portions of the Potatoes, steep them for some time in salt and water, then pack them in a metal pot, in layers, with cabbage leaves, sprinkling salt over each layer, and cook them as above directed; if found necessary, a little Bran or Oatmeal may be added.

Derryluskan, 1st December, 1845.

E. WOODS. PRINTER, CLONMEL.

(National Archives, Relief Commission Papers, 676.)

III

RELIEF UNDER THE CONSERVATIVES

In the autumn of 1845, when it became obvious that a serious disease was affecting the potato crop, there were many calls for the government to intervene. The government had provided relief in previous food crises and, indeed, the Prime Minister, Sir Robert Peel, had administered £250,000 in relief works during the partial famine of 1816-17 when he was Chief Secretary for Ireland. The situation was almost certain to require government intervention, as the only state welfare available was that provided under the Poor Law Act of 1838, that is, the hated workhouse system. To avail of this form of relief, one had to live in a workhouse, and perform tedious work. The capacity of the workhouses was limited, but adequate in the period prior to the Famine, as only the utterly destitute had recourse to a workhouse.

In 1845, Peel and the Conservative party (Tories) were unpopular with Irish nationalists due to their resolute opposition to repeal of the Union, which culminated in their jailing of Daniel O'Connell and other activists the previous year. Peel, however, was familiar with conditions in Ireland and was well aware that a widespread failure of the potato crop could be devastating. In devising relief measures, he faced a formidable political problem. Personally, he believed that to provide relief for the numbers likely to need it would necessitate importing cheap corn, which could be done economically only if import duties were lifted. But tampering with the Corn Laws was anathema to the Conservatives, as British consumers and farmers were protected by tariffs, and believed they would suffer if free trade in foodstuffs was allowed. Faced with this difficulty, Peel quietly arranged for the importation of a quantity of Indian corn from the United States, a commodity in which there was little trade and which was largely independent of the Corn Laws.

In November, Peel established the Relief Commission to plan and administer the relief. It included representatives of the various agencies which were to have a role, namely, the constabulary, the army commissariat, the coastguard, the Board of Works, and the Poor Law Commission. It was to operate partly through local committees, some of which had already been established. Their role was to raise subscriptions, organise employment schemes, and arrange for the purchase of cheap food, which they would sell or, in cases of real hardship, dole out free.

In 1845-46 and indeed throughout the Famine, the general problem was not that there was an absolute shortage of food but rather that a large percentage of the population did not have the money to buy what was available. Early in 1846, the situation was exacerbated because dealers put their prices up to levels which were beyond the reach of those most in need. In the winter and early spring, there was little employment, especially in the countryside, and money was scarce. To remedy this situation, the Government provided loans for public works, but worthwhile schemes proved difficult to get under way; only a small percentage of the destitute derived any benefit from the works schemes in the spring or summer of 1846.

Peel's supplies of corn eventually arrived and were stored in commissariat depots. The corn was sold by commissariat officials or local relief committees at a price calculated to recover costs. To conserve stocks, some depots did not open until as late as May, when people were already virtually starving; even then supplies were inadequate, especially in remote areas in the south-west and west. The total quantity was not very significant and has been estimated to amount to an iron ration of a pound of meal a day for half a million people for three months. But Peel's imports had an important secondary role in that they stabilised prices for other foodstuffs such as flour and oatmeal.

In June 1846, Peel eventually succeeded in virtually eliminating import duties on corn products. But he immediately paid the price when a group of aggrieved Conservatives failed to support him in a crucial vote. He went out of office, however, in the knowledge that few, if any, had died of starvation during his management of the crisis. But, in the great tragic drama then unfolding, the season 1845-46 turned out to be merely the prelude.

1. Peel's dilemma

The potato blight was first reported in August 1845, but it was only when the digging of the main crop began in October that the full extent of the loss become apparent. The news was conveyed to Peel by the Lord Lieutenant, Lord Heytesbury, and they exchanged letters setting out their views on the situation and on possible courses of action. The Lord Lieutenant was the representative of the Crown in Ireland; in practice, he was responsible for implementing government policy. The administration was based in Dublin Castle and was directed by the Chief Secretary and the Under Secretary.

Letter of Sir Robert Peel to Lord Heytesbury.

Drayton Manor, 15 October 1845.

My Dear Lord Heytesbury,

The accounts from Ireland of the potato crop, confirmed as they are by your high authority, are very alarming… The remedy is the removal of all impediments to the import of all kinds of human food – that is, the total and absolute repeal for ever of all duties on all articles of subsistence.

I believe that, practically, there would be no alternative. To remit the duty on Indian corn expressly for the purpose of averting famine would make it very invidious to retain a duty on other species of corn more generally applicable to the food of man. You might remit nominally for one year; but who will re-establish the Corn Laws once abrogated, though from a casual and temporary pressure? I have good ground, therefore, for stating that the application of a temporary remedy to a temporary evil does in this particular case involve considerations of the utmost and most lasting importance.

You must therefore send us from time to time the most authentic information you can. There is such a tendency in Ireland to disregard accuracy and to exaggerate, that one is unwilling to give hasty credence to Irish statements. There can, however, I fear, be no reason to doubt that the failure of the potato crop will be very general.

Has the recent fine weather (which has, I presume, extended to Ireland) had a favourable effect? What is the price of potatoes in the different markets? Is that price rapidly increasing? I fear the lowness of price – even if it exist – might be no indication of abundance. There might be an undue quantity of inferior potatoes sent for sale, for fear of rapid decay if they were kept on hand. Can you employ any persons to collect information to be relied on, in the chief potato-growing districts in Ireland? Would a person of intelligence specially sent to Galway, Cork, etc., etc., have better means of ascertaining the facts and the prospects of the failure than can be derived from written reports from stipendiary magistrates or others?

I need not recommend to you the utmost reserve as to the future, I mean as to the possibility of government interference. There would be none without summoning parliament to adopt measures or confirm those of the executive.

(*Memoirs of Sir Robert Peel by Lord Mahon and Edward Cardwell*, London, 1856-57, II-III, p.121-3.)

Sir Robert Peel (1788-1850). (Hulton-Deutsch Collection.)

Letter of Lord Heytesbury to Sir Robert Peel.

Vice-Regal Lodge, 17 October.

My Dear Sir Robert,
I have to acknowledge yours of the 15th, which I have communicated most confidentially to Sir Thomas Fremantle [Secretary at War].

We are very fully impressed with the immense importance of the question, and the consequences to which it may lead. Our attention has been earnestly directed to it, ever since the reports from the provinces have been so unsatisfactory. These reports continue to be of a very alarming nature, and leave no doubt upon the mind but that the potato crops have failed almost everywhere. I enclose an abstract of those received yesterday. A more favourable account indeed has been received by Mr. A'Court [Private Secretary] from the Dean of Ossory [Rev. Charles Vignoles], whose letter I also enclose; but I must observe that the Dean, though a sensible, is a somewhat sanguine man, and is apt to view matters in the most favourable light.

I am not inclined to think that a special commission would be able to collect more accurate information than that which is furnished by the several county inspectors. When the potato-digging is a little more advanced, we might move the lieutenants of counties to call meetings of the resident landholders, with a view to ascertaining the amount of the evil, and their opinion of the measures most proper to be adopted...

Even if the crops would turn out to be as bad as is now apprehended, it is not thought that there will be any immediate pressure in the market. There will be enough saved for immediate consumption. The evil will probably not be felt in all its intensity till towards the month of February, or beginning of spring. I am assured that there is no stock whatever of last year's potatoes in the country. Gloomy as all this is, it would be hardly prudent to adopt any very strong or decisive measures till the final result of the potato harvest can be fully ascertained. The digging will not be all over till about the second week in November.

I may refer you for what was done upon a former occasion to various proclamations of Lord Cornwallis in the years 1800-1, and to Acts, 41 George III, chapter 36, renewed by 43 George III, chapter 13. These acts are no longer in force, having only been passed to meet the difficulties then existing. [The acts prohibited the exportation of corn, potatoes and provisions from Ireland.]

(*Memoirs of Sir Robert Peel*, II-III, p.123-5.)

'The Minister's Dream'; a cartoon depicting Peel wrestling with the problems posed by potatoes and corn, and beset with political opponents, including Daniel O'Connell. (*The Pictorial Times*, 22 Nov. 1845; courtesy of NLS.)

2. Quantifying the loss

It was difficult to get accurate information on the extent of the potato failure as the disease seemed to strike at random and the pattern was not uniform around the country. To ascertain the likely deficit in the crop, the government asked for weekly reports from the constabulary, and information was also forwarded by various officials and community leaders. The army commissariat which was involved in managing the relief depots eventually tabulated and published the data. Among those who reported on the situation was the board of guardians of the Tralee Poor Law union (the area serviced by the Tralee workhouse).

Report from Tralee board of guardians, 11 November 1845.

This board, having anxiously sought and obtained what they consider accurate information relative to the disease so general thro' the potato crop within their union (one of the largest in Ireland), offer the following as the result of their enquiries and of their own inspection and observations in different localities, without any intention on the one hand of creating unnecessary alarm, or on the other of withholding such information as may induce the adoption of measures calculated to guard against the worst.

It is then the opinion of this board that one-third, at least, of the crop, which however exceeded an average one, has been totally lost, and it appears that the white [Lumper] potato, that which our peasantry consume, has suffered most, but all kinds have suffered more or less, and no locality, that we can ascertain, has escaped.

We trust that, under providence, much of the remaining part may be saved, but it is our opinion that, even supposing such to be the case, the price will rise to such a height as must render the substitution of other foods indispensably necessary for the support of human life.

The farmers are now using every precaution, such as ventilation and separation of the sound from the unsound potatoes – they have no other means in their power, as few, if any of them, have house-room for more than perhaps a week or ten days consumption. Since these precautions have been taken, the disease, it would appear, has been very much checked, except in cases where the potatoes were pitted, and it is to be hoped that, under providence, a considerable portion of the remaining will be saved.

When we consider that our peasantry are entirely dependent on the potato for food, we cannot but feel that even the slightest indication to failure must create alarm; but in the present case, alarm to a considerable extent is warranted, taking into consideration the loss already sustained, and the uncertainty which prevails as to the safety of the remaining part of the crop.

Finally, and upon mature consideration, we feel it our duty to state that, in our opinion, every precaution should be taken in time for the substitution of human foods which the prevalent disease in the crop so urgently calls for. We do not now advert to another calamity which, we much fear, will also result from the present failure, which is the supply of seed for the ensuing season.

This report is made up to the present day only, and this board has to observe that a great portion of the crop remains still in the ground.

Signed,

John Hurley, Chairman,

24 guardians being present.

(National Archives, Relief Commission Papers, 215700.)

Return showing the proportion of actual crop lost.

| | | | | Proportion of actual crop lost in electoral divisions | | | | | | | | | | Number of electoral divisions not yet returned | Total number of electoral divisions |
| | | None | Not Exceeding | Exceeding $^1/_{10}$ | Exceeding $^2/_{10}$ | Exceeding $^3/_{10}$ | Exceeding $^4/_{10}$ | Exceeding $^5/_{10}$ | Exceeding $^6/_{10}$ | Exceeding $^7/_{10}$ | Exceeding $^8/_{10}$ | Exceeding $^9/_{10}$ | | |
			$^1/_{10}$	Not Exc. $^2/_{10}$	$^3/_{10}$	$^4/_{10}$	$^5/_{10}$	$^6/_{10}$	$^7/_{10}$	$^8/_{10}$	$^9/_{10}$	$^{10}/_{10}$		
Ulster	Antrim	...	...	...	4	35	50	8	20	11	4	...	...	132
	Armagh	...	...	3	11	24	6	...	...	...	...	...	...	44
	Cavan	...	...	...	5	5	10	...	...	3	...	...	23	46
	Donegal	3	7	20	13	29	21	...	...	3	...	...	1	103
	Down	...	...	4	16	40	27	2	4	3	...	...	...	96
	Fermanagh	...	18	4	6	8	3	...	4	...	...	...	...	43
	Londonderry	...	11	...	29	17	24	...	1	4	...	...	...	86
	Monaghan	...	3	5	2	11	17	2	15	6	...	...	...	61
	Tyrone	4	53	22	15	11	23	...	2	2	...	...	...	132
Munster	Clare	...	...	3	1	11	25	...	10	4	...	...	...	54
	Cork	...	...	16	25	91	43	...	2	1	...	...	...	178
	Kerry	...	2	3	13	29	15	...	4	1	...	...	...	67
	Limerick	1	...	5	9	19	25	...	9	5	...	...	...	73
	Tipperary	1	...	12	15	33	63	1	7	5	...	...	...	137
	Waterford	...	...	...	3	4	18	...	9	14	...	...	1	49
Leinster	Carlow	...	...	...	...	...	...	...	...	...	...	...	14	14
	Dublin	...	2	3	4	12	8	...	1	8	...	...	1	39
	Kildare	...	4	6	7	29	4	...	1	1	...	...	...	52
	Kilkenny	...	...	...	...	9	19	...	6	...	...	...	...	34
	King's [Offaly]	...	...	2	4	19	6	...	1	...	...	...	21	53
	Longford	...	...	5	6	10	11	...	2	...	...	...	...	34
	Louth	...	...	...	4	4	23	...	3	10	...	...	...	44
	Meath	...	...	2	11	11	27	1	3	7	...	...	...	62
	Queen's [Laois]	...	2	...	5	11	5	1	3	...	...	...	...	27
	Westmeath	...	...	1	7	3	6	1	1	...	...	...	26	45
	Wexford	...	1	5	9	20	18	...	4	...	...	...	...	57
	Wicklow	...	1	6	10	17	6	...	2	...	...	...	...	42
Connaught	Galway	...	1	5	6	26	31	...	6	1	...	...	...	76
	Leitrim	...	...	3	8	15	11	...	...	1	...	...	...	38
	Mayo	...	3	12	11	6	15	...	3	1	...	...	12	63
	Roscommon	...	2	...	1	20	25	...	2	2	...	...	...	52
	Sligo	...	...	...	9	3	11	...	...	...	...	...	...	23
	Gross Total	9	110	153	269	582	596	16	125	93	4	...	99	2056

(*Correspondence explanatory of the measures adopted by H.M. government for the relief of distress ...* p. 36; P.P. 1846 (735) XXXVII.)

3. *Indian corn*

*I*n previous food crises, Indian corn had been imported as it was cheap and was considered suitable for feeding large numbers in time of emergency. Peel was already well aware of its merits, but in a letter of 5 November Commissary-General Hewetson brought it to his notice and recommended its use. Peel acted swiftly and without waiting for cabinet sanction commissioned the London bankers, Baring Brothers, to arrange the purchase and importation of £100,000 worth of Indian corn from the United States. An additional £45,000 was spent in the United Kingdom and the total cost amounted to £152,000. While significant, this expenditure was minimal considering that the deficit in the potato crop was estimated to have cost three million pounds.

Letter of Commissary-General Hewetson to Peel and Peel's reply.

Southampton, 5 November 1845.

Trusting the subject of this communication will apologise for my presumption in addressing the first minister of the Crown, I beg leave most respectfully to bring under your notice, with reference to the want to be apprehended among the labouring classes in this country and Ireland, arising out of the disease so generally fatal to the potato crops, that a cheap, nutritious, and excellent substitute for the potato, viz, Indian corn-meal, can be procured in great abundance in the United States of America, at a cost, in comparison with other substitutes, exceedingly low. My long residence in North America as a public officer enables me to state, with great confidence, that should Her Majesty's government contemplate the formation of magazines in this country and Ireland for the supply, in the course of the winter, of food to the destitute classes, Indian corn-meal would be the cheapest substitute for the potato, equally, if not more substantially, nutritious, and as simple in its mode of preparation. Its use in the United States is most universal among the peasantry and labouring people. Should its introduction by Her Majesty's government into this country for this specific purpose be deemed expedient by prompt and secret measures, it can be cheaply and readily purchased to any extent, and shipped from the ports of New York and Baltimore so as to arrive here in January 1846; the arrangement would, of course, be temporary to meet an emergency; and should such an emergency be proved, I have no hesitation in adding that Indian corn-meal in every point of view, with great economy

as a leading feature, is one of the best descriptions of supply that can be laid in for gratuitous distribution. Whatever prejudices, if any, may exist as to its use as an article of food in this country, will, I should say, on trial, with simple directions for its preparation, immediately cease.

Respectfully soliciting to apologise for intruding this letter.

Whitehall, 9 November.

Sir Robert Peel presents his compliments to Mr Hewetson, and is much obliged by the communication which Mr Hewetson has very properly addressed directly to Sir Robert Peel.

(*Correspondence explanatory ... distress ...* p. 1; P.P. 1846 (735) XXXVII.)

Indian corn and Indian corn-meal imported by Baring Brothers.

Indian corn. (*The Pictorial Times,* 28 Feb. 1846; courtesy of NLS.)

Per Adirondack	Cargo	£6,985	18	4
	Freight and charges	1,842	4	5
Per Atlas	Cargo	8,584	12	2
	Freight, &c.	2,062	16	5
	Ditto underclaimed	3	15	11
Per Rainbow	Cargo	3,907	7	11
	Freight, &c.	987	1	7
Per Winnipiac	Cargo	4,402	13	7
	Freight, &c	1,126	17	10
Per Elsinore	Cargo	6,403	8	10
	Freight, &c.	1,566	4	11
Per Harriet Rockwell	Cargo	4,455	3	6
	Freight, &c.	1,391	2	5
	Demurrage &c.	127	12	1
Per Arab	Cargo		(Lost)	
Per Ohio	Cargo	3,923	15	4
	Freight, &c.	1,024	7	4
Per Trident	Cargo	3,807	11	6
	Freight, &c.	966	14	3
Per Liberty	Cargo	7,258	5	3
	Freight, &c.	1,436	1	4
Per Edinburgh	Cargo	3,476	6	0
	Freight, &c.	874	2	4
Per Empire	Cargo	12,134	7	9
	Freight, &c.	1,976	16	0
Per Cornelia	Cargo	11,758	6	8
	Cargo and freight	2,000	0	0
	Balance of ditto	215	15	9
Per Almade	Cargo	4,795	17	7
	Freight, &c.	1,02	9	11
Total from United States		**£105,256**	**8**	**8**

(*Correspondence explanatory ... distress ...* p. 249; P.P. 1846 (735) XXXVII.)

4. *The local relief committees*

The Relief Commission was first established in November 1845 and was reconstituted the following February. The new chairman was Sir Randolph Routh, Commissary-General. The Commission co-ordinated the efforts of local relief committees, of which there were 648 by August 1846. Some, however, had difficulties in raising subscriptions and many were ineffective and merely nominal. The Commission published guidelines for their operation, sections of which are reproduced here. It received numerous letters relating to the affairs of the local committees, such as that of the parish priest of Kilgeever, Co. Mayo, the text of which is given on the next page.

Extracts from instructions for relief committees.

The Commission having had under their consideration the necessity of establishing local committees, properly organized in the several districts where destitution is likely to prevail, through whose superintendence the approach and progress of distress in such localities may be watched, and the means of relief administered according to the instructions of government:

It is resolved,

1. That lieutenants of counties be requested to form committees for conveniently-sized relief districts, in those cases where it shall be established on good and sufficient grounds that very considerable loss of the potato crop has been sustained, and that extreme distress is near at hand. That these committees be comprised of the following classes:

Lieutenant or deputy lieutenant of the county.

Magistrates of petty sessions.

Officer of Board of Works.

Clergymen of all persuasions.

Chairman of Poor Law union of the locality.

Poor Law guardians of electoral district or districts.

Coastguard officer, where available.

Resident magistrate,

and such other active and intelligent gentlemen as the lieutenant may select.

5. That the measures to be adopted by the officers of government are to be considered merely as auxiliary to those which it is the duty of the persons possessed of property in each neighbourhood to adopt. That the local committee should, therefore, put themselves in communication with such persons, and should solicit subscriptions from them proportioned to their means and to the extent of distress in the locality to which they belong.

In cases where there may arise a scarcity of food within a district, or the price of food may have been artificially raised, the government will be prepared to transmit to the local committee, at cost price, including the expense of carriage, a quantity of food corresponding to the amount of the subscriptions paid in for that purpose, and to place that food in the hands of the local committee for distribution on their own responsibility, at cost price, or as wages of labour to destitute persons employed on local works, or when absolute destitution is united with inability to labour, in gratuitous donations.

6. That some few and very particular instances may occur in which the necessary relief cannot be afforded by funds derived from the proprietors, or voluntary associations, of the district. In such instances, stations will be established in the distressed localities for the distribution of relief, subject to the rules hereafter detailed. The distribution of such relief will be conducted by the Commissary-General, through the agency of the commissariat, of the coastguard, or of the constabulary, with the co-operation of the local committee of the district, whose duty will be particularly directed to the selection of proper objects for relief, the preservation of the stores, and the accurate account of their appropriation, which will be duly entered on their records.

7. That in cases wherein any assistance is afforded by government, either in aid of local subscriptions, or otherwise, the following rules are to be invariably observed in the administration of relief:

1st – A task of work shall be required from every person capable of giving it, who applies for relief.

4th – Gratuitous relief shall be afforded only to those persons who are entirely incapable of giving a day's work, and who have no able-bodied relative on whom they are dependent, and these cases only in which their reception in the workhouse of the union to which they belong, is, from want of room, impracticable.

John Pitt Kennedy, Secretary.

Castle, Dublin, 28 February 1846.

(NLI Ms 8474(6), Sir Richard Bourke Papers; a slightly variant text is in a Treasury minute in *Correspondence explanatory ... distress ...* p. 249; P.P. 1846 (735) XXXVII.)

Letter of parish priest of Kilgeever, Co. Mayo to Relief Commission.

Louisburgh, Westport, 27 April 1846.

Sir, I beg to acknowledge the receipt of your letter of the 24th instant conveying to me the request of the Commissioners to communicate with the Lieutenant of the County Mayo with a view to his appointing a committee of relief for this distressed district.

I beg to state for the information of the Commissioners that we do not know the address of the Lieutenant of this county; we are informed that he is, at present, in some part of England. I beg further to say that I deplore the existence of any necessity to urge the Commissioners to give such directions, as the destitution and wretchedness of the people are so very close upon us, and have been already felt by many of the people, that relief should be given promptly and immediately; the small quantities of potatoes that are for sale have reached already a famine price. Typhus fever, diarrhoea and dysentery are rife amongst the people, many of whom have fallen victims to their virulence. There is but one resident gentleman in this parish – Mr James Garvey of Tully; there are no magistrates, none but the clergy to convey the wants of the people. Under these circumstances, a committee has been formed today, composed of individuals best qualified to administer to a suffering people the relief of government, viz: Mr James Garvey, Doctors Fergus and Durkin, Messrs John Comber, George Lynch and Michael Carroll, along with the local clergy.

Now, I beg most earnestly to submit that we have done every thing in our power to meet the reasonable wishes of the Commissioners. In the absence of any of the magistracy – in the absence of the Lieutenant of the county, and with absentee landlords, we do not see what else we could do but what we have done. We beg, therefore, most earnestly of the Commissioners not to suffer the people to starve. We seek not alms, we solicit employment. But, whatever the mode of relief be, we again repeat our hope that the people will not be allowed to starve.

I have the honour to be,

Sir, your obedient servant, Patrick MacManus, Parish Priest of Kilgeever.

(National Archives, Relief Commission Papers, 1884.)

5. *The arrival of Indian corn*

The first of Peel's Indian corn was offered for sale at Cork, Clonmel and Longford on 28 March, but some depots did not open until the middle of May. Moreover, it proved difficult to supply remote areas where the need was greatest. The general operation of the scheme was erratic and patchy, which accounts for mixed reports. For example, Cork City was close to source and was reasonably well supplied. The views of the Cork City Grand Jury given here may not, however, represent the general feeling in Cork City; contemporary reports on many aspects of the Famine were often coloured by political or class prejudice.

Resolutions of the Grand Jury of the City of Cork.

Resolved unanimously,

That the sincere and grateful acknowledgments of the Grand Jury of the City of Cork be respectfully presented to the Right Honourable Sir Robert Peel and the members of Her Majesty's late government, for the timely and judicious aid afforded to the distressed population of Ireland, during a period when the deficiency of their ordinary food threatened them with serious privations, but which the wise arrangements of the government, aided by the generous contributions of our benevolent fellow-citizens and other charitable individuals, have, under providence, happily averted, and the beneficial effects of which may be traced in the diminution of disease, the lightness of the criminal calendar, and the peaceful demeanour of the people.

Resolved,

That having too much reason to apprehend a similar cause for the active agency of the government during the ensuing year, we would respectfully direct the attention of Her Majesty's present Ministers to the impending calamity, and respectfully suggest that extensive employment for the labouring classes, by the construction of useful public works, is the means best adapted to alleviate that privation and distress, which must otherwise inevitably follow a deficiency in their ordinary food.

Signed for self and fellows, Thomas S. Reeves,

City Grand Jury Room, Cork, 25 July 1846.

(*Correspondence relating to measures adopted for the relief of the distress in Ireland,* p.3; P.P. 1847 (761) LI.)

Schull, a coastal village in west Cork. Throughout the Famine, remote areas such as Schull did not always get their fair share of government relief. (*The Illustrated London News,* 13 Feb. 1847.)

'Government sale of Indian corn at Cork'. (*The Illustrated London News*, 4 April 1846.)

Report on the sale of Indian corn in Cork.

On Saturday last, the government sales of Indian corn and meal commenced in Cork. Immediately on the depots being opened, the crowds of poor persons who gathered round them were so turbulently inclined as to require the immediate interference of the police, who remained there throughout the day. Among the poor, who were of the humblest description and needing charitable relief, the sales were but scanty. The occasion had become of necessity; for potatoes have risen to 11d market price for 14lbs; and, some of the leading commercial men in Cork have made a calculation which shows that the government can afford to sell the Indian corn at a much cheaper rate. Our artist at Cork [James Mahony] has sketched the crowd immediately on the opening of the store.

We feel gratified to learn that a steamer has been despatched from Cork to Dublin, laden with 600 sacks of Indian meal. One half, by the orders, is to be despatched by the Royal, and the other by the Grand Canal, to the interior. It must be acknowledged that Her Majesty's government are executing their duty promptly and with energy. The *Cork Examiner* of Tuesday contains the following account of the sale:

'The bakers in Dublin are selling India-meal bread in large quantities to the better classes, as well as to the poor, and all consider it more palatable than the ordinary whole-meal, or brown bread. The price fixed on it was one penny per pound. The result of the day's sale is sufficient to dissipate all further doubt, and to demand the most serious attention of the citizens of Cork. We understand that 4,480lbs of the corn-meal were sold on Saturday, at one penny per pound.

'The committee waited this morning on Mr Hewetson [Commissary-General], to grant them a further supply; they of course, offering to pay the full price for it; but Mr Hewetson was compelled to refuse the request, he having no order from the government to that effect. The people, supposing that the supply would be continued, assembled in hundreds round the depots; but were informed of the fact of there being no more for sale. Considerable excitement was occasioned by the announcement, and the Mayor, fearing that a disturbance might arise in consequence, published a public notice, stating that when the order, which was daily expected, should arrive, further supplies would be distributed'.

(*The Illustrated London News*, 4 April 1846.)

6. A diet of Indian corn

A problem with alternative foodstuffs was that many of those who subsisted on boiled potatoes had little experience of cooking anything else. They had no ovens and few utensils, and generally did not know how to make the best use of Indian corn. The Relief Commission published instructions but these did not always reach the more remote areas, and many people could not read English. Another problem was that the corn had an extremely hard shell and was difficult to grind into edible meal. Ideally, the meal should be used with a mixture of flour or oatmeal, but these were beyond the means of the poor. The result was that it caused severe stomach problems; this, together with its yellow colour, led to its becoming known as 'Peel's brimstone'.

Memorandum on Indian corn sent by Routh (Relief Commission) to Trevelyan (Treasury), 31 July 1846.

Various manners of using Indian corn for human food.

Suppawn, or porridge, that is to say, boiling milk, broth, or water, thickened with Indian corn-meal, in the same way that people in the south of England thicken them with wheat flour, and that people in the north thicken with oatmeal. Put into water, this is a breakfast, supper, or dinner for little children; put into milk or broth, it is the same for grown people. It is excellent in all disorders arising from bad digestion. In milk or broth it is a good strong meal, sufficient for a man to work upon.

It takes about three pounds and a half of Indian corn-flour to make porridge for ten persons, less than half a pound of corn-flour for a meal for one man, and a warm, comfortable meal that fills and strengthens the stomach. Three pounds and a half of wheaten flour would make four pounds and a half of bread, but it would be dry bread, and bread alone, and not affording half the sustenance or comfort of the porridge.

Mush: Put some water or milk into a pot and bring it to boil; then let the corn-meal out of one hand gently into the milk or water, and keep stirring with the other until you have got it into a pretty stiff state; after which, let it stand ten minutes or a quarter of an hour, or less, or even only one minute, and then take it out and put it into a dish or bowl. This sort of half-pudding half-porridge you eat either hot or cold, with a little salt or without it. It is eaten without any liquid matter, but the general way is to have a basin of milk, and taking a lump of the mush you put it into the milk and eat the two together.

Samp, though not in such common use as porridge or mush, is very much used. The husk or skin of the corn is scalded off, or dipped in hot lye, or beaten off as we do the skin of oats. This is put into a pot with pork or fat, and boiled just in the same manner as the people in the country make pease porridge; but the samp is more wholesome and more nutritious.

Correspondence explanatory ... distress ... p. 226; P.P. 1846 (735) XXXVII.)

Instructions issued by the Relief Commission on the use of Indian meal.

As it is important to pursue the most economical mode of using Indian meal, the following receipt [recipe] for cooking it into porridge, which has been in use for some time in an extensive establishment, may be useful:

In five pints of boiling water mix one pound of Indian meal, which afterwards boil for half an hour on the evening previous to the porridge being required. The following morning, add a little hot water, and when it comes to a boil, let it boil slowly for at least half an hour. If a larger quantity be made, it must be boiled for a longer time both in the evening and morning.

The weight will be increased six-fold; that is to say, seven pounds of Indian meal will produce at least forty-two pounds of substantial porridge.

The salt should not be added until near the time for using it.

It is important to mention that an increase of quantity is found to take place in the cookery of Indian-meal porridge by the above mode of boiling it twice; that is, once overnight, and again when giving it out the following morning. A party who has adopted this plan states that an increase of one-fifth is thus effected, and that the boiling, previous to its being cooked for use, gets rid of much of the raw taste which has been objected to.

(National Archives, M 3486.)

'Beggars and peasants assembled for Indian meal, July 1847'; (NLI Sketch-Book 2018 TX; the volume has five pencil drawings, signed 'LLDB', showing people queuing for food, mainly at Poulacurra House, which has not been identified.)

7. Starvation

Throughout the Famine, the government always did too little, and too late. Food relief was eventually provided, but not enough in the most severely affected areas. Relief works designed to provide employment were also slow in getting started and they employed only a small fraction of those looking for work. By late spring and early summer of 1846, there were no potatoes, food prices had soared, and many people had no money to buy the cheap relief corn. While the destitute were supposed to get it free, that did not always happen in practice. The result was that there was considerable hardship, and the use of the term 'famine' began to become commonplace in the newspapers.

Report in *The Freeman's Journal,* **7 May 1846.**

State of the South – Famine.
From our special reporter, Tulla, County Clare,
1 May 1846.

I have just concluded a tour of over sixty miles in this county; but previous to my entering on particulars I must give you the state of things about Limerick. My first visit was to the village of Doonass, about eight miles from Limerick, where I had been informed there was great misery and want. About a mile to the Limerick side is a place called Gurtnaglee, over against Mount Catherine, the residence of Mr Lloyd. There are about thirty houses here, and not a single potato (if I except a few remaining rotten ones) with any of the people. They at present subsist on Indian meal purchased in Limerick; but the means of the people are nearly exhausted, and they are in the utmost consternation at the prospect of utter destitution which is staring them full in the face.

The greater portion of the property about here belongs to Sir Hugh Massey. At the village of Doonass, I found over 300 families – principally women, young and old – assembled round the petty sessions home, where the Rev. Mr McMahon, P.P., and one of his assistant curates, with two gentlemen belonging to the neighbourhood, were giving out Indian meal to the starving people. It was a melancholy sight, and perhaps one of the most touching I have yet beheld. There were the representatives of at least over 1,000 human beings collected about the place, all eager to get their bags filled with meal, in order to carry it to their famishing children and families. Would that some landlords and legislators had witnessed the scene. The faithful clergy assisting their flocks in the trying hour of need, whilst the landlords, who are morally bound to take care of the persons from whom they derive their incomes, remain in listless apathy, and leave the people to their fate. There are in the parish of Doonass over 250 families utterly destitute of food or the means of procuring it, and were it not for the exertions of the Catholic clergy these unhappy people would at the present moment be without even the scanty allowance which is afforded them. I cannot omit mentioning a gratifying fact, namely, the Rev. Mr Allen, a Protestant clergyman, has been most active in this parish in assisting the Rev. Mr McMahon and his curates...

I have never witnessed anything like the scene that was presented at Doonass: the creatures crowded round the windows of the house – the doors had to be closed; it was pitiable to hear the implorings of the mothers and daughters beseeching the reverend gentlemen to let them go at once as their children, fathers, or families were waiting at home for food.

Official reports on distress in spring 1846.

Co. Tyrone; Clerk of Clogher Poor Law union to Poor Law Commissioners:

Guardians are of opinion that no sound potatoes will remain after seed time.

Co. Dublin; J. O'Ferrall, Esq., Kingstown, 28 March:

Report states that 695 persons are now suffering privation from the high price of provisions; 317 are in extreme distress, their means of buying food being more inadequate than that of the others.

Co. Kilkenny; Rev. Luke Fowler, Barony of Cranagh, Freshford, 28 March:

Distress is daily spreading in village of Freshford, amounting to all but starvation; writer's house daily beset by starving people; impossible to provide even a scanty supply for the numbers famishing.

King's Co.; Dean Hawkins, Moneygall, 28 March:

The potatoes of many poor people of neighbourhood are all consumed; many poor people would gladly walk to Roscrea (5 miles) for Indian flour at famine price.

Queen's Co.; Extract from guardians' minutes of 20th instant, Mountmellick Poor Law union, 28 March:

That a number of decent women with families, amounting to 80 human beings, apply to the guardians for relief, they being without food or sufficient employment; these applicants form but a small proportion of those actually subsisting on food made from 'the wash' of the starch yard [liquid waste left when starch is extracted from corn or potatoes], food but indifferently suited for pigs.

Co. Westmeath; Queries of Poor Law Commissioners, answered by W. Fetherstone, Esq., Mullingar Poor Law union, 28 March:

Conacre holders suffer most; poorhouse fuller than in summer months; poor labourers' supply of potatoes in many instances already exhausted, and unless immediate relief is given, the consequences will be awful; 350 labourers are unemployed in barony.

Co. Leitrim; Lord Clements, Mohill Poor Law union, 28 March:

Minutes state that the cottiers at present are almost destitute; Lord Clements states that parties have visited the houses of dealers in oatmeal for the purpose of forcing them to lower their charges.

(*Correspondence explanatory ... distress...* p. 223-5; P.P. 1846 (735)XXXVII.)

Beggars on the O'Connell
estate at Derrynane,
Co. Kerry.
(*The Pictorial Times,*
14 Feb. 1846; courtesy
of NLS.)

8. The Spectre

S *tages of the Famine are graphically represented in a publication consisting of three plates and four accompanying verses by H.D. (unidentified), published by Thomas McLean, London, 1851. The preface states: 'In Ireland's late calamity, the earnest endeavour of Englishmen of all ranks to alleviate, by vast pecuniary contributions, the suffering of her starving sons, spoke, so as not to be mistaken, the sympathy of brothers'. Plate I may be taken as representing the situation in the early summer of 1846, towards the end of Peel's term of responsibility. At that stage, the second failure of the potato crop was on the horizon and absolute famine was about to take hold.*

THE SPECTRE.

STANZA I.

Far West a grim shadow was seen, as 'tis said,

Like a Spectre from Famine and Pestilence bred;

His gaunt giant-form, with pale Poverty wed,

    Meteor-like, fraught with awe, flashed in view:

Some exclaim'd it was naught but a shadow of night,—

Some derided the Seer who proclaim'd its dread might,—

But at length all confess'd his forebodings were right;

    The event quickly prov'd them too true.

IV

RELIEF UNDER THE LIBERALS

Prior to the appearance of the blight in 1845, disease seldom struck the potato crop in two successive years; people expected that once they weathered the hungry spring and summer of 1846, they could look forward to a normal crop that harvest. But in July, blight was again reported and this time it was far more widespread and uniform. The result was that only a quarter of the normal crop was saved. Apart from the many individuals who lost practically their entire crop, a deficit of three-quarters was a catastrophic loss for the country as a whole.

Peel's government had saved the country from the worst effects of the shortage of 1845-46, and the people now looked to his successor, Lord John Russell, who became Prime Minister at the end of June. Unlike Peel, Russell was well regarded by nationalists, and O'Connell and the Repealers had supported the Liberals at various times over the years. Expectations were high, but, as was the case with Peel and the Corn Laws, Russell was constrained by economic and political considerations. The Liberals were resolutely committed to free trade and were opposed to interfering with normal commerce, either by importing cheap foodstuffs or, as was done in previous crises, by preventing the export of food. They believed that either course would be disastrous; government imports would discourage commercial importers; prohibiting exports, they felt, would depress Irish agriculture and result in higher prices for the British consumer.

Moreover, in economic matters, Russell relied heavily on the Chancellor of the Exchequer, Sir Charles Wood, and on Charles Trevelyan, the permanent head of the Treasury, both of whom believed in policies of *laissez faire* and minimal government intervention. But while such doctrinaire economic theories may have been valid in normal circumstances, the situation in Ireland in the late summer of 1846 required pragmatic action. In August, however, when Russell outlined his relief measures in the House of Commons, it became clear that there would be no dramatic intervention, and that his policy would be less remedial than that of Peel. The government would not restrict exports or become involved in the import or sale of cheap corn, but it would provide employment on a large scale through a new round of public works schemes. These, however, would ultimately have to be paid for entirely from Irish resources. In effect, despite the Union, Ireland in her time of crisis would largely have to work out her own salvation.

On the outbreak of blight in August 1845, Peel had six months in which to lay contingency plans. In the autumn of 1846, however, the situation was much more urgent. Many people had lost their entire crop and all potatoes would be consumed by the end of the year. Due to the shortage, food prices escalated and many people were actually starving. Belatedly, the government decided to purchase Indian corn, but apart from a considerable delay in arriving at the decision, delivery took up to three months and worthwhile supplies did not materialise until December. But even then, the corn was not doled out free except to the absolutely destitute. By and large, it was sold at prevailing prices, as the government was unwilling to undercut the dealers and so interfere with normal trade. Dealers cynically exploited the shortage and prices soared, thereby forcing up the price of the corn and meal provided by the government depots. On the issue of price control, Russell's policy can be contrasted with that of Peel. Russell allowed the importers and dealers to determine prices, whereas Peel, by selling the government imports at cost, forced a general drop in prices. In effect, Peel controlled the situation, but Russell allowed vested interests to dominate. This was partly because Russell's personal authority in the cabinet was weak.

In the autumn and early winter of 1846, famine set in and deaths were widespread in the west and south-west. For most people, the only hope of salvation lay in the relief works, but schemes took a long time to organise, and the winter was already under way before significant numbers were employed. But even for those, the respite provided by the relief works proved to be but temporary and wholly inadequate.

1. *The blight reappears*

The potato crop promised to be exceptionally good in 1846 but the blight reappeared in July, a month earlier than the previous year. Years later, William Steuart Trench, the farming speculator who outlined his method of planting (p. 14-15), recalled his dismay at the sudden destruction of his crop. As everybody then knew from the bitter experience of the previous year what the failure could mean, there was widespread consternation. In a letter to Trevelyan, Father Theobald Mathew, 'the Apostle of Temperance', voiced the general concern. As Trevelyan was involved in the remedial measures of the previous year, Father Mathew flatteringly attributed the credit to him.

Memories of the second onset of the potato blight.

Each day, from the time I first heard of the disease, I went regularly to visit my splendid mountain crop, and each day saw it apparently further advanced in course of arriving at a healthy and abundant maturity.

On August 6, 1846 – I shall not readily forget the day – I rode up as usual to my mountain property, and my feelings may be imagined when before I saw the crop, I smelt the fearful stench, now so well known and recognised as the death-sign of each field of potatoes. I was dismayed indeed, but I rode on; and as I wound down the newly-engineered road running through the heart of the farm and which forms the regular approach to the steward's house, I could scarcely bear the fearful and strange smell, which came up so rank from the luxuriant crop then growing all around; no perceptible change, except the smell, had as yet come upon the apparent prosperity of the deceitfully luxuriant stalks, but the experience of the past few days taught me that all was gone, and the crop was utterly worthless.

I need not tell how bitterly I was disappointed, overthrown as all my anticipations of profitable results were by this great calamity. Not only did I foresee the loss of my £3,000 – no small sum to a man who had just surrendered an agency of £1,000 per annum; but I felt also that the hopes of future success, on which I had expended a large capital and much time and thought for years, were gone, that it would be

madness ever to venture on the trial of such a crop again, and that all my labour and patient experiments, which had hitherto turned out so completely successful, were, by this new and fearful calamity sent by the special hand of God, and the like of which had never appeared in nature before, utterly blasted.

But upon this I will not dwell. It is enough to say that the luxuriant stalks soon withered, the leaves decayed, the disease extended to the tubers, and the stench from the rotting of such an immense amount of rich vegetable matter became almost intolerable. I saw my splendid crop fast disappearing and melting away under this fatal disease. I tried to dig the potatoes rapidly, in the hope of saving something; and, in accordance with the advice of Sir Robert Kane and others, I set up a temporary machine for the conversion of the tubers into starch. But the final result was that the produce of the entire crop yielded about forty pounds in starch, whilst the cost of grinding the pulp, and erecting machinery, amounted to about twice that sum! My plans, my labour, my £3,000, and all hopes of future profit by these means were gone!

But my own losses and disappointments, deeply as I felt them, were soon merged in the general desolation, misery, and starvation which now rapidly affected the poorer classes around me and throughout Ireland.

(Trench, *Realities of Irish life*, 1868, p. 101-3.)

Rev. Theobald Mathew (1790-1856). (NLI P&D.)

Letter of Rev. Theobald Mathew to Trevelyan.

Cork, 7 August 1846.

It is not on matters personal to myself I now take the liberty to address you; yet my heart is so full of your unmerited kindness, I cannot commence the subject without repeating my most grateful thanks for your goodness to my orphan nephew.

I am well aware of the deep solicitude you felt for our destitute people, and your arduous exertions to preserve them from the calamitous effects of the destruction of the potato crop last season. Complete success has crowned your efforts. Famine would have desolated this unhappy country were it not for your wise precautions.

Divine providence, in its inscrutable ways, has again poured out upon us the viol [*sic*] of its wrath. A blot more destructive than the simoon of the desert has passed over the land, and the hopes of the poor potato-cultivators are totally blighted, and the food of a whole nation has perished. On the 27th of last month I passed from Cork to Dublin, and this doomed plant bloomed in all the luxuriance of an abundant harvest. Returning on the 3rd instant, I beheld, with sorrow, one wide waste of putrefying vegetation. In many places the wretched people were seated on the fences of their decaying gardens, wringing their hands and wailing bitterly the destruction that had left them foodless.

It is not to harrow your benevolent feelings, dear Mr Trevelyan, I tell this tale of woe. No, but to excite your sympathy in behalf of our miserable peasantry. It is rumoured that the capitalists in the corn and flour trade are endeavouring to induce government not to protect the people from famine, but to leave them at their mercy. I consider this a cruel and unjustifiable interference. The gentlemen of the trade have nothing to do with Indian corn; it is, I may say, a creation of the government, a new article of food, wisely introduced for the preservation and amelioration of the people of Ireland. Insidious efforts were even made to prejudice the people against this new food. Thank God they were in vain, and it is now a favourite diet; and ten thousand blessings are hourly invoked on the heads of the benefactors who saved the miserable from perishing.

(*Correspondence ... distress ...*, p. 9; P.P. 1847 (761) LI.)

Searching for potatoes in west Cork: 'Boy and girl at Cahera'. (*The Illustrated London News*, 20 Feb. 1847.)

2. Lord John Russell's policy

In a speech in the House of Commons on 17 August 1846, the Prime Minister outlined his plans for dealing with the new emergency. His tone was sympathetic but he did not seem to comprehend the gravity of the situation. He proposed to provide public works so that people could earn enough to support themselves. He did not, however, intend to import cheap food and believed that commercial traders would import all that was necessary. A Treasury minute written later that month indicates that officials at the highest level were obsessed with ensuring that the interests of traders and shopkeepers were protected.

Speech by Lord John Russell.

Having already stated the evils which have in practice arisen from interference by the government with the supply of the public food, I have only to add that we do not propose to interfere with the regular mode by which Indian corn and other kinds of grain may be brought into the country. We propose to leave that trade as much at liberty as possible. But there may be particular cases, as there were in 1836 and 1839, where, in consequence of the part of the country where the famine prevailed being very inaccessible, it became necessary to employ the commissariat officers. As a general rule, however, we shall still take care not to interfere with the regular operations of merchants for the supply of food to the country, or with the retail trade, which was much deranged by the operations of last year. With regard to relief committees, we propose that they should for a time be constituted, taking care to avoid those errors which have hitherto ensued from want of experience, and guided by the lights we have received from the practice as hitherto established. In

Lord John Russell (1792-1878). (Hulton-Deutsch Collection.)

particular, we shall endeavour to avoid the giving of tickets, by members of the relief committees, to persons who are not in need of relief...

Sir, as I stated at the commencement, this is a special case, requiring the intervention of parliament. I consider that the circumstances I have stated, of that kind of food which constitutes the subsistence of millions of people in Ireland being subjected to the dreadful ravages of this disease, constitute this a case of exception, and render it imperative on the government and the parliament to take extraordinary measures for relief. I trust that the course I propose to pursue will not be without its counterbalancing advantages; that it will show the poorest among the Irish people that we are not insensible, here, to the claims which they have on us as the parliament of the United Kingdom; that the whole credit of the Treasury and means of the country are ready to be used as it is our bounden duty to use them, and will, whenever they can be usefully applied, be so disposed as to avert famine and to maintain the people of Ireland; and that we are now disposed to take advantage of the unfortunate spread of this disease among the potatoes to establish public works which may be of permanent utility. I trust, Sir, that the present state of things will have that counterbalancing advantage in the midst of many misfortunes and evil consequences. I know that I need not detain you any longer than to assure the Committee and the House that we consider that our predecessors in office did show a very laudable anxiety to meet the evil – that the remedies they applied were suited to the occasion – that we shall endeavour to imitate the spirit in which they acted, while we shall endeavour to take advantage of their experience to correct errors which were inevitable in consequence of such unforeseen difficulties.

(*Hansard*, House of Commons, 17 August 1846.)

Treasury minute regarding relief policy.

In order to keep in check, as far as possible, the social evils incident to an extensive system of relief, it is indispensably necessary that the relief committees should not sell the meal or other food provided by them, except in small quantities to persons who are known to have no other means of procuring food; that the price at which the meal is sold should, as nearly as possible, be the same as the market prices which prevail in the neighbourhood; that the committees should not give a higher rate of wages, nor exact a smaller quantum of work on any works carried on by them from funds at their own disposal than is the case in respect to the works carried on under the superintendence of the Board of Works, and that works should be carried on by them only to the extent to which private employment is proved not to be available.

The serious attention of every person who will have to take a part in the measures of relief rendered necessary by the new and more complete failure of the potato crop would be particularly called to this important fact, that the limitations and precautions which have been prescribed to the government boards and officers in carrying out the relief operations, with the object of rendering the necessary interference with the labour and provision markets productive of the smallest possible disturbance of the ordinary course of trade and industry, will be rendered nugatory if the same prudence and reserve are not practised by the relief committees in the administration of the funds placed at their disposal by private or public benevolence; and their Lordships therefore feel it to be their duty earnestly to request that every person concerned, will, to the extent of the influence possessed by him, endeavour to secure such a restriction of the measures of relief to cases of real destitution, and such a just consideration for the interests of merchants and dealers, in the free exercise of whose callings the public welfare is so deeply concerned, that instead of the habitual dependence upon charitable aid which might otherwise be apprehended from the extensive measures of relief in progress, every description of trade and industry may be stimulated by them...

My Lords have considered with the careful attention which the importance of the subject demands, the measures proper to be taken with a view to continue the late commissariat operations to the extent which may be absolutely necessary for the purpose of providing supplies of food for sale in districts to which the ordinary operations of the provision trade cannot be expected to extend, the strictest regard being at the same time paid to the pledge which has been given, not to interfere in any case in which there is a reasonable expectation that the market will be supplied by mercantile enterprise; and they will proceed to state the course which appears to them to be the best adapted to secure the important object in view.

(Printed Treasury minute, *c.* 21 August 1846; NLI Ms 8474, Sir Richard Bourke Papers.)

'Political economy, or, Lord John in Peel's clothes. The Queen: "Well! It is not the best fit in the world, but we'll see how he goes on"'! Russell was a much smaller man than Peel, and there was speculation that he might also fail to measure up as Prime Minister. (*Punch*, 26 July 1846.)

3. Trevelyan's attitude

The official mainly responsible for relief, Charles Edward Trevelyan, had patronising views on the Irish. In particular, he believed that the chronic distress was largely due to the landlords' failure to manage their estates efficiently and provide responsible leadership. He regarded the Famine as divine intervention and believed that in the long term it would prove a blessing by eliminating dependence on the potato, by reducing the population, and by forcing landlords and people to take control of their own destiny. His philosophy is revealed in letters to Sir Randolph Routh, chairman of the Relief Commission, and to Lord Monteagle [Thomas Spring-Rice], an enlightened Co. Limerick landlord and a former Chancellor of the Exchequer.

Letter of Trevelyan to Routh.

Treasury, 3 February 1846.

I feel satisfied that you will concentrate your whole energies on the direct and practical measures for the relief of the suffering to be anticipated from the impending scarcity. Whether we regard the possible extent of that suffering, the suddenness with which it may come upon us in various points, or the fearful consequences of its not being promptly relieved, the subject is one which calls for all our foresight and power of arrangement.

That indirect permanent advantages will accrue to Ireland from the scarcity and the measures taken for its relief, I entertain no doubt; but if we were to pursue these incidental objects to the neglect of any of the precautions immediately required to save the people from actual starvation, our responsibility would be fearful indeed. Besides, the greatest improvement of all which could take place in Ireland would be to teach the people to depend upon themselves for developing the resources of their country, instead of having recourse to the assistance of the government on every occasion. Much has been done of late years to put this important matter on its proper footing; but if a firm stand is not made against the prevailing disposition to take advantage of this crisis to break down all barriers, the true permanent interest of the country will, I am convinced, suffer in a manner which will be irreparable in our time.

Up to the present date, nothing has, so far as I am aware, been done which should prevent a perfectly sound line from being taken, and one which will bear looking back upon, after the excitement arising from present circumstances shall have passed away.

(*Correspondence explanatory ... distress ...*, p. 25; P.P. 1846 (735) XXXVII.)

Thomas Spring-Rice, 1st Lord Monteagle (1790-1866). (NLI PA 1425.)

Letter of Trevelyan to Lord Monteagle.

To the Right Hon. Lord Monteagle.

My Dear Lord,

I have had the pleasure of receiving your letter dated 1st instant, and before proceeding to the subjects more particularly treated in it, I must beg of you to dismiss all doubt from your mind of the magnitude of the existing calamity and its danger not being fully known and appreciated in Downing Street.

The government establishments are strained to the utmost to alleviate this great calamity and avert this danger, as far as it is in the power of government to do so; and in the whole course of my public service, I never witnessed such entire self-devotion and such hearty and cordial co-operation on the part of officers belonging to different departments met together from different parts of the world, as I have on this occasion.

My purchases are carried to the utmost point short of transferring the famine from Ireland to England and giving rise to a counter popular pressure here, which it would be the more difficult to resist because it would be founded on strong considerations of justice.

But I need not remind your lordship that the ability even of the most powerful government is extremely limited in dealing with a social evil of this description. It forms no part of the functions of government to provide supplies of food or to increase the productive powers of the land. In the great institution of the business of society, it falls to the share of government to protect the merchant and the agriculturist in the free exercise of their respective employments, but not itself to carry on those employments; and the condition of a community depends upon the result of the efforts which each member of it makes in his private and individual capacity...

In Ireland the habit has proverbially been to follow a precisely opposite course, and the events of the last six weeks furnish a remarkable illustration of what I do not hesitate to call this defective part of the national character. The nobility and gentry have met in their respective baronies, and beyond making the presentments required by law, they have, with rare exceptions, confined themselves to memorials and deputations calling upon the government to do everything, as if they have themselves no part to perform in this great crisis of the country. The government is expected to open shops for the sale of food in every part of Ireland, to make all the railroads in Ireland, and to drain and improve the whole of the land of Ireland, to the extent of superseding the proprietor in the management of his own estate, and arranging with his tenants the terms on which the rent etc. is to be adjusted...

I must give expression to my feelings by saying that I think I see a bright light shining in the distance through the dark cloud which at present hangs over Ireland. A remedy has been already applied to that portion of the maladies of Ireland which was traceable to political causes, and the morbid habits which still to a certain extent survive are gradually giving way to a more healthy action. The deep and inveterate root of social evil remains, and I hope I am not guilty of irreverence in thinking that, this being altogether beyond the power of man, the cure has been applied by the direct stroke of an all-wise providence in a manner as unexpected and unthought of as it is likely to be effectual. God grant that we may rightly perform our part and not turn into a curse what was intended for a blessing. The ministers of religion and especially the pastors of the Roman Catholic Church, who possess the largest share of influence over the people of Ireland, have well performed their part; and although few indications appear from any proceedings which have yet come before the public that the landed proprietors have even taken the first step of preparing for the conversion of the land now laid down to potatoes to grain cultivation, I do not despair of seeing this class in society still taking the lead which their position requires of them, and preventing the social revolution from being so extensive as it otherwise must become.

Believe me, my dear lord, yours very sincerely,

C.E. Trevelyan. Treasury, 9 October 1846.

(NLI Ms 13,397, Monteagle Papers.)

4. The operation of relief committees

*I*n the autumn and winter of 1846 and into 1847, the local relief committees found it difficult to raise subscriptions. In this second season of hardship, people were less generous as the effects of the scarcity were felt higher up the social scale and all classes were under pressure. While most of the local committees did extremely valuable work, some members abused their trust, and there were widespread allegations of favouritism. Insights into this and other aspects of the Famine are provided in a 391-page manuscript by Hugh Dorian, 'Donegal, sixty years ago', written in 1896. His main sources for the Famine period were the recollections of living witnesses.

AN APPEAL
TO THE LANDED PROPRIETORS,
AND OTHERS IN THE
DISTRICT OF CASTLEISLAND.

THE RELIEF COMMITTEE recently appointed for the Parishes of CASTLEISLAND, KILLEENTIERNA, DYSART, and BALLINCUSHLANE, beg once more respectfully to address the several Landed Proprietors of the District, and all those to whom GOD has graciously afforded means to contribute to the Relief of a People on the very verge of FAMINE.

A solemn and imperative duty lies upon such to come forward freely and liberally —a duty for the discharge of which they are responsible to Almighty GOD. The necessity is extreme, the call, therefore, upon those who are bound to meet it is most urgent.

Indian Corn Meal—now the principal resource of the poor—and all other Bread Stuffs, have reached a price which makes it impossible for a labouring man—even if in full employment—to sustain a family ; whilst under existing circumstances—no public works being as yet in progress—he is rendered altogether unable to purchase Food almost at any price.

Unless, therefore, the most speedy and effectual means are instantly adopted, to cheapen FOOD, and to counteract monopoly, the most disastrous consequences must necessarily ensue.

The Committee being fully and fearfully convinced of this, hesitate not to repeat, that it is a sacred duty imperative upon all who are interested in the district—Landed Proprietors and others—cheerfully and heartily to meet the present dreadful emergency —to stay the progress of destitution, and to afford effectual relief to their poor brethren, in this their time of difficulty and distress.

REMEMBER—"*It is more blessed to give, than to receive.*"

WILLIAM MEREDITH,
Chairman.

F. R. MAUNSELL,
Rector of Castleisland,
Secretary and Treasurer.

Castleisland Committee Room,
October 19, 1846.

(NLI Proclamations Collection.)

Memories of the relief committees.

On other days the committee meet; the doors are closed, but occasionally a side door opens to admit some one in authority who, by this device, escapes the attention of crowds outside. Inside, they consult and issue tickets but, on every occasion, unfortunately, the supply of Indian meal at their disposal is not enough to meet the pressing demand. The day's work of the gentry over, they are on the way of dispersing, but how to get away, for not a tithe of the expectant multitude outside get the expected token, that is, a ticket, or, as they called it 'line', for as much as a morsel. It may then be easily imagined, the pangs of the already hungry parent, waiting all day, made his wants, his grievances known, as much so as language in his power lay; but so disappointed in the evening and returning home hungry, vexed, with no word of consolation on his lips, only to view the sad scene, the agonizing scene of the family before him still more hungry. Oh! can we imagine his feelings, his sufferings.

On leaving the place and gaining the outside, a rush is made at the committee men; the skirts are nearly pulled off their coats at the attempts to get some words from them, and it is with the greatest difficulty they can make their way, everyone asking, 'can you do nothing for me, your honour, or your reverence'? For we must not forget that the 'Soggarth aroon' felt inclined to go there too, and though his influence was not the greatest, still he went there, and on the jostling and pulling, his garments also got their share like another. From one, and another, comes the lamentation, 'I am here all day'. 'How can I go home now, for I did not leave as much as a spoonful of food behind me with Molly and the children, and I did not tell you that before, as I thought you would do something for me, after keeping one here all day, and how can I go home wanting'?

The manner of the consoling replies to such appeals would be in the shortest words: 'nothing can be done for *you* this day. Come back next week and we will try'. Good encouragement indeed for an empty stomach, to live, to do or to die, during a week. Other committee men were entrusted with small sums of money and at their direction divided [it] among those supposed most in need, and if they had not the necessary goods to give in lieu themselves, they were watchful to find out a friend who had and put the money in his way. The applicant for relief presented himself at the committee man's dwelling, got an hour or so at some job, then was supplied with the desired ticket drawn out in favour of some petty shopkeeper at some distance, and having reached that place, have to await turn. All this circuitous way of doing good was more like hard labour or convict punishment...

This was the way in which a great deal of the relief fund, not all English money, of course, entrusted to those worldly-minded men, was smuggled and converted into other uses, and yet such men were looked upon as good men, because they gave employment, for their own benefit, on the charitable money bestowed by others, in America or Australia perhaps. Such imputations may, to the reader, seem rather harsh, when we refer to men who should have better feeling towards the weak and the hungry. Yet such was the undoubted fact, and therefore it is no way trespassing the rules of charity to relate the same. Nor could it be given half in its true light, how the poor were treated and despised as if they were beings of quite a different creation. The satiated never understands the emaciated.

(Hugh Dorian, 'Donegal, sixty years ago: a true historical narrative', 1896; photostat copy in National Library, Ms 2047; original in St Columb's College, Derry; reproduced by kind permission.)

5. The export of food

Throughout the Famine, there were demands that the export of foodstuffs be prohibited. The government claimed that it would be counter-productive, as it would retard Irish home production and inhibit imports; such reasoning did not impress people who were literally starving. In the autumn of 1846, a number of violent protests took place, the most notable at Dungarvan, Co. Waterford. The police fired on a crowd attempting to prevent grain leaving the port; several people were injured and one man died of his wounds. While imports far exceeded exports for the period of the Famine as a whole, there was an acute shortage of food in late 1846 and early 1847. An absolute ban at that time would have reduced prices and would probably have saved lives.

Editorial, *The Waterford Freeman*, 3 October 1846.

Riot in Dungarvan – Food for the Poor – Exportation of Food.

When famine is spreading its pall over the land, and death is visiting the poor man's cabin, it is not meet that the food of millions should be shipped from our shores. It is indispensably necessary that the grain should remain in the country while scarcity is apprehended. Will not a starving population become justly indignant when whole fleets, laden with the produce of our soil, are unfurling their sails and steering from our harbours, while the cry of hunger is ringing in their ears? It is beyond human endurance to suffer it; and a wise government should at once issue an order prohibiting the exportation of provisions from this country until the wants of the people shall have been sufficiently provided for.

A report had gone abroad that ships were freighted to convey grain from Dungarvan for England on last Monday, and this rumour had the effect of arousing the fears of the people; consequently, large masses flocked to Dungarvan for the purpose of preventing such exportation. It is evident that they did not intend to commit any violence, as they came unarmed. Their only object was to make such a demonstration as would prevent the shipping of grain. The force of public opinion was the only weapon they meant to use, for they carried neither pike nor gun. A collision took place between these defenceless and unfortunate people, and several were wounded...

If provision depots be not immediately formed in order to reduce the markets to a reasonable price, and the exportation of grain prohibited, it is hard to say what desperation and despair may not do.

'Food riot in Dungarvan'. (*The Pictorial Times*, 10 Oct. 1846; courtesy of Birmingham Library Services.)

A cartoon inspired by the famine in Galway and Mayo in 1831 (due to the failure of the potato crop the previous year). It was equally relevant to the situation in 1846. (By Robert Seymour, *The Looking Glass*, July 1831; courtesy of Glin Castle.)

But, above all things, the prohibition of exporting grain from this country is imperatively called for. When Indian corn and meal is purchased for our support, and carried across half the globe for our use, is it not a most unaccountable anomaly – a monstrous reality – that we are sending our wheat, corn, meal and flour out of the country? The government should act boldly, promptly, and wisely, and lay an instantaneous embargo on the exportation of Irish food. If they refuse to do this, the consequences may be both melancholy and dangerous. The necessity for immediately establishing provision depots in every principal town in Ireland cannot be too frequently or too forcibly pressed on the government.

Merchants are closing their stores, already counting their gains, and gloating over the misery by which they hope to enrich themselves. If provision depots were thought necessary last season, how much more so are they needed now, when there is scarcely a single sound potato in the land.

We are aware that our excellent and humane Lord Lieutenant [the Earl of Bessborough] is making every exertion in his power to aid the people. The Prime Minister, of course, will listen attentively to his remonstrance, and we think that we may calculate with certainty on the establishing of provision depots, both for the purpose of feeding the destitute poor and of reducing the price of food so as to place it within the reach of the labouring classes. But a day, an hour, a moment should not be lost in carrying those vitally important regulations into effect. Famine will not accommodate itself to the tardy movements of a cabinet council. The circular of a premier will not stop its fell progress. There must be acts as well as words. It cannot be concealed that the country is in a most disturbed state. The women assembled in Dungarvan on Thursday, and prevented the loading of the vessel with grain. They did this in the presence of the military, and in defiance of the civil authorities. Do not such acts speak volumes to the government?

6. *Crime and food*

The rate of crime doubled during the Famine, but the increase mainly consisted of crimes against property. The focus was on food or the money to provide it; crime ranged from poaching or siphoning blood from cattle, to burglary, attacks on shops and armed robbery. The authorities took strong action and the army and constabulary were employed in guarding food depots and protecting produce in transit. In December 1847, the Crime and Outrage (Ireland) Act provided for more police and additional powers for the authorities.

Report from *The Pictorial Times*, **30 October 1847.**

Famine in Ireland.

The contrast of the two plates in this page suggests reflections anything but complimentary to Irish gratitude. On the one hand, we behold the operation of the arrangements of a wise and humane government for supplying a destitute and famine-stricken population with the means of existence. The wheels of the meal cart creak under the burden which is to relieve hundreds of human beings from the horrors of starvation. A gallant and devoted body of Light Dragoons are taken from their ordinary duties to escort the supply in safety to its destination. Look on that picture – and on this. A band of lawless ruffians, who prefer the wages of crime to the fruits of honest industry – who would rather spill human blood to purchase a meal than till the generous earth for the sake of its abundance; this band, armed with such weapons of offence as violence or robbery have placed within their reach, positively await the coming of the supplies that they may feed their own wants, even at the risk of their lives, and despoil the famished creatures for whom the succour is intended. We fear such spectacles are more frequent than even the reports from Ireland lead us to suppose. They present a very gloomy picture of the state of society, and almost serve to justify the penuriousness that would deny assistance to one-half of Ireland, on the grounds of the crimes and indolence of the other half.

'Irish armed peasants waiting for the approach of a meal cart'. (*The Pictorial Times*, 30 Oct. 1847; courtesy of NLS.)

'Meal cart under military escort proceeding to a relief station in Clonmel'. (*The Pictorial Times*, 30 Oct. 1847; courtesy of NLS.)

Report on food riots in Dublin.

There was some rather serious rioting at Dublin yesterday week. About nine o'clock in the morning, a body of men, apparently railway labourers, tolerably well clad, assembled at the foot of Summer Hill, adjoining Lower Gardiner Street, Dublin, and they were not long there when two bread carts approached. A portion of the party, armed with large sticks, drew out towards the carts, addressed threatening terms to the men in charge, while the rest of the mob deliberately rifled all the contents of the carts. Some three or four policemen were attracted to the spot by the commotion, but, from the attitude assumed by the fighting section of the plunderers, they did not consider themselves warranted in attempting the arrest of any of the party; all, in consequence, escaped.

About two hours afterwards, a party, supposed to be the same gang, attacked the shop of Mr Campbell of Marlborough Street, and carried off all the bread in his shop. They proceeded down Marlborough Street to Eden Quay, and again stopped before the door of Mr Coyne, the bread and biscuit baker residing there, and repeated their demand for bread; but, on seeing the police approaching, they retired and passed over

Carlisle [O'Connell] Bridge in the direction of Westmoreland Street. A mob surrounded the shop of Mr Jeffers, baker, of Church Street; but, the police being in the vicinity, they were called on, and succeeded in dispersing the mob. Several bread carts were stopped in the outlets of the city, and their contents taken.

There were more bread riots on Tuesday morning. At daybreak, a body of about 300 men collected at the Broadstone and, having arranged their plans, rushed down Dominick Street into Dorset Street, where they attacked a bread cart and in an instant seized its contents. Shortly afterwards they attacked a second cart, when five or six mounted policemen, and about the same number of foot police, came upon them. A scuffle ensued and the police succeeded in arresting eight of the plunderers. These persons were brought before the magistrates of Henry Street police office, and from their statements it appeared they were with one exception from the counties of Wicklow, Wexford, Kildare, and one was from the county of Clare. The leader of the mob was arrested. His name is Murphy, a native of Dublin, and on his person was found the sum of 2s 5d.

(*The Illustrated London News*, 16 Jan. 1847.)

V

RELIEF WORKS

Lord John Russell and his Liberal colleagues subscribed to the strict Protestant ethic of their day. They believed in charity for the deserving poor, but set much greater store on the virtues of hard work, thrift and self-reliance. They regarded the Irish poor as indolent and feckless, and over-dependent on charity. This attitude influenced their strategy for dealing with the situation in Ireland. Accordingly, in the measures announced in August 1846, the emphasis was on public works schemes; the Irish poor would not get handouts but would have to work for their bread. Apart from providing people with a means of salvation, the relief works would foster habits of industry and a spirit of self-reliance in the workforce.

The new series of relief works was to be organised along more cost-effective lines than was the case with those organised under Peel. Responsibility for the approval of schemes was entrusted to the Board of Works, and the method of financing was drastically changed. Up to half the cost of the previous series had been met by the government; now, apart from areas of extreme distress, each county was to pay the entire cost of its schemes. In the present crisis, the government was willing to advance loans, but these were to be repaid in full, and at 3½% interest to boot. In effect, Irish ratepayers were to pay for the relief works: 'Irish property must support Irish poverty'.

The strategy for the new series of public works was mainly devised by Trevelyan and the scheme was outlined by Russell in the House of Commons on 17 August. Legislation was speedily enacted as the Poor Employment Act, 1846 (9 & 10 Victoria, chapter 107). The procedure for getting schemes approved was extremely bureaucratic, with the result that the winter was setting in before worthwhile numbers of workers were taken on.

The new series of works was again mainly devoted to making or repairing roads. To ensure value for money, a regime of task-work was introduced so that pay would relate to performance. Task-work was unpopular but, as the crisis deepened over the winter of 1846-47, the numbers of those applying for work increased dramatically. Poor people had no money to buy food, and for many the public works were the only possible means of earning enough to stay alive. Humane Board of Works officials found it hard to resist pleas from starving people and they allowed women and, eventually, children onto the schemes. By December, the numbers had swollen to 441,000, and in March they peaked at 714,000, a total of wage-earners which must have supported close to three million. As the numbers grew, the Board of Works could no longer manage the situation. By the early spring of 1847, the whole system was in virtual chaos.

Belatedly, the government decided to phase out the relief works and adopt a new approach. The core problem with the relief-works strategy was that it was not designed for the situation that developed during the winter of 1846-47. If the distress had been less severe, the works could have served a useful function by providing employment for perhaps up to a quarter of a million people. As the situation was allowed to develop, however, with dealers forcing up prices, even the families of those employed on the works were starving, as the average wage of 10d a day was not enough for survival at the current inflated prices.

The consensus now regarding the relief works of the winter of 1846-47 is that they were ill-conceived. Admittedly, they employed over 700,000 at peak, thereby helping to maintain up to three million people. But people who were half-starving were forced to do hard labour, and endure the attendant misery of long journeys to and from the works during a cold and wet and particularly severe winter. It was harsh, especially considering that the average earnings did not amount to a living wage for a family. There was little productive benefit and the costs were high – £4,848,235. With hindsight, it would have been more cost-effective, and certainly more humane, to have devoted the money to providing subsidised or free food.

1. *Organising relief works*

The Lord Lieutenant and his staff decided on the areas where schemes were needed and called presentment sessions of local ratepayers at which projects were presented and adopted. Those approved by the Board of Works were then transmitted to the Treasury for sanction. As the number of presentments from some areas proved overwhelming, only a fraction of them secured official sanction, as was the case with those from the barony of Moyashel and Magheradernon, Co. Westmeath. Only 14 of the 38 proposals were approved by Richard Griffith and Thomas Larcom, special commissioners of the Board of Works. Local relief committees were again established and their main function was to compile lists of people eligible for employment.

Extracts from instructions for relief committees.

1. The relief act recently passed, 9 and 10 Vic., chapter 107 (August 1846), directs that when the public works for which it provides become requisite in any barony extraordinary presentment sessions are to be assembled.

16. The employment provided by law must be of a public nature; and the owners and occupiers of land in Ireland are, by the Act 9 and 10 Vic., chapter 107, charged with the expense of such works as are indispensably necessary for the subsistence of the destitute poor.

18. When public works of relief are to be executed, the several relief committees in the barony are to supply to the officers of the Board of Works appointed to conduct them lists of persons requiring relief by employment, made up from registers of applicants for relief in the following order, and not containing a greater number of persons than the officers of works shall propose to employ from each relief division of the barony, having regard to the extent of the labouring population requiring relief in such division:

    a. Persons destitute of means of support who have the largest families wholly depending on them.

    b. Persons with smaller families wholly depending on them.

    c. All other persons requiring employment on public works, for whose support it is actually necessary.

19. A book for the registry of applicants for employment will be supplied to each committee. As the applications are received, inquiry should be made to ascertain the real condition of every applicant, and none should be registered but such as shall appear to be in actual necessity of relief, having no other resource or means of acquiring subsistence than employment on public works.

20. When lists of applicants are supplied to the officers of the Board of Works, they will issue work tickets to the persons who are to be employed; and when the lists shall not contain all the applicants registered, this should be stated at foot, giving there the number still requiring employment.

29. The books, correspondence, papers, and accounts of the relief committees should at all times be open to the inspection of government officers who will be appointed to visit each barony, and who should be furnished with copies of any documents or accounts they may require. Detailed accounts of receipts and expenditure, in the form of an account current, should be kept, and certified copies of them will be required after the 15th of August 1847.

(Correspondence ... distress in Ireland, p.490-2; P.P. 1847 (761) LI.)

<u>38</u> Works applied for £ *1923=14=6*

<u>14</u> Recommended = £ *574=15=10*

D 831

OFFICE OF PUBLIC WORKS,

11th January 1847

SIR,

WITH reference to the Schedule of Works presented by the Justices and associated Cess-payers of the

Barony of *Moyashel & Maghuederuson*

County of *Westmeath*

Dated *28th december* 1846

And signed by *Sir R Levinge Bart,* Chairman,

under the Provisions of the Act, 9 & 10 Vict., ch. 107, We have had a Report thereon by *Florence Mahony Esqr*

and having had same under our consideration, are enabled to advise the Lord Lieutenant, to recommend for the sanction and approval of the Commissioners of Her Majesty's Treasury the following Works, amounting in the whole to the Sum of *Five Hundred and twenty Four Pounds, Fifteen Shillings and Six Pence ——*

18	*A road to be repaired in Wirstown*	12	9	"
26	*A road to be repaired leading to Robinstown Tynell ——*	50	—	"
37	*A Road to be repaired from Saunders Bridge to Turnpike*	60	"	"
38	*A Footpath to be made from Saunders Bridge to Boardstown* £	52	6	6
		574	15	6

We are

Sir,

Your Obedt servts

R Griffith

Wm A Larcom

(National Archives, Distress Papers 1847, D 831.)

2. The engineering of roads

The relief works of 1846-47 were primarily devoted to the making of new roads or the improvement of existing ones. Following the act of 5 March 1846, the Board of Works issued technical specifications for the guidance of their engineers and supervisors, and these were largely followed in the new series of works that began in the autumn of that year. The vast majority of the people employed on the relief works were labourers. An outline of their duties and the system of task-work is provided in an account by William Henry Smith, an English engineer employed on the schemes.

Instructions for the guidance of engineers, etc., 5 March 1846.

For engineers, for the laying out and constructing new lines of road, or the improving of existing roads by cutting down hills and filling hollows.

With respect to construction: In all cases of formation through arable land, the vegetable soil should be removed from beneath the metalling, and where practicable (within a reasonable limit as to cost) the whole surface of the formation should be ballasted with rough rubble stones about six inches in depth, on which the metalling is to rest. This ballast will form an effective system of underdrainage for the road, without which the cost of maintenance will be much increased; free egress must also be given to the drainage water into the side ditches or fences, the grips of which should be so formed as to levels that the water without accumulation may run freely off; by adopting these means, the ditches tend to drain the land as well as the road. The sketch gives a good form of cross-section for roads and fences.

Where side-cutting is taken for trunking or forming the road, the soil should be stripped from off the land wanted, and the excavation taken so as to allow of the lands being reformed and cultivated when the soil is restored. The same practice should be adopted in spoil-banks; the soil should be taken off where the excavated earth is to be laid, and the surface of the spoil-bank, when properly formed with slopes of 6 to 1, resoiled and returned to the farmer...

In the formation of roads through moors or shallow bogs, the elastic matter should be removed where the cost would not be too great, an inflexible base being of the first consequence in road constructing. When the cost becomes too heavy from the depth of the bog, the first operation should be drainage, so as to remove the stagnant water from off the line. These drains, which are to cross the road at interstices of about 40 feet, should be so made of dried turf properly moulded, as to remain permanently open, and the side or fence drains, in all cases and at all times, for these cross drains to discharge into. The formation may then be proceeded with; the filling in of all the hollows to be done with virgin bog, chopped and firmly trodden. The crowning of the roadway to be then formed with dried peat scraps; those are sods cut about 16 inches by 12 inches, and 9 inches in depth, laid evenly over the whole breadth of the carriageway, in two layers; on this formation a soaling [sealing ?] of tenacious clay, 9 inches in uniform depth, should be placed, on which the metalling, either fine broken stones, or, what is better for bog roads, adhesive gravel, is to be placed, averaging 8 inches in thickness. The equilibrium of a bog road is its greatest security.

To increase the means of extending employment to the poor in cutting down hills and filling hollows, long wheeling even to the extent of from 150 to 200 yards may be encountered sooner than employ horses, as the hire of two horses will absorb the wages of seven men at least.

John MacMahon, C.E., Office of Public Works.

(*Correspondence explanatory ... distress*, p.297-8; P.P. 1846 (736) XXXVII.)

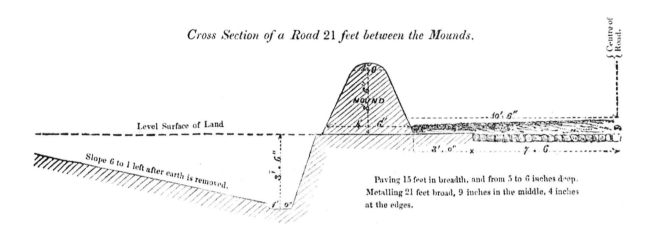

Cross Section of a Road 21 feet between the Mounds.

Paving 15 feet in breadth, and from 5 to 6 inches deep.
Metalling 21 feet broad, 9 inches in the middle, 4 inches
at the edges.

Duties of labourers employed on road works.

This class were at first generally employed by day-work; afterwards, a system of task was adopted, each gauger and his men having allotted to them a portion of a road to cut away, for which they were given a certain price per cube yard as it was removed; the maximum rate being 1s 6d *per diem*. This system was obviously most difficult, and led to much scheming and imposition. In the first place, it was frequently impossible to find a sufficient number of persons competent to measure up work, and even where these persons were obtained, a correct system of task-work could not in many cases be adopted.

Remarks: For instance, supposing a hill required to be cut down, and two gangs placed at equal distances from the top, on the opposite ascents; the men are to cut twenty yards forward, and one yard deep, at 6d per yard, the road being ten yards in breadth; to all

appearance, this work will be fairly and equally allotted; yet, on the one side, they might earn 2s or 2s 6d *per diem*, and on the other, they would not make 6d. This arises from the difference of stratification; on one side might be found nothing but sand or sand and gravel, whilst on the other, large blocks of boulders might appear that would

require breaking, or even blasting up, ere they could be removed; nor could this be remedied, as was suggested, by first breaking into the ground; every yard might vary from rock to sand, as is frequently the case. It was strictly enjoined that animal labour, as far as possible, was to be prohibited, in lieu of which wheelbarrows were to be employed, as giving a greater amount of labour.

(William Henry Smith, *A twelve months residence in Ireland during the Famine and the public works, 1846 and 1847*, London, 1848, p. 57-9.)

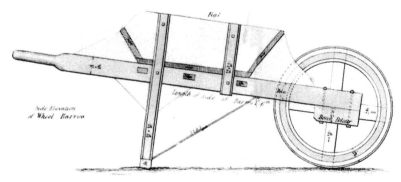

'Plans and description of economic implements used in the execution of public works'.
(*Correspondence from July 1846 to Jan. 1847 relating to the measures adopted for the relief of distress*, Board of Works series, facing p. 217; P.P. 1847 (764) L.)

3. Piers and harbours

Arelatively small relief operation was devoted to the construction or improvement of piers and harbours. The main legislation was enacted by Peel on 5 March 1846 as, 'An act to encourage the sea fisheries of Ireland by promoting and aiding with grants of public money the construction of piers, harbours and other works' (9 Victoria, chapter 3). The amount of money made available was small and under Peel amounted to just over £10,000. After the main relief works were suspended, however, these works were continued under new legislation and, together with other fishery initiatives, such as the establishment of fish-curing stations on the south and west coasts, proved worthwhile and ultimately productive.

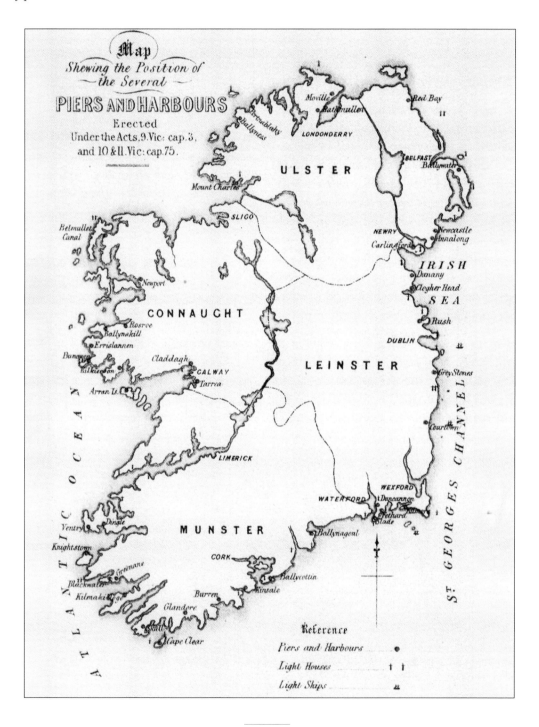

Schedule of projects towards the cost of which grants were sanctioned.

Name and description of work	County	Applicants	Estimate		
			£	s	d
Annalong – Harbour improvement, wharf and breakwater	Down	Inhabitants	2,490	0	0
Aran Island – Pier and landing slip	Galway	John Digby, Esq.	2,400	0	0
Brandon – Rebuilding the pier	Kerry	Inhabitants, per James Hickson, Esq.	600	0	0
Ballycottin – Pier	Cork	M. Longfield, Esq.	2,840	0	0
Ballyness – Pier	Donegal	W. Olpherts, Esq.	640	0	0
Bunowen – Pier	Galway	John A. O'Neill, Esq.	6,400	0	0
Ballynakill – Landing slip and wharf	Galway	Francis J. Graham, Esq.	900	0	0
Belmullet – Canal	Mayo	W. H. Carter, Esq.	9,000	0	0
Bunatruhan – Landing slip	Donegal	Rev. G. H. Tredennick	500	0	0
Ballynacourty – Extension of pier	Waterford	Thomas Wyse, Esq.	500	0	0
Blackwater – Pier and roadway	Kerry	Rev. Denis Mahony	900	0	0
Ballywalter – Pier and roadway	Down	Andrew Mulholland, Esq.	4,500	0	0
Ballynagaul – Pier and landing slip	Waterford	J. W. Strangman, Esq.	1,800	0	0
Burren – Pier and landing slip	Cork	Lord Bernard	1,100	0	0
Carlingford – Pier and Broadway	Louth	R. McNeill, Esq.	3,350	0	0
Courtown – Screw-pile pier	Wexford	Lord Courtown	4,570	0	0
Cape Clear – Landing place and pier	Cork	Sir W. W. Becher, Bart	460	0	0
Claddagh – Quay	Galway	Rev. J. R. Rush and others	4,000	0	0
Clogher Head – Harbour improvements	Louth	Owners of Land	750	0	0
Cushendall – (Red Bay) Pier	Antrim	John McNeill, Esq.	5,000	0	0
Dingle – Extension of pier	Kerry	Inhabitants, per James Hickson, Esq.	3,000	0	0
Dunany – Extension of pier	Louth	A. B. Bellingham, Esq.	543	12	9
Duncannon – Pier and approach	Wexford	A. Stephens, Esq., and others	6,000	0	0
Errislannan – Dock	Galway	John S. Lambert, Esq.	843	10	9
Fethard – Repairs of pier &c.	Wexford	J. W. Webb, Esq.	63	0	0
Grey Stones – Landing wharf	Wicklow	W. R. La Touche, Esq.	1,200	0	0
Greenane – Pier	Kerry	John Mahony, Esq.	300	0	0
Glandore – Harbour improvements	Cork	James R. Barry, Esq.	220	0	0
Helvick Head – landing slip and improvements to basin	Waterford	Lord Stuart De Decies	450	0	0
Kilkieran – Pier	Galway	Waste Land Society	3,000	0	0
Knightstown (Valencia) – Extension of pier and breakwater	Kerry	Knight of Kerry	2,700	0	0
Kilmakilloge – Pier	Kerry	Marquis of Lansdowne	2,200	0	0
Kilmore – Pier	Wexford	Inhabitants	6,210	0	0
Moville – Pier	Donegal	William Hazlett, Esq.	5,900	0	0
Newport – Quay wall and deepening channel	Mayo	Sir Richard O'Donnell, Bart	1,200	0	0
Newcastle – Pier and breakwater	Down	Lord Annesley's Representatives	9,400	0	0
Portnablahy – Pier	Donegal	Alexander Stewart, Esq.	1,900	0	0
Rosroe – Pier	Galway	General Thompson	800	0	0
Roundstone – Repairing pier	Galway	Thomas Martin, Esq.	1,200	0	0
Rush – Rebuilding pier	Dublin	Sir Roger Palmer	1,400	0	0
Sea View – (Mount Charles) Pier	Donegal	L. Cornwall, Esq.	2,675	0	0
Slade – Pier	Wexford	Inhabitants	1,400	0	0
Skull – Pier and approach	Cork	Inhabitants	2,400	0	0
Tarrea – Pier and approach	Galway	M. Blake, Esq.	2,235	0	0
Ventry – Pier and landing slip	Kerry	James Hickson, Esq., and others	2,200	0	0

Note: In addition to relief works from 1846-47, the list and map include works up to December 1851. (*Twentieth report from the Board of Public Works, Ireland*, appendix G; P.P. 1852-53 (1569) XLI.)

4. *Farmers employed on relief works*

A problem with the relief works was ensuring that employment was given only to the needy. The local relief committees were responsible for nominating people and naturally they were subject to various forms of pressure, in some cases amounting to outright intimidation. Relatively independent farmers were often taken on in preference to paupers who had nobody to make representations on their behalf. An unfortunate result was that some farmers neglected their land and their planting; in a time of food scarcity, this was obviously short-sighted.

Letter from Trevelyan to Richard Pennefather, Under Secretary.

Treasury Chambers, 26 June 1846.

Sir, With reference to their Lordships' minute dated 16th instant, on the third monthly report of the Commissioners of Public Works, a copy of which was forwarded to you with my letter of the same date, I am commanded by the Lord Commissioners of Her Majesty's Treasury to state that, having reason to believe that numerous persons who do not really stand in need of relief are employed on the works which have been sanctioned under the Act, 9 Victoria, chapter 1 [March 1846], for the relief of the people suffering from scarcity, and that rates of wages are given exceeding what is required for providing subsistence for the workpeople and their families, and holding out a temptation to engage in the works carried on under the above mentioned act in preference to other means of employment which are open to them, their Lordships request that you will suggest to the Lord Lieutenant that the Board of Works and the Relief Commission should be directed to issue such instructions to the superintendents of the works and to the local relief committees, as will secure a due observance of the rules which have been laid down for the proper administration of the funds provided for the relief of the people suffering from the late failure of the potato crop in Ireland.

I am, etc., C.E. Trevelyan.

(National Archives, Relief Commission Papers, 3816.)

A relief committee certificate.
(National Archives, Relief
Commission Papers, 3485.)

No. _____

We, the undersigned, certify that from the best inquiries we have been able to make

_____

has lost his Stock of Potatoes by the prevalent Disease, and is a proper object for employment on the Roads carried on by the Board of Works.

Dated at _____ this_____
day of_____ 1846.

Members of Committee.

By Authority—A. Thom, 87, Abbey-street, Dublin.

NOTICE.

CAVAN RELIEF COMMITTEE.

The Relief Committee have received numerous complaints of persons having obtained employment in the Public Works in this district, who do not come within the description laid down in the instructions issued by Government to the Relief Committees, that is " persons who are destitute of means of support, or for whose support such employment is actually necessary."

It is obvious that Pensioners at a shilling a day, Farmers (or their sons) possessing a cart and horse, and several cows, with stacks of oats in their haggard, cannot be included in this description ; and yet many such, it is stated to the Committee, are at present employed.

When such persons once take into consideration that, as employment obviously cannot be afforded to all, their obtaining it throws out of the work poor destitute and starving people, the Committee confidently trust they will voluntarily withdraw and give up their tickets.

The Committee, however, will continue to receive complaints ; and if the party complained of does not withdraw of his own accord, he will be called upon to shew upon what grounds he claims to be employed on the Public Works.

The Committee will not recommend for employment Servants or Labourers who are actually engaged, or those who leave their employers without consent.

When any Gentleman or Farmer requires Labourers, to be paid at the same rate adopted in the Public Works, if he will notify to the Committee the names of those he wishes to hire, they shall be immediately struck off their Lists so long as they are thus required ; the Committee being authorised to afford employment to those alone who cannot obtain it elsewhere.

The Commitee are informed that Carts and Horses belonging to wealthy farmers are employed at the Public Works. This they consider quite unjustifiable.—There are persons holding little or no land, who keep a Cart and Horse entirely for hire, and actually live by it. Of such, a list might, without much difficulty, be made ; and the Committee think that such might fairly obtain employment at the usual wages, of 2s. 6d. per day, under the Board of Works, provided they cannot procure it elsewhere. But if it shall be found necessary to employ the Carts of persons not in want, the Committee recommend that they shall receive three men from the Public Works in exchange, or if they prefer it, two men, and the wages of the third in cash ; but that in no case, shall the wages of 2s. 6d. a day for man, cart, and horse be paid, unless to those included in the list before mentioned.

The Committee are of opinion that, for the future, Overseers and Check Clerks, as far as may be found practicable, should be selected from persons at present in the Public Works; their merit might be judged from their conduct while employed, and if any should be found deserving of promotion, it would be a great incentive to others, and would also be a saving of the Public Money.

FARNHAM, *Chairman.*

November 10, 1846.

JOHNSTON, PRINTER, CAVAN,

(National Archives, Relief Commission Papers, Cavan.)

5. The numbers employed

The map showing the numbers employed on relief works in 1846-47 does not quite represent the distribution of distress, as the provision of relief works did not necessarily reflect the level of distress in an area. For instance, remote areas with scattered populations often did not have leadership to press their case; also, ratepayers were slow to propose works as they would ultimately have to pay for them. Some of the workers' problems are referred to by William Edward Forster, an English member of the Society of Friends (the Quakers), who made an important contribution as a relief worker and publicist. As Chief Secretary in 1880-82, he was nicknamed 'Buckshot' by Parnell for his repressive policies.

Extracts from W.E. Forster's narrative, January 1847.

Early next morning we proceeded to the small village of Leenane [Co. Galway], where we found a large body of men engaged in making a pier under the Labour Rate Act [Poor Employment Act]. This village appeared to be, comparatively speaking, well off, having had in it public works for some weeks, and the wages at pier-making being rather better than those earned on the roads. Still, even here the men were weak, evidently wasting away for want of sufficient food...

I here met with a striking instance of the patience of these sufferers. The Bundorragha men had been at work for three weeks on the roads, and the men at a neighbouring village for five weeks; owing to the negligence or mistake of some officers of the works, with the exception of two of the gangsmen who had gone themselves to Westport the end of the previous week, no wages had until this morning been received. While I was there, the pay-clerk sent a messenger over, but still only with wages for a few; and it was wonderful, but yet most touching, to see the patient, quiet look of despair, with which the others received the news that they were still left unpaid. I doubt whether it would have been easy to find a man who would have dared to bear the like announcement to starving Englishmen.

On recrossing the water, I found my father [William Forster] waiting for me on a car on which we proceeded to Clifden, which we did not reach till after nightfall. Near the Kylemore Lake, under that grand chain of mountains, the Twelve Pins, we found full a hundred men making a new road. After long cross-questioning, we learned that their wages did not average, taking one with another and allowing for broken days, more than four shillings and sixpence per week per head, and this we found confirmed by our inquiries in other districts; in fact, for the more distressed localities of Mayo and Galway, I should consider this too high an average.

To get to their work, many of the men have to walk five, even seven Irish miles. The sergeant of a police station by the roadside told us that the custom of these men was to take a little meal-gruel before starting in the morning, taking but one meal one day and treating themselves with two the next. He mentioned cases in which they had worked till they fell over their tools. Four and sixpence per week thus earned, the sole resource of a family of six, with Indian meal their cheapest food, at 2s 10d to 4s per stone! What is this but slow death, a mere enabling the patient to endure for a little longer time the disease of hunger? Yet even this was the state of those who were considered well off – provided for; and for this provision the people were everywhere begging as for their lives. In some districts there were no public works; and even where there were, we found that though the aim was to find employment for one man to every five or six souls, it really was not given to more than one man in nine or twelve...

In many of the more remote and distressed – because neglected – districts, where the inhabitants have hitherto subsisted upon potatoes, a retail trade in provisions is altogether novel to their habits; and so complete is the absence of capital, that there is no probability (at least this year) of its overtaking the demand. Often the poor people have, after earning their wretched pittance at the public works, to walk ten, twenty, even thirty miles to the nearest store to get a stone of meal, or to buy it off the small hucksters at an advance of as much as thirty per cent above the market price.

(Distress in Ireland: Extracts from correspondence published by the Central Relief Committee of the Society of Friends, II, p. 35-36, 1847.)

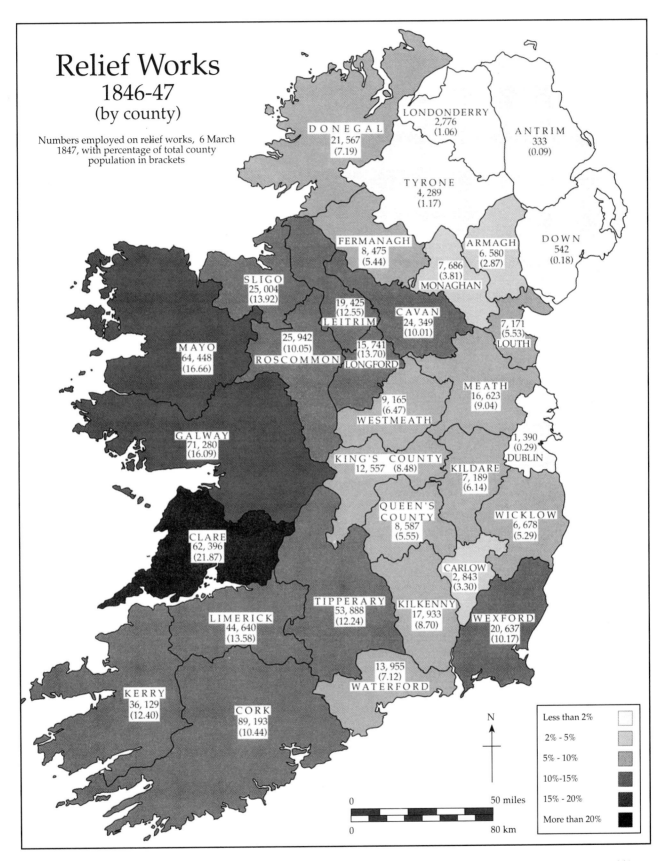

Relief Works
1846-47
(by county)

Numbers employed on relief works, 6 March 1847, with percentage of total county population in brackets

LONDONDERRY
2,776
(1.06)

ANTRIM
333
(0.09)

DONEGAL
21,567
(7.19)

TYRONE
4,289
(1.17)

DOWN
542
(0.18)

FERMANAGH
8,475
(5.44)

ARMAGH
6.580
(2.87)

7,686
(3.81)
MONAGHAN

SLIGO
25,004
(13.92)

19,425
(12.55)
LEITRIM

CAVAN
24,349
(10.01)

7,171
(5.53)
LOUTH

25,942
(10.05)
ROSCOMMON

15,741
(13.70)
LONGFORD

MAYO
64,448
(16.66)

MEATH
16,623
(9.04)

9,165
(6.47)
WESTMEATH

GALWAY
71,280
(16.09)

1,390
(0.29)
DUBLIN

KING'S COUNTY
12,557 (8.48)

KILDARE
7,189
(6.14)

QUEEN'S
COUNTY
8,587
(5.55)

WICKLOW
6,678
(5.29)

CLARE
62,396
(21.87)

CARLOW
2,843
(3.30)

TIPPERARY
53,888
(12.24)

KILKENNY
17,933
(8.70)

WEXFORD
20,637
(10.17)

LIMERICK
44,640
(13.58)

13,955
(7.12)
WATERFORD

KERRY
36,129
(12.40)

CORK
89,193
(10.44)

N

Less than 2%	
2% - 5%	
5% - 10%	
10%-15%	
15% - 20%	
More than 20%	

0 ——— 50 miles

0 ——— 80 km

(*Sixteenth report from the Board of Public Works, Ireland,* appendix R1; P.P. 1847-48 (983) XLXVII; redrawn by Brian MacDonald.)

6. *Reviewing the relief works*

The organisation most directly involved with the relief works of 1846-47 was the Board of Works. The Board was generally acknowledged as having acquitted itself well in an impossible situation which was foisted on it and over which it did not have full control. The Board's views of the whole episode were conveyed in a report to the Treasury in September 1847 when the enabling act expired. The folk-memory of the public works and those who master-minded them is well represented in Hugh Dorian's account, written just fifty years later.

Recollections of the relief works.

After a good deal of unsuccessful petitioning on the part of the starving people and many delays and many unfulfilled promises on the part of the upper class, the government was moved at last to extend relief by giving employment in the shape of making 'broad roads', as they were called. Government engineers were sent out at a good salary to mark out the new lines of roads, through rocks and bogs and every other impediment. The greatest engineering and ingenuity used in laying out these were to find out the most difficult routes, impossible to make and impossible to tread. Then pay-clerks, check-clerks, overseers and gangs-men or gaffers were appointed according as they had real or supposed knowledge, or better still through intercession; and at long last, the hungry and the naked, in the cold depth of winter, were set to work; and a selection of those was made, those and those only, who were known to be in extreme necessity, and their daily wages fixed at not even that valuable coin – one shilling – oh no! but exactly nine pennies per day.

In any work that ever was attempted, this was the most useless, for the reason that the roads were never completed, and at this day, would remind the historian of like traces left by the hands of the Romans in the Ages of Invasion. They can and will, in after ages, be traced in most places from the pieces here and there partly constructed; and, following the course of the lines, can be seen the gravel-hole, the quarry, or the shattered rock, from which more than one poor man had to crawl to his home, such as it was, overpowered with hunger, fainting through weakness, make for his bed, such as it was, lie down, and die.

The ideas [*sic*] of the efforts to construct the new lines of roads served but one end and that was they being the means of sending many a poor honest man to the untimely grave through hunger and cold, for he was restricted in such a manner that if he did not put in an appearance on the ground in all kinds of weather, no matter what the distance might be, or if he was not present at every roll-call, his pay, small as it was, was reduced one-half or one-fourth. Every man, therefore, who was fortunate enough to get his name on the list, did his utmost to appear, but to work was not able, nor yet much inclined. While on the ground and apparently working, a man in every gang, or as they were called 'squads', kept a lookout for the approach of the 'gaffer', whilst the rest of the gang sat or stood idle, and when under the eyes of the gaffer itself, their efforts were such that the slowest manoeuvres of a new 'Corporation-Brigade' man were swift motion in comparison.

Here is where the government advisers dealt out the successful blow and it would appear premeditated, the great blow for slowly taking away human life, getting rid of the population and nothing else, by forcing the hungry and the half-dead men to stand out in the cold and in the sleet and rain from morn till night for the paltry reward of nine pennies per day. Had the poor pitiful creatures got this allowance, small as it was, at their homes, it would be relief, it would be charity; it would convey the impression that their benefactors meant to save life, but in the way thus given, on compulsory conditions, meant next to slow murder.

(Hugh Dorian, 'Donegal, sixty years ago', 1896; photostat copy in NLI Ms 2047.)

Report by the Board of Works to the Treasury.

The first step was the resumption of the roads which had been left unfinished at the close of the former season; and the next, to adopt such of the numerous roads presented at the various sessions as were nearest to the seat of distress in each particular district, and which offered the least prospect of ultimate inutility. The scarcities which occurred in former years were local and confined to the western counties, in which there was great need of new roads. In 1846, however, the famine was general throughout Ireland, and there was no alternative but to adopt the presentments for repairs, small deviations, and improvements or hill-cuttings, when road-work became indispensable in the better-conditioned counties.

The distress became rapidly severe and more general; with the failure of the potato, the labour as well as the food of the humbler classes was gone. The farmers and gentry were unable to afford them ordinary employment; and public works, of the limited nature we have described, became the means of procuring food. The utility of the work was soon lost sight of in the struggle for life which rapidly ensued when public work of any kind became necessary as its sole condition, and our duties assumed another form; we were, in fact, no longer Commissioners of Public Works, but the administrators of outdoor relief to nearly a million of families, encumbered with the necessity of providing labour, tools and materials for its execution, officers for its superintendence and for the control of the mass of people thus brought together, and, finally, a machinery for the payment of the whole body in money wages.

The work was chosen for the people, not the people for the work; and with this reversal of the natural conditions of the effects of labour, the whole machinery was reversed, and that which in other circumstances would have facilitated our labours, acted of course in the contrary direction. The presentment sessions, which should have been deliberative bodies composed of proprietors and occupiers interested in the country, able to project and consider what works could be executed in their neighbourhood with the quantity of labour suddenly placed at their disposal, were, from the circumstances of haste and pressure, in all respects the reverse. They met in most cases wholly unprepared with projects of utility and unable to resist the absurd or improper projects which were thrust upon them by interested parties, first throwing the origination of projects on the officers of the government, who were generally strangers among them, and whose functions should have been wholly executive; and then leaving to the Board in Dublin the task of sifting the whole; in fact, the presentment sessions became worse than useless, the responsibility of all fell on the Board of Works, but deprived of that freedom of action which would have resulted from the legal adoption of the course into which matters virtually fell, viz, that the Board should be entrusted with a sufficient fund to meet the distresses of the district, and themselves originate the works, subject to the approval of your Lordships.

When this delay had been encountered, the executive part began; and here another body, the relief committees, appeared, whose duties should have been to investigate distress and prevent improper persons from forcing themselves on the works, but who, in too many instances, confined their attention to swelling the lists for relief, or constituted themselves into courts of grievance, for receiving and supporting complaints of every description...

We are anxious to say a few words on the present state of the relief works, so many of which are left in an unfinished state, and respecting which very serious complaints are made. It was our effort in the opening of the season to examine and consider every project and undertake only those which were of a useful character, but this caution soon became impracticable; work was required by the magistrates and clergy to be found for the destitute poor at the doors of their cabins, and the state of a particular locality as to distress was the only consideration. Doubtless, therefore, many roads were broken up which in their present state are worse than they were before... They remain a constant and unsightly monument of a disastrous period. Much consequent injury has also been done by cutting off farmers from their fields, which in many cases, indeed, are left unfenced. Gateways and cottages are left on the summits of cuttings, and retaining walls buried beneath the fillings below.

(Signed) H.D. Jones, Richard Griffith, John Radcliff, W.T. Mulvany, T.A. Larcom; 1 March 1849.

(Final report of the Board of Public Works, Ireland, relating to measures adopted for the relief of distress, July and August 1847, p.6; P.P. 1849 (1047) XXXIII.)

7. The Spectre

By the winter of 1846 absolute famine had taken hold in many parts of the country. A notable feature of the Famine, however, was that it was a regional phenomenon. Connacht, west Munster, south Ulster and west Leinster were the regions worst affected. The potato-dependent areas came off worst; local conditions obviously varied and there were marked discrepancies even within counties. Another feature of the Famine was that all classes did not suffer equally. Even in the worst areas, the large farmers escaped relatively unscathed and, in some cases, they actually prospered due to better prices for produce.

STANZA II.

———

The fell Spectre advanc'd,—who the horrors shall tell

Of his galloping stride, as he sounded the knell

Of thousands on thousands who 'neath his eye fell?

    Death cast the sure dart at his nod:

Now to low feeble moan sinks the sufferer's last cry,

As the pestilent fiend to each victim draws nigh,

Swift the death-smitten body is laid out hard by ;—

    'Tis a dread visitation of God.

VI

SOUP KITCHENS

In food emergencies, soup has often been utilised as a cheap and practical means of feeding large numbers of people. In the early nineteenth century in Britain, soup was distributed to the poor by various charitable organisations, most notably by the Society of Friends (the Quakers). In Ireland, as the crisis deepened in the autumn of 1846, certain organisations and private individuals, particularly relief committees and landlords' wives, began to provide soup for the local poor. The ingredients varied according to what was cheaply available; the soup was often based on meal and was more in the nature of stirabout or gruel. It was generally sold at a halfpenny or a penny a quart, but was given free to the destitute.

These local initiatives were *ad hoc* responses to the crisis, but in November the Irish Quakers became involved in relief efforts in an organised way. They adopted a systematic approach to the provision of relief and set up a number of soup kitchens along the lines suggested by Quakers in England. These proved popular and successful, and it soon became apparent that soup kitchens were an extremely practical means of providing relief. Simultaneously, the government was losing faith in the public works. Overwhelming numbers were flooding onto the works, administration was breaking down, and costs were escalating. Moreover, in many parts of the country, there was an alarming increase in mortality from starvation, fever and other diseases.

In the spring of 1847, the government radically changed its relief strategy, and transferred the main responsibility for relief to the Poor Law unions and the workhouses. To allow time for the change to be implemented, and to take the people through the hungry months until the next harvest, it decided to phase out the relief works and establish a system of free soup kitchens. Legislation was enacted in February 1847, and a new Relief Commission was established in Dublin under the direction of an experienced administrator, Sir John Burgoyne. The scheme was to be funded by the Poor Law rates and by local subscriptions which would be matched with government grants; to expedite matters, the government provided loans which were to be repaid from the rates.

The local relief committees were reconstituted to administer the scheme. As with the previous committees, they drew up lists of people entitled to relief. The destitute got the soup free; those earning wages insufficient for their needs were allowed to purchase it. The numbers employed on the relief works were gradually reduced and most people were laid off in the period from March to June. The soup kitchens, however, were only slowly established due to bureaucratic regulations, and there was considerable hardship in the interim period. But by August, up to three million people were receiving soup daily. The scheme made a very significant contribution to relief and saved the lives of many thousands.

The idea of taking free government soup was abhorrent to many people but it soon became popular. Commentators noted that there was a marked improvement in the appearance of the destitute in areas where soup kitchens were in operation. The scheme, unfortunately, was terminated in September; the rationale was that as the potato crop was relatively unaffected by blight in 1847, the crisis was over. Thereafter, official policy dictated that the state should have minimal involvement with relief, other than ensuring that the Poor Law unions fulfilled their responsibilities.

The government decision to abandon the relief works in favour of the free soup scheme was influenced by the fact that farm labourers and small farmers were being employed on the works, which would result in less cultivation and continue the cycle of famine. That turned out to be the case. In 1847, the potato crop was generally free of blight, but only a small acreage had been planted, due to the general disruption, shortage of seed, demoralisation and despair. On average, the eventual yield was not much more than a quarter of pre-Famine levels, and, in effect, the Famine raged unabated.

1. *Relief committees distribute soup*

With the deteriorating situation in the latter months of 1846, many relief committees began to provide soup or stirabout for the destitute in their areas. It was generally sold, but there were various systems whereby the charitable could sponsor the food for those who could not afford to pay for it, as was the case at Cloone, Co. Leitrim. Most relief committees were short of funds; Major Sterne of the Brookeborough Relief Committee wrote to the Chief Secretary, Henry Labouchere, for assistance: 'anything from a penny postage stamp to £100'. The only response, however, was the promise of 'the formula of a soup which can be provided at a very moderate price'.

CLOONE SOUP-SHOP.

Days of Distribution:

WEDNESDAYS AND SATURDAYS,

WEEKLY.

RULE 1.—That Mrs. HOGG be requested to act as Treasurer, and superintend the management of the Cloone Soup Shop.

2.— That Soup be sold to the destitute at 1d. per Quart.

3.—That, in order to provide some Subsistence for the totally destitute, who are *wholly* without means, a copy of these Rules be sent to the Clergy, Gentry, and Farmers of the Parish of Cloone, to afford them an opportunity of supporting this benevolent object, and providing substantial relief for the Poor in their localities.

4.—That each Subscriber shall have power to recommend persons for gratuitous *weekly* supplies of Soup, according to the following order:

Subscribers of £1, to dispose of 16 Quarts of Soup, weekly, for 16 weeks, on Recommendation Tickets, to be supplied by the Treasurer.

Subscribers of 10s., to dispose of 8 Quarts, weekly, for 16 weeks, &c.

Subscribers of 5s., to dispose of 4 Quarts, weekly, for 16 weeks, &c.

Subscribers of 1s., to dispose of 2 Quarts, weekly, for 6 weeks.

The Glebe, Cloone,
December, 1846.

P.S.—Bailiffs to have power to recommend on the Subscriptions of absentee Landlords, as above.

[BRENNAN, Printer, Ck.-on-Shannon.

(National Archives, Relief Commission Papers, 10,120.)

The Brookeborough Relief Committee soup kitchen.

To the Editor of *The Fermanagh Reporter.*

Dear Sir,

My soup shop is now in full operation, and any poor person can be relieved at one halfpenny per quart. Sir A. B. Brooke is, I understand, about to open one likewise, so that I trust the poor in our parish will be amply supplied; it is open to any one to visit and witness the ingredients of which it is composed. The following is about the cost of 20 gallons; we may have occasion to vary it a little according to circumstances as we go on:

	£	s	d
Boiler, made of best block tin, with sheet-iron cover	0	12	0
Iron stand, measure, ladle, etc.	0	8	0
	1	0	0
Six pounds of meat, cow's head or otherwise @ 3d	0	1	6
Ten pounds of oatmeal	0	1	8
Onions, or leeks	0	0	6
Turnips, cabbage, and carrots	0	0	3
Pepper and salt	0	0	3
Cook and fire	0	1	0
	0	5	2
Eighty quarts, at ½d	0	3	4
Loss	£0	1	10

Perhaps the meat may be something more, and the meal something less, by and bye; say a loss on each boiling of two shillings, so that a fund of £10 or £20, with care and management, will last for a considerable time.

Major W. Sterne, Chairman, Brookeborough Relief Committee.
Gola, 7 December 1846.

(National Archives, Relief Commission Papers, 8614.)

'A sketch of the poor assembled for soup at Poulacurra House on the 22nd of February, 1847'. (NLI Sketch-Book 2018 TX, p.23.)

2. Landlords and soup kitchens

The National Library's collection of estate papers from the O'Hara estate at Annaghmore, Co. Sligo includes a letter by Major Charles O'Hara in response to a request from Lady Louisa King-Tenison of Kilronan Castle, Keadue, Co. Roscommon, for advice on setting up a soup kitchen. His reply attests the inflated price of foodstuffs in the winter of 1846-47. While soup provided by landlords and other groups was often of poor quality, being sometimes watery and almost invariably over-cooked, the health of those receiving it generally improved. The benefits conferred by the soup kitchens were, however, largely counteracted by a widespread fever epidemic in the first half of 1847.

Draft of Major O'Hara's reply to Lady King-Tenison.

I had the honor to receive your ladyship's letter this day when engaged with our clergyman in discussing the 'Means to procure cheap food', distributed by the Relief Commission, Dublin, which he found at Thom's, 87 Abbey Street [Dublin]. I regret I have not one to send your ladyship as it gives the best information I have seen on soup and provisions shops and I beg to refer you to it. Provisions shops are most essential; our country folk are bad cooks and know not how to turn food to the best advantage. The *Sligo Journal* was incorrect, as it generally is, in reporting my recent return from Liverpool. I went there in October to look for food in consequence of the destitute state of the markets in Sligo, and I succeeded in purchasing a cargo of Indian corn, coming from Trieste, on advantageous terms, which has since arrived and is nearly consumed. I also purchased flour and other bread stuffs, as they are termed, as I thought cheap, but expense of package and storage on arrival made them very expensive. Prices of all things have risen enormously; and to judge from the papers and market reports there is little advantage derivable from going to Liverpool. Sir Robert Gore-Booth, by means of his brother, a shipowner, has ordered several cargoes from America direct to Sligo, giving those who pleased a portion of them; and I think he said on Tuesday he should continue to order so long as there were candidates for the cargoes, and that he expected that the last cargo of Indian corn ordered was to cost at Sligo only £12 a ton; the price now charged in Sligo is £19 – and in Liverpool little less. This might be your ladyship's best course. You will find him an honest merchant and Henry Gore-Booth a good supercargo [supervisor]. I am now busied in establishing four soup shops on different works so as to enable the labourers [to get] a warm meal of soup or hot porridge at a cheap rate: a halfpenny for a pint of soup or porridge, whereas the wretches were in the habit of bringing with them in the morning a little raw meal or flour and diluting it with cold water – their only food. A great point is to teach them to cook, and by the shops afford them the means of doing so at home. I sell Indian meal, oatmeal, flour, peameal (excellent for soup), rice, American beef, and peppers and spices, onions, carrots and turnips when procurable. My working parties amount to near 1,500 men daily and consume 12 ton a week of meal.

4 January 1847.

(NLI Ms 20,320, O'Hara Papers.)

Report by an estate steward to his landlord.

[Spelling as in the manuscript.]

Sir,

I received yours this morning and am desired by Mrs Meall to give you the following receipt [receipt i.e. recipe] as the way she makes our soup.

Quantity of water	190	quarts
Beef	30	lb
Barley	8	lb
Peas to be stiped the night before	8	lb
Turnips	3	stone

5 pennyworth of vegatables, leeks, greens and cellery, adding salt to taste.

Fire lighted at ½ past 5 o'clock.

Beef cut up very small and bones all well broken; barley put in with the water, cold beef and other ingredients as soon as it boiles. Keep up the boil till ¼ before 12 o'clock noon, when it will turn out 144 quarts of good soup. These quantitys has been all exactly misured and weighted today that we might be correct in our statement; and the soup is very good.

You will see by the above statement that we are using more barley and peas than we did at the commensment, as we have no carrot or parsnips or onions now. Kelly gave up the contract he mead with me about the beef. I have contracted with another for 2¾d. Mrs Meall would like to trye the Ameracan peas as they are cheap and would help greatly to thiken the soup.

There was one of the pay masters of the publick works robbed near Castleconnel yesterday about noon, opsite Lady Massey, and I here £380 was taken in notes, silver and coper. There was another atempt to rob another paymaster about Cappawhite; one policeman shot, but the horse in this case took fright and run off with the driver and money.

Owing to this robbrey the workmen has not been paid this week and they are crying out bitterly, poor men.

I remain, Sir, Your obedient humble servant,
George Meall.
Raheen, 23 January 1847.

Letter of George Meall to Sir Richard Bourke, Raheen, Co. Limerick [formerly governor of New South Wales]; (NLI Ms 8474(4), Sir Richard Bourke Papers.)

'A group of peasants and beggars assembled in the kitchen garden of Poulacurra House, May 1847'. (NLI Sketch-Book 2018 TX, p.26.)

3. The Society of Friends

In November 1846, a group of local Quakers established a soup kitchen in Cork. When the Central Relief Committee of the Society of Friends was established later that month, it decided on soup kitchens as one of its principal strategies. In addition to setting up a number of soup kitchens run by Quakers, it provided funds to local relief committees, especially in the west, for the purchase of soup boilers. The success of the Quaker scheme impressed the local officials involved in relief, and was an important factor in influencing the government to undertake the distribution of free soup on a national basis. The Quakers' soup kitchens saved many lives, especially in the early months of 1847 before the state scheme was fully operational.

The Quaker soup kitchen in Charles Street, Dublin.

This institution was opened on the 23rd of first-month, and is under the care of a joint committee of men and women Friends, several of whom attend in rotation to superintend the delivery of the soup. It is capable of making 2,400 quarts per day. There are three wooden vats in which the soup is boiled by steam, each containing about 200 gallons, also an iron boiler of about 80 gallons. The distribution takes place twice in the day, viz, from half-past seven till nine in the morning, and from twelve to three in the afternoon; and it is open on every weekday.

The soup is sold at 1d per quart, or with a piece of bread at 1½d, and it is a satisfaction to the committee to observe how desirous the poor are to avail themselves of the facility it affords them to procure a good and nutritious food at a moderate price. It is now about a month since its commencement, and during this period about 12,500 quarts have been purchased by this class. The committee also dispose of the soup by tickets, which are sold at the same price to those who wish to distribute them gratuitously. The average distribution has been more than 1,000 quarts per day, but the number applying for it appears to be increasing; on some days there have been more than 1,500 quarts distributed.

The soup has for the past few weeks been made according to the following proportions; and although the committee are far from believing that it is not susceptible of improvement, yet the statement may be useful, as it has been found to supply an excellent and nutritious soup:

Receipt for 200 gallons.

Beef	150	lb
Peas	70	lb
Oatmeal	42	lb
Scotch barley	42	lb
Ground pepper and allspice	½	lb
Salt	¼	stone

To make the soup, fill the vessel about half-full of water; when boiling, put in the meat, having been previously cut into small pieces about the size of a walnut, and the bones broken small. An hour after, put in the peas, first dividing them into bags containing about 14lb each and tied at the top, but leaving sufficient room for the peas to swell. In about four hours afterwards, take out the bags and turn the peas into a tub; have them bruised into a paste, and put them back into the boiler along with the barley. Keep it boiling gently for four or five hours, then put in the oatmeal, which should be first blended with cold water, and fill the boiler with water to the quantity required. Put in the salt and spices an hour after the oatmeal; keep all well stirred for about half an hour, when it will be ready for delivery.

The committee are fully aware that a very palatable soup could be made at a much lower cost; but at a time when the poor are without the means of supplying themselves with really nutritious food, and from this cause are increasingly liable to the attacks of diseases now so prevalent, they believe it to be of some importance to supply this deficiency by placing within their reach a description of food which may counteract these tendencies.

(Correspondence published by the Central Relief Committee of the Society of Friends, 1847, p.41.)

A Quaker soup kitchen in Cork.

The illustration shows a benevolent attempt to mitigate the suffering in the city of Cork, viz, the Society of Friends' Soup House. There are many similar establishments in operation through the county; but, we prefer the annexed, because the idea originated with the Society of Friends. The funds for its support are chiefly raised among this charitable class; and we are happy to state that the establishment is now in a position to supply 1,500 gallons of soup daily, at a loss, or rather cost, of from £120 to £150 per month to the supporters of the design. The present calls are for from 150 to 180 gallons daily, requiring 120 pounds of good beef, 27 pounds of rice, 27 pounds of oatmeal, 27 pounds of split peas, and 14 ounces of spices, with a quantity of vegetables. Tickets, at *one penny each*, are unsparingly distributed; on presenting one of which, each poor person receives one quart of soup, with half a small loaf of bread; and both are of good quality.

In the making of the soup, the greatest possible cleanliness is observed; attention is paid to the poor who throng the place daily for their cheap supply of food, as well as to the visitors, who go to see the soup made and who are requested to test its quality and suggest any improvement. The vats, which are shown in the sketch, are worked by a steam engine in an adjoining house; and, to ensure cleanliness as well as sweetness, they are used alternately.

'The Cork Society of Friends' Soup House'. (*The Illustrated London News*, 16 Jan. 1847.)

4. *Legislation*

The government's decision to set up a national free soup scheme was influenced by the belief that it would be cheaper than the relief works. As it turned out, it cost less than anticipated as substantial quantities of food were imported in the spring and summer of 1847, and prices dropped considerably. On 25 January, the Prime Minister, Lord John Russell, outlined the scheme in the House of Commons; the legislation was passed speedily and it became law on 26 February. The aim was for a network of soup kitchens sufficiently close to each other that people would not have to walk more than four miles there and back.

Extract from Lord John Russell's speech.

The opinion of the government was ... that the system [relief works] had become so vast, and, at the same time, the destitution and the want of food had so greatly increased, that it was desirable to attempt some other temporary scheme, by which, if possible, some of the evils which they have now to meet might be mitigated, and with so vast an expenditure of money that more effectual relief should be afforded. It has appeared to us that it will be desirable to form in districts, say electoral districts, relief committees; which relief committees shall be empowered to receive subscriptions, levy rates, and receive donations from the government; that by means of these they should purchase food and establish soup kitchens in the different districts; that they should, so far as they are able, distribute rations with this purchased food to the famishing inhabitants; and that, furnishing that food, they should not require as indispensable the test of work, but that labouring men should be allowed to work on their own plots of ground or for the farmers, and thus tend to produce food for the next harvest and procure, perhaps, some small wages to enable them to support their families.

After we considered this scheme, I communicated it to the Lord Lieutenant of Ireland [Lord Bessborough]. We have consulted the various officers of the Board of Works and at the head of the commissariat. They are prepared to consider it favourably; and we shall endeavour, first by a preparatory measure and next by a bill to be proposed to parliament, to carry into effect this arrangement. There is a person in this country conversant with Ireland, having been long engaged in the public works of that country, who earned not only the general esteem of the governments he has served but of the people among whom his operations were carried on. The person to whom I allude is Sir John Burgoyne ... He will be in communication with the Lord Lieutenant, and will have the co-operation of Colonel Jones and the Board of Works, of the commissariat, the head of the Poor Law Commission, the chief of the constabulary, and of other persons who are competent and ready to give him assistance. In proposing this measure, with the view of affording, if possible, more efficient means of relieving the poor people who now are in want of food, and, at the same time, of setting loose great numbers of persons for the ordinary operations of agriculture, we must take care – and the Lord Lieutenant is prepared to take care – that the substitution of this system for public works shall be made as easy in the transition as possible.

I do not despair of Ireland; I say there is no reason ... why Ireland may not at a future day rise to a state of great happiness and prosperity.

(*Hansard*, House of Commons, 25 January 1847, 435-6.)

Report in *The Pictorial Times* on food imports.

The government has wisely suspended all other business to direct more effectually the measures proposed for the alleviation of the misery and distress that is now depopulating Ireland. Our sympathies, in common with those of the inhabitants of all England, go with Ministers in their object and their endeavours. Party spirit is hushed, public opinion undivided, when the necessity is urged of immediately and sufficiently supplying the wants of our suffering fellow-countrymen, unable from their situation and circumstances to do aught in favour of themselves. To help them now, indeed, is our immediate duty; to teach them better habits, a wiser social economy, and a less selfish nationality, must be reserved for more fortunate times, when, perchance, our readiness to assist them in adversity will have prepared even the most prejudiced against us to receive our advice without questioning our sincerity.

That the government is active in performing what it proposes is evident. A fleet is already engaged in conveying provisions to Ireland. The *Avenger*, steam-frigate; the *Geyser*, steam-sloop; the *Rattler*, steam-sloop; the *Emerald* and *Mercury*, tenders; and the *Lively* and *Devon*, lighters, have arrived at Cork with provisions from the English ports, and have been ordered to their respective destinations on the Irish coast.

We can well understand with what feelings of joy the famished inhabitants of these districts must behold each fresh arrival of provisions for their sustenance. They will not, at least, curse us whilst they receive our bounty. There must be some truce to national jealousy and misguided prejudice, when they see such ample proof of our sympathy and social affection. False prophets may indeed interrupt or suspend amicable feeling for a time between the inhabitants of the two countries; but if the Irish can distinguish between bread and stone, the experience of the present time must for the future enable them to perceive who are Ireland's best friends, and who her most dangerous enemies.

Measures are also in progress for the establishment of soup kitchens throughout the country. According to a statement of Lord Bernard [James, Earl of Bandon, Lieutenant of Co. Cork], on Tuesday night in the House of Commons, no less a number than 3,000 persons receive gratuitous relief in Skibbereen every week; this is but one of some thirty food depots which had been opened during the last four weeks in the west of Ireland alone. In a few days these will be quadrupled. A steamer has been especially despatched with a large supply of boilers for preparing soup, which will be distributed throughout the counties where such aid is most required.

'Relief for Ireland'. (*The Pictorial Times*, 30 Jan. 1847; courtesy of Birmingham Library Services.)

5. *Eligibility for soup*

Burgoyne's Relief Commission stipulated three categories eligible for free soup: 1) destitute helpless persons; 2) destitute able-bodied persons without land; 3) destitute able-bodied with a small piece of land. A fourth category, those earning wages insufficient for their support, were allowed to purchase the soup or food. The local relief committees were responsible for drawing up lists of those eligible and ration cards were issued. It took some months to get the scheme fully operational, but by the end of May a million people were getting daily rations; by August the number had grown to an astonishing three million.

Ration cards issued by the Relief Commission; the half ration was for children under nine. (Brother Allen Library.)

The French chef at London's Reform Club, Alexis Soyer, was invited to Dublin by the Lord Lieutenant to install a model soup kitchen. The kitchen provided 8,750 rations a day; the government handed it over to the relief committee of the South Dublin Union. A decade later Soyer gained international fame for reforming the diet and victualling of the British army in the Crimea. (*The Illustrated London News*, 17 April 1847.)

Letter of Drogheda Relief Committee to the Relief Commissioners.

Gentlemen,

In obedience to your order, I send you the query-sheet herewith filled; and also one of our tickets for bread and soup rations. Parchment is selected in preference to paper and card, as the tickets remain in the possession of the poor persons and get rumpled and soiled in their keeping, circumstances which would be destructive to paper or card. They were issued to last six months.

In the house selected for the distribution, three or four of the soup committee attend daily. To one of them the poor person hands the ticket and gives the vessel for soup to an assistant. The committee man calls out 5, or 4, or 6, as the case may be, and makes a puncture with a large awl on the date, as you will perceive on this, March the 12th. This prevents the return of the ticket for the day, whilst the ticket still remains good. The number 200 or 100, as the case may be, refers to a corresponding number in the registry book in which the particulars on the heading are recorded, and by practice the distribution is rapid; reference to the registry book being unnecessary except in doubtful cases, few of which occur.

To avoid the danger of dysentery, white bread is generally used, and for the same reason beef is preferred to pork, although good American pork could be procured. The mixture of Indian meal with the rice gives satisfaction. No soup is allowed to remain over, lest the vegetables might ferment and occasion disease. The soup is nutritive and conducive to health. The poor look better since we commenced distribution, now about eight weeks. I am of opinion that if arrangements could be made to sell soup at cost price to persons in employment on railways, public or private works, it would improve their capability of working as they have not the utensils nor the knowledge necessary to prepare wholesome and nutritive food economically; coal, besides, is dear

No. *200.* **Soup Ticket.**

Name,.... *Pat Rogers*
Residence,.... *Morgans Lane*
No. in Family for Relief,.... *five*

	JANUARY.						APRIL.			
Su.	3	10	17	24	31	Su.	4	11	18	25
Mo.	4	11	18	25		Mo.	5	12	19	26
Tu.	5	12	19	26		Tu.	6	13	20	27
We.	6	13	20	27		We.	7	14	21	28
Th.	7	14	21	28		Th. 1	8	15	22	29
F. 1	8	15	22	29		Fr. 2	9	16	23	30
S. 2	9	16	23	30		Sa. 3	10	17	24	

	FEBRUARY.						MAY.			
Su.		7	14	21	28	Su.	2	9	16	23	30
Mo.	1	8	15	22		M.	3	10	17	24	31
Tu.	2	9	16	23		Tu.	4	11	18	25	
We.	3	10	17	24		W.	5	12	19	26	
Th.	4	11	18	25		Th.	6	13	20	27	
Fri.	5	12	19	26		Fr.	7	14	21	28	
Sa.	6	13	20	27		S. 1	8	15	22	29	

	MARCH.						JUNE.			
Su.		7	14	21	28	Su.		6	13	20	27
Mo.	1	8	15	22	29	Mo.		7	14	21	28
Tu.	2	9	16	23	30	Tu. 1	8	15	22	29
We.	3	10	17	24	31	W. 2	9	16	23	30
Th.	4	11	18	25		Th. 3	10	17	24	
Fr.	5	12	19	26		Fr. 4	11	18	25	
Sa.	6	13	20	27		Sa. 5	12	19	26	

and they have no other fuel. There are three or four factories, for instance, here, in which large numbers of females and children are employed. Their wages are small and by the loss of potatoes they can barely find themselves sufficient food. If a boiler was opened near each factory, these persons could be better fed, and as cheaply as now, by getting bread and soup at cost price. The arrangements however would be too complex for a relief committee who have a great deal of private and other public business to attend to.

I have the honour to be, gentlemen,
Your obedient servant, Patrick Marron, Secretary;
Relief Committee Rooms, Tholsel, Drogheda,
12 March 1847.

(National Archives, Relief Commission Papers, 14,241.)

6. *Soup and souperism*

While the Society of Friends and other groups provided soup and relief in a spirit of Christian charity, irrespective of the religious denomination of the recipients and with no claims on their allegiance, a number of evangelical missionary groups made relief conditional on conversion to the Protestant faith. Among the most controversial proselytisers were Rev. Edward Nangle who established a missionary colony on Achill Island, Co. Mayo in 1831, and Rev. Alexander Dallas who established schools in Connemara during the Famine. They attracted some hundreds of converts, but their strident propaganda caused great resentment among the Catholic clergy. 'Souperism' remains an abiding image in popular folklore.

Views of a 'liberal' Protestant couple on the Achill mission.

We consider every conscientious accession to the Protestant faith as a contribution in aid of the well-being of the state and the prosperity of Ireland more especially; but such experiments as that at Achill will be made in vain. We have shown that here it has been a complete failure; the principles upon which it has been conducted have not been in accordance with the divine precept of 'charity', nor has the clergyman under whose control the settlement is placed been an example of that gentle, peace-loving, and persuasive zeal, that 'meek and unaffected grace', which should distinguish a humble follower of 'The Lord and Master'.

One word more and we dismiss this subject: it was impossible not to appreciate the magnanimity of the poor, miserable, utterly destitute and absolutely starving inhabitants of Achill, who were at the time of our visit enduring privations at which humanity shudders, and to know that by walking a couple of miles and professing to change their religion they would have been instantly supplied with food, clothes and lodging. Yet these hungry thousands – for it would be scarcely an exaggeration to say that nine-tenths of the population of this island were, in the month of July last, entirely without food – preferred patiently to endure their sufferings, rather than submit to what they considered a degradation... But we have deemed it our duty to submit the case fully to our readers, with a view, particularly, to invite the consideration of English subscribers to 'The Mission'.

(Mr and Mrs S.C. Hall, *Ireland: its scenery and character, &c.*, London, 1841-3, vol.II, p.167-9.)

'The Protestant missionary settlement at Isle of Achill'; A contemporary lithograph. (NLI 1493TA.)

→

'Ballinaboy School [Co. Galway], near the monastery, 10th August, 1850', established by the Rev. Dallas. (NLI 2003TX, a sketch-book illustrating the work of Rev. Dallas and his followers.)

Letter of Father William Flannelly to Dr Daniel Murray, Archbishop of Dublin.

Ballinakill, Clifden, Co. Galway, 6 April 1849.

My Lord,

I beg most respectfully to claim your lordship's indulgence for presuming to submit the following observations to your judgement. The enemies of the faith are now endeavouring by all means to proselytise the people, have money to no end, and apostate priests and laics are the instruments selected to conduct this impious crusade. It cannot be wondered if a starving people would be perverted in shoals, especially as they go from cabin to cabin, and when they find the inmates naked and starved to death, they proffer food, money and raiment, on the express condition of becoming members of their conventicles. Scurrilous tracts are scattered in thousands among the poor by those emissaries of discord, and they go so far as to send the Catholic clergyman a copy of those pamphlets through the post office.

They are in the habit of saying to the poor people, 'why not go to your priests and get money from them'; but they take care to conceal the fact that there was a period when the priests had both lands and money, and in trust for the poor of God; but persecution unjustly transferred those Catholic treasures to others, who, instead of complying with the charitable intentions of the original donors, revel in the profligate enjoyment of their sacrilegious plunder.

Should the faithful have placed any charities at your grace's disposal, as there is now absolute necessity for external aid to carry on the ordinary duties of the mission, I presume to express the hope your grace will be so kind as to appropriate some portion of them to meet the extraordinary spiritual and temporal wants of this part of Connemara. In fact, I think the deplorable state of all Connemara should be brought under the notice of the Society of the Propagation of the Faith, in order, if possible, to check the wicked course of these evil men.

I can assure your grace that a mile of the public road cannot be travelled without meeting a dead body, as the poor are houseless and daily turned out of the poorhouse whenever they exhibit any symptoms of sickness. There is not a hut without fever and dysentery, the sure precursors of cholera, which I fear is the next ordeal through which the poor Irish must pass...

William Flannelly, Catholic Curate.

(Dublin Diocesan Archives, Murray Correspondence 121.)

VII

THE WORKHOUSE

In the first two years of the Famine, the government placed little reliance on the state welfare service, that is, the workhouse system provided under the 1838 Poor Law Act. Instead, it provided relief by various special measures. The reason was that the workhouses were designed to cater for a relatively small population of paupers, and did not have the capacity for the massive numbers requiring support from the spring of 1846 onwards. Their total capacity amounted to about 100,000 places, but they were so unpopular that at the beginning of the Famine they housed only 38,000. With the crisis, however, the numbers increased, and by January 1847 amounted to over 100,000.

Early in 1847, the government decided to abandon special relief measures and to transfer responsibility for relief to the Poor Law system. In arriving at that momentous decision, it was influenced by a number of considerations, mainly financial. The government was committed to policies of financial stringency, and British taxpayers were becoming increasingly opposed to subsidising relief in Ireland on an on-going basis. To enable the Poor Law system to cope with the crisis situation, the government arranged for an expansion and some reorganisation of the service.

Legislation enacted in June and July 1847 empowered boards of guardians to provide outdoor relief for the first time. Those eligible were 'the impotent poor' (the aged and infirm), and widows with two or more children. In addition, it enabled the Poor Law Commissioners to authorise outdoor relief in the form of food for able-bodied men for periods of up to two months. An important restriction known as 'the Gregory clause' rendered those holding more than a quarter of an acre of land ineligible for any relief under the Poor Law; this had cruel repercussions in that many smallholders who needed relief were forced to give up their holdings and become long-term paupers. To oversee the system, a separate Poor Law Commission was established for Ireland; additional inspectors, relieving officers and other officials were appointed. Stringent control, however, was maintained by Trevelyan and the Treasury.

As might be expected, the demand for admission to the workhouses far exceeded their capacity, especially in the areas where the crisis was most intense. There was considerable overcrowding, conditions were insanitary and disease was rampant. The situation was aggravated by a serious fever epidemic early in 1847. The average weekly mortality escalated from four per thousand inmates in October 1846 to twenty-five the following April, with the result that people looked for refuge in the workhouse only as a last resort. Extra accommodation was gradually provided by opening auxiliary workhouses, by extending existing buildings, and by creating additional unions with new workhouses. By the end of 1849 total capacity amounted to over 250,000.

The government was determined to keep the numbers on outdoor relief to a minimum, as otherwise the costs would be more than the rates could support, unions would become bankrupt, and the government would again be forced to finance special relief measures. In spite of the restrictions, 800,000 were receiving outdoor relief by June 1849; it was not until 1852 that outdoor relief was virtually phased out.

Many of the unions were seriously under-financed as ratepayers were under pressure and it was difficult to collect rates. The problem was especially acute in the congested west and south-west, where the numbers requiring relief were greatest and rateable valuations were lowest. To enable the system to cope, the government assisted the destitute unions by means of loans and money raised by the British Relief Association. In 1849, in an attempt to distribute the burden of rates more equitably, the government instituted a 'rate-in-aid' on property throughout the country. Ratepayers in the more prosperous areas of Leinster and Ulster resented this, especially as the new rate was not extended to Britain. But, notwithstanding the Act of Union, which it was determined to maintain, the government was resolute that the burden of maintaining the Irish poor should be borne by Ireland alone and would not be shared by the British taxpayer.

1. Government policy on Poor Law relief

Though technically a mere executive, Trevelyan had considerable influence on government policy and was largely responsible for the decision to transfer the onus for relief to the Irish Poor Law and the ratepayers. He believed that the causes underlying the crisis – uneconomic holdings, congestion and the generally backward state of agriculture – were all attributable to the neglect and mismanagement of the landlords. The landlords were the main ratepayers and he hoped that by making them largely liable for the costs of relief, they would be forced to eradicate the root causes of poverty, and eventually effect a reform and a transformation of the Irish rural economy.

Trevelyan's outline of the Poor Law system.

Three things had become apparent before the close of the year 1846. The first was that if these gigantic efforts were much longer continued they must exhaust and disorganize society throughout the United Kingdom, and reduce all classes of people in Ireland to a state of helpless dependence. The second was that provision ought to be made for the relief of extreme destitution in some less objectionable mode than that which had been adopted, for want of a better, under the pressure of an alarming emergency. The third was that great efforts and great sacrifices were required to provide another and a better subsistence for the large population which had hitherto depended upon the potato.

Upon these principles the plan of the Government for the season of 1847-8, and for all after-time, was based. Much the larger portion of the machinery of a good Poor Law had been set up in Ireland by the Irish Poor Relief Act which was passed in the year 1838. The island had been divided into unions, which were generally so arranged as to secure easy communication with the central station; and these had been subdivided into electoral districts, each of which appointed its own guardian, and was chargeable only with its own poor, like our parishes. A commodious workhouse had also been built in each union by advances from the Exchequer, and rates had been established for its support. No relief could, however, be given outside the workhouses, and when these buildings once became filled with widows and children, aged and sick, and others who might with

equal safety and more humanity have been supported at their own homes, they ceased to be either a medium of relief or a test of destitution to the other destitute poor of the union.

To remedy this and other defects of the existing system, three acts of parliament were passed in the session of 1847, the principal provisions of which were as follows: destitute persons who are either permanently or temporarily disabled from labour, and destitute widows having two or more legitimate children dependent upon them, may be relieved either in or out of the workhouse, at the discretion of the guardians. If, owing to want of room, or to the prevalence of fever or any infectious disorder, adequate relief cannot be afforded in a workhouse to persons not belonging to either of the above-mentioned classes, the Poor Law Commissioners may authorize the guardians to give them outdoor relief in food only; the Commissioners' order for which purpose can only be made for a period of two months, but, if necessary, it can be renewed from time to time. Relieving officers and medical officers for affording medical relief out of the work-house are to be appointed; and in cases of sudden and urgent necessity, the relieving officers are to give 'immediate and temporary relief in food, lodging, medicine, or medical attendance' until the next meeting of the guardians. After the 1st November, 1847, no person is to be relieved either in or out of a workhouse, who is in the occupation of more than a quarter of an acre of land.

(C.E. Trevelyan, *The Irish crisis*, 1848, p. 151-4.)

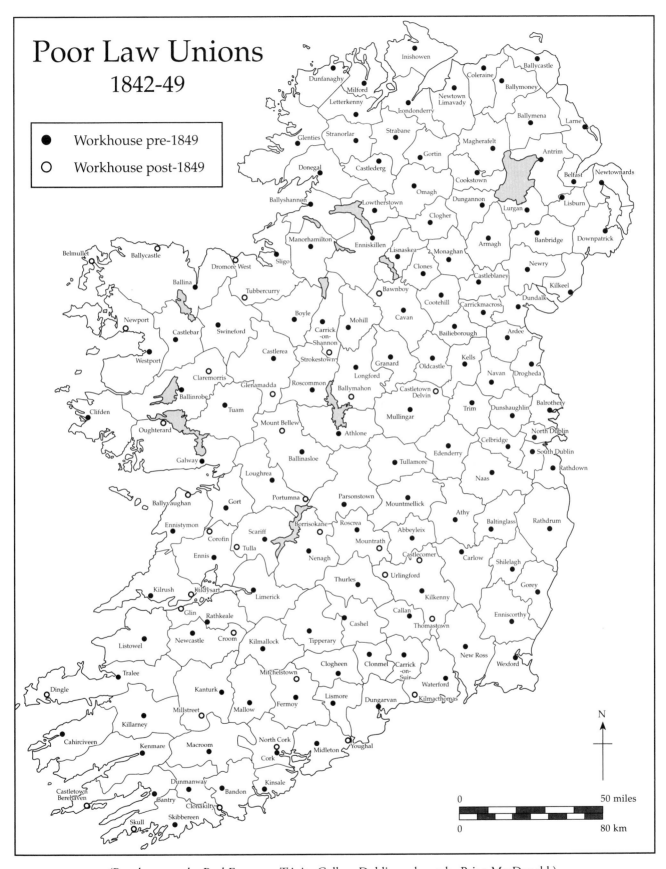

Poor Law Unions
1842-49

●   Workhouse pre-1849

○   Workhouse post-1849

Belmullet
Ballycastle
Dunfanaghy
Inishowen
Milford
Coleraine
Ballycastle
Ballymoney
Letterkenny
Newtown Limavady
Londonderry
Ballymena
Larne
Glenties
Stranorlar
Strabane
Magherafelt
Antrim
Donegal
Castlederg
Gortin
Cookstown
Belfast
Newtownards
Ballyshannon
Omagh
Dungannon
Lurgan
Lisburn
Lowtherstown
Clogher
Dromore West
Sligo
Manorhamilton
Enniskillen
Lisnaskea
Monaghan
Armagh
Banbridge
Downpatrick
Ballina
Tubbercurry
Bawnboy
Clones
Castleblaney
Newry
Kilkeel
Dundalk
Newport
Boyle
Mohill
Cavan
Cootehill
Carrickmacross
Ardee
Castlebar
Swineford
Carrick-on-Shannon
Bailieborough
Westport
Castlerea
Strokestown
Granard
Oldcastle
Kells
Navan
Drogheda
Claremorris
Glenamadda
Roscommon
Longford
Castletown Delvin
Trim
Dunshaughlin
Balrothery
Ballinrobe
Ballymahon
Clifden
Tuam
Mount Bellew
Mullingar
North Dublin
Oughterard
Athlone
Celbridge
South Dublin
Galway
Ballinasloe
Edenderry
Rathdown
Loughrea
Tullamore
Naas
Ballyvaughan
Portumna
Parsonstown
Mountmellick
Gort
Mountrath
Athy
Rathdrum
Ennistymon
Scariff
Borrisokane
Roscrea
Abbeyleix
Baltinglass
Corofin
Tulla
Nenagh
Castlecomer
Carlow
Shilelagh
Ennis
Thurles
Urlingford
Kilrush
Kildysart
Limerick
Kilkenny
Gorey
Glin
Rathkeale
Callan
Enniscorthy
Listowel
Newcastle
Croom
Kilmallock
Tipperary
Cashel
Thomastown
Tralee
Mitchelstown
Clogheen
Clonmel
Carrick-on-Suir
New Ross
Wexford
Dingle
Kanturk
Lismore
Waterford
Millstreet
Mallow
Fermoy
Dungarvan
Kilmacthomas
Killarney
Macroom
North Cork
Midleton
Youghal
Cahirciveen
Kenmare
Cork
Castletown Berehaven
Dunmanway
Kinsale
Bantry
Bandon
Clonakilty
Skull
Skibbereen

N

0   50 miles

0   80 km

(Based on map by Paul Ferguson, Trinity College Dublin, redrawn by Brian MacDonald.)

2. The workhouse buildings

Under the Poor Law Act of 1838, a total of 130 workhouses were planned. They were all built and operational by the end of 1846. All but five were new buildings; the construction of such a large number of substantial public institutions in such a relatively short space of time was a considerable achievement. The government provided loans and each board of guardians was responsible for the erection of its workhouse. They were constructed according to standard designs prepared by George Wilkinson, an architect who had been involved in workhouse projects in England. Their construction provided considerable employment; 11,000 men and 10,000 horses and carts were involved at peak periods.

A description of the workhouse buildings.

Of the character of the buildings generally, this 'bird's-eye view' will convey a sufficiently accurate idea. There are, however, several houses with elevations differing from the one here given – intended to diversify the appearance of these structures in different localities. The workhouse may be considered to consist of four separate structures, containing as follows:

1) The entrance building, which contains the waiting hall for paupers applying for admission, and the porter; the board room on the upper floor, in which the guardians meet and determine the admission of applicants for relief; the probationary wards, with four separate yards for containing those paupers when admitted, and who are here examined by the medical officer and washed in a bath supplied with hot and cold water.

Paupers affected by any disease are retained in these wards until in a fit state to go into the body of the house. Previously, however, they are deprived of their old clothes, which are fumigated and deposited for return (if required), and they are then dressed in a comfortable suit of the workhouse clothing.

2) The main building contains, in the centre, the master's and matron's apartments, around which are the store rooms, the kitchen and workhouse, the schoolrooms for boys and girls separate, and the several wards, to which they command immediate access.

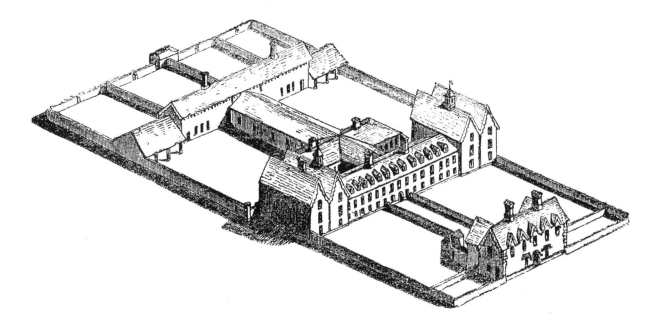

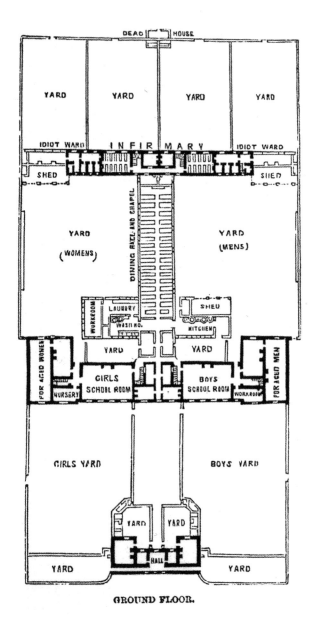

GROUND FLOOR.

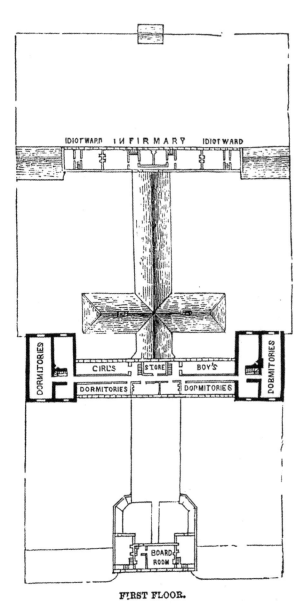

FIRST FLOOR.

3) The third division contains the dining-hall, and kitchen and washhouse; buildings which are all arranged in connection with the yards of the paupers employed or having access thereto, so as to avoid passages and other separations which interfere with proper classification.

4) The infirmary is a distinct building, and conveniently placed for access; on each side is a building reserved for male and female idiots – a class of inmates unprovided for in buildings of the kind in England, and whose location here greatly relieves the lunatic institutions of the country.

The upper floor of the buildings contains dormitories, from which the paupers are excluded in the daytime. The arrangement for sleeping is entirely novel, and for such large buildings infinitely beyond the arrangement of bedsteads – the advantages of which are detailed in the architect's report to the Poor Law Commission ... in which the bedsteads that are used are also described, and are of a kind different from those used in any other buildings, and very conducive to order and cleanliness.

(Hall, *Ireland*, 1841-43, III, p. 343-6.)

3. The landlords and the workhouse

The landlords were the main financiers of the Poor Law system; in addition to rates on their own buildings and demesnes, they were liable for the entire rates of holdings valued at under £4 (about ten acres), and for half the rates of all other properties. They also controlled the system, as they constituted a majority on most of the boards of guardians which administered the workhouses. As the main ratepayers, landlords had a vested interest in keeping costs to a minimum; in some cases, boards dominated by landlords restricted admission to the workhouse and did not actively pursue defaulting ratepayers. An extreme example was the board of the Castlebar union in Co. Mayo, which was alleged to be both incompetent and corrupt. It was eventually dissolved, and replaced by paid officials known as vice-guardians.

Report on the state of the Castlebar workhouse.

Castlebar, 17 January 1847.

Gentlemen,

In reference to the letter of the Rev. Richard Gibbons, P.P., Castlebar, to T. N. Redington, Esq., Under Secretary for Ireland, forwarded to me on the 14th instant, with a request that I should report as to it, I have the honour to inform you that I arrived in Castlebar late on the eve of the 15th instant; that I attended the board of guardians yesterday, and made inquiries in reference to the state of the workhouse and the letter of the Rev. Mr Gibbons, and I regret to have to report that the statements in Mr Gibbon's letter are true, and so far from being exaggerated, hardly come up to the facts of the case.

Since the 21st of last November, the paupers were left without any breakfast (the master having no fuel to cook it), on three days, viz, the 1st of January and the 4th and 15th instant; but in all cases they got one meal. Lord Lucan, through his agent, supplied meal, but he did not supply bread since the 26th of December, and only now and then supplied turf; and the master did not get one-third as much turf as was required, and had to leave the paupers some days in bed for heat. There was no regularity as to meals, owing to the irregularity of the supplies, and the inmates were left without any meal on the 15th instant until half-past two o'clock.

The coffin contractor would not supply coffins, money being due to him (for although he got checks, he could get no money for them), and the master of the workhouse had, as he informs me, to advance money out of his own pocket to procure coffins to bury the dead in. I enclose you copies of the observations of the medical officer of the workhouse (in the medical return book, form 18) since he wrote the letter of the 19th of December, which was placed on the minutes, and which you are aware of. These observations will show you better than any of mine could do, the state of this workhouse, and the privations the inmates have suffered, and the consequences. Not only have the inmates had their meals of stirabout irregularly served, and been left without breakfast on some days, and on all days without a sufficiency of fuel, but the sick in hospital, in their utmost need, have been left without the diet and necessaries prescribed for them by their medical attendant. Since the 21st of November the inmates have been left solely dependent on the supplies sent in by the Earl of Lucan (the guardians having no funds, refusing to strike a rate, not taking steps to collect the arrears, and not even holding regular meetings). When Lord Lucan, at the meeting of the guardians of the 21st, opposed the striking of a new rate and the admission of more poor, it was understood that his Lordship would provide for the wants of the then inmates; and yesterday a resolution was passed, calling the attention of Lord Lucan's agent to the reports of the medical officer, and requesting his attention thereto.

In my report of the 27th *ultimo* I informed you of the rate struck by this board of guardians, the amount of arrears, and as to the insufficiency of the excuses for their non-collection. After the meeting of the board of guardians was over yesterday, I had an interview with one of the collectors, and examined his books, and of the amount of rate now uncollected, viz, £1,079, I find that nearly two-thirds are due by persons who are rated as immediate lessors [landlords or middlemen]. The rate rated on the Earl of Lucan, as immediate lessor, is marked as unpaid in many cases; that, I saw in the books, and the rate-collector informed me that he had not paid any of the rate for which he is rated as immediate lessor in any part of the union, and that the rate I saw marked as paid in the books, for which his Lordship appeared rated as immediate lessor for persons valued at and under £4, was paid by the occupiers themselves.

Sir Samuel O'Malley, it also appears, has not paid any of the rates for which he is rated as immediate lessor. Lord Kilmaine has not paid a large portion of the rate for which he is rated as immediate lessor. Mr Kearney, vice-chairman of the board of guardians, has not paid the rate rated on him as immediate lessor, and many other persons of rank and property that it would be of no further use to enumerate.

It is needless, gentlemen, to enlarge on such facts as these; a workhouse closed at such a time, in a wretched town and county, where some of the people have died of starvation, and where two-thirds of the rates due (amounting to £1,079) are due by immediate lessors, persons of the largest property in the union; and while the few inmates who are allowed to be in the house (123 yesterday) are left in the state that is described by this report, by the observations of the medical officer, and the letter of the Rev. Mr Gibbons; it will, however, I hope, at last show the necessity for some compulsory and easily available means of compelling boards of guardians, from time to time, to strike sufficient rates (whenever the state of their finances show the necessity for new rates being struck) being as soon as possible enacted.

G. C. Otway, Assistant Poor Law Commissioner (*Correspondence relating to the state of union workhouses in Ireland*, p.49-50; P.P. 1847 (766) LV.)

A view of the workhouse at Lismore, Co. Waterford, by Robert Armstrong, 1842. The birds overhead provide a key: *one*, 'infirmary and idiot wards'; *two*, 'male and female wards, dormitories, etc.'; *three*, 'porter's lodge and boardroom'. (NLI 1956TX.)

4. *The workhouse diet*

From the introduction of the Poor Law in 1838, official policy was to keep costs to a minimum. This was mainly achieved by making conditions in the workhouses so restrictive as to deter all except those in dire distress. The policy was to maintain diet at a level inferior to that of the poorest labourer, lest he might be seduced into giving up his employment and seeking refuge in the workhouse. In normal times, this draconian policy worked to the extent that in the period immediately before the Famine less than half the available accommodation was taken up. From the summer of 1846 onwards, however, workhouse fare was far superior to that of some millions of the population and the numbers seeking admission escalated.

Dietary of the Ballina workhouse, Co. Mayo.

ABLE-BODIED

Breakfast
8 ounces of oatmeal and Indian meal in stirabout, and 1 pint buttermilk or molasses.

Dinner
12 ounces of bread or biscuits and 1 quart pea soup for four days in the week; 10 ounces of rice and Indian meal in stirabout for remaining three.

INFIRM ADULTS

Breakfast
4 ounces rice and Indian meal in stirabout and ½ pint sweet-milk or mollasses.

Dinner
8 ounces bread and 1 pint of pea soup four days in the week; for remaining three days, 5 ounces of Indian meal and rice and 1 pint buttermilk.

Supper
8 ounces bread or biscuit and ½ pint of sweet-milk.

CHILDREN UNDER 15

Breakfast
4 ounces Indian meal and rice and ½ pint of buttermilk or molasses.

Dinner
6 ounces bread and 1 pint pea soup for 4 days; 5 ounces rice and Indian meal, and ½ pint of buttermilk or molasses for remaining 3 days.

Supper
¼ lb of bread or biscuits and ¼ pint of sweet-milk or molasses.

INFANTS UNDER 2 YEARS

½ lb bread and 1 pint of sweet-milk. The proportion of rice and Indian meal to be equal.

THE SICK

Full diet
1 lb bread, 1 pint new-milk with rice-water for drink.

Half diet
½ lb bread, 1 pint new-milk with rice-water for drink.

Spoon diet
Rice or barley water with arrowroot, sago or tapioca, as the cases may require, say, ½ ounce sago, ½ ounce arrowroot or ½ ounce tapioca.

(Minute book of Ballina union, 18 March 1848; NLI Ms 12,204.)

An official view on workhouse dietaries, 1840.

The essential principle to be attended to in framing a dietary for a workhouse appears to be, that the food of a pauper, maintained at the public cost, should not be more abundant or better than that of the poor man maintaining himself in independence by his industry... And yet, exactly in proportion to the difficulty of adjusting the diet according to this principle, is the necessity of being careful to do so; because where subsistence is precarious, scanty, and unwholesome, and, such as it is, not to be obtained without severe exertion, there, a supply of food, even of tolerable quality and in moderate quantity, yet provided regularly and without fail, becomes almost irresistibly attractive to the poor. Where such is the case, there is great danger of those tests becoming ineffectual whereby some security is given that none

but the actually destitute are relieved; and when once pauperism becomes on the whole, and in the estimation of a large portion of the poorer classes, more eligible than independence, evils, which cannot be contemplated without dread, are sure to follow.

It is a matter of notoriety that meat is rarely, if ever, tasted by the Irish peasant; and the fact of its being almost universally excluded from the dietaries of public institutions shows that the change in his habits and circumstances in life, that a man undergoes when he becomes an inmate of any of them, does not render a change of diet necessary for his well-being.

Report by Richard Hall, Assistant Poor Law Commissioner, 20 March 1840.

(*Sixth annual report of the Poor Law Commissioners,* appendix D, p. 238-9; P.P. 1840 (245) XVII.)

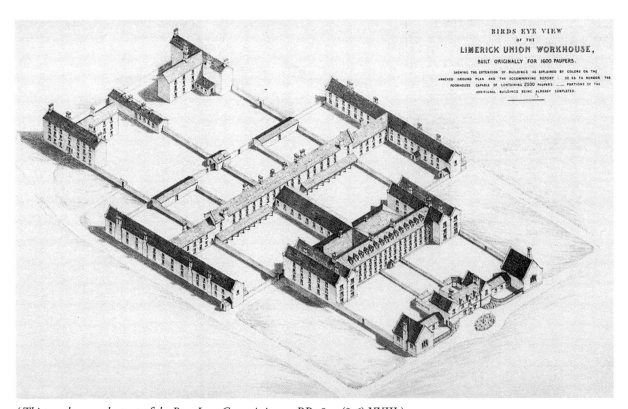

(*Thirteenth annual report of the Poor Law Commissioners*; P.P. 1847 (816) XXIII.)

5. *The workhouse and work*

The Poor Law ethic required that those receiving relief should perform work for the benefit of the workhouse and as an exercise in character-formation. The regime centred around labour; apart from the sick and the very young, nobody was allowed to remain idle. The policy of making the workhouse as unattractive as possible extended to the matter of work, and the tasks assigned were monotonous and tedious. The men broke stones, ground corn and laboured on the workhouse land. The women also did heavy manual labour; in addition, they unravelled oakum or coir (fibre), did needlework, washed the linen, scrubbed the floors, and took care of the old, the sick and the children.

Report on quilt-making in Athlone workhouse.

We have to acknowledge the receipt of yours of the 25th instant, on the subject of quilts made in this workhouse, and in reply, beg to state that the quilts in question are made of linen and woollen thread – linen warp and woollen weft; size, two-and-a-half yards by two. The material is all spun in the house by females, dyed and wove out of it at a cost of 6d per yard. They are lined with the old blankets in this way; we are using old rugs for same purpose. The worsted with which they are quilted was also prepared in the house; it is of a peculiar twist.

80 are now finished and in use, 130 more are in hands, and materials wove for 220. We have found it very difficult to procure flax for the last two months;

but have ordered another dozen of spinning-wheels for wool, and are preparing friezes, of which we stand in need just now.

The quilts will stand us in about 5s 3d each, and we are assured will last twenty years; the contract existing for rugs on our arrival here was 5s each, and two years is the utmost they could stand. We have not an idler in the house, except in sickness.

Edward Wall and John A. Drought, Vice-guardians of Athlone union, Co. Westmeath. To the Poor Law Commissioners, 26 October 1848.

(Second annual report of the Commissioners for Administering the Laws for the Relief of the Poor in Ireland, p. 148; P.P. 1849 (1118) XXV.)

No illustration of people in an Irish workhouse around the time of the Famine has yet been discovered. This view is probably of a women's dormitory in an English workhouse, but it may give some indication of life in the Irish equivalent. (Courtesy of Gill & Macmillan.)

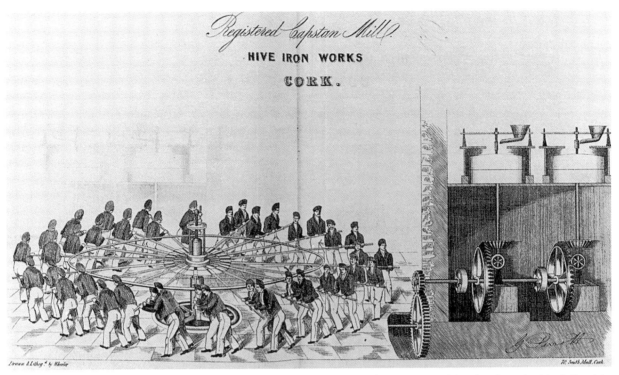

Capstan mills were used for grinding corn in a number of workhouses. Turning the capstan was tiring, but the authorities believed it induced discipline. (National Archives.)

A Scottish writer's account of workhouse work.

One little Captain Something, an intelligent commonplace little Englishman (just about to quit this horrid place, and here for the second time), does attend us, takes us to Westport workhouse, the wonder of the universe at present.

Human swinery has here reached its acme, happily: 30,000 paupers in this union, population supposed to be about 60,000. Workhouse proper, I suppose, cannot hold above 3,000 or 4,000 of them, subsidiary workhouses, and outdoor relief the others. Abomination of desolation; what can you make of it! Outdoor quasi-work: 300 or 400 hulks of fellows tumbling about with shares, picks and barrows, 'levelling' the end of their workhouse hill; at first glance you would think them all working; look nearer, in each shovel there is some ounce or two of mould, and it is all make-believe; 500 or 600 boys and lads, pretending to break stones. Can it be a charity to keep men alive on these terms? In face of all the twaddle of the earth, shoot a man rather than

train him (with heavy expense to his neighbours) to be a deceptive human swine.

Westport union has £1,100 a week from government (proportion rate-in-aid), Castlebar has £800, some other has £1,300 etc., etc.; it is so they live from week to week. Poor rates, collectible, as good as none. (£28 14 0 say the books); a peasant will keep his cow for years against all manner of cess-collection; spy-children tidings run, as by electric wires, that a cess-collector is out, and all cows are huddled under lock and key – unattainable for years. No rents; little or no stock left, little cultivation, docks, thistles; landlord sits in his mansion, for reasons, except on Sundays. We hear of them 'living on the rabbits of their own park'. Society is at an end here, with the land uncultivated, and every second soul a pauper. 'Society', here, would have to eat itself, and end by cannibalism in a week, if it were not held up by the rest of our empire still standing afoot!

(Thomas Carlyle, *Reminiscences of my Irish journey in 1849*, London, 1882, p. 201-2.)

6. No room in the workhouse

*M*any *people seeking refuge were refused admission. Apart from cases where the guardians restricted entry to keep down the rates, many workhouses had legitimate reasons as they were overcrowded to the extent of having to sleep three or more people to a bed. As it was difficult to collect rates, a number of workhouses became bankrupt and were forced to expel inmates. In addition, people were refused admission because they could not prove that they were destitute. For example, the 'Gregory clause' excluded those with more than a quarter of an acre, a disqualification which originally extended to dependants. Descriptions of scenes at workhouse gates are provided by two English Quakers, Joseph Crosfield and James Hack Tuke.*

Report by Joseph Crosfield.

Boyle, 5th of twelfth-month, 1846.

In this place, the condition of the poor previously to their obtaining admission into the workhouse is one of great distress; many of them declare that they have not tasted food of any kind for forty-eight hours; and numbers of them have eaten nothing but cabbage or turnips for days and weeks. This statement is corroborated by the dreadfully reduced state in which they present themselves; the children especially being in a condition of starvation, and ravenous with hunger. Last year there were no such cases as these; the poor coming into the workhouse then from the pressure of temporary difficulties, and remaining there a comparatively short time.

Carrick-on-Shannon, 6th of twelfth-month, 1846.

At this place our first visit was to the poorhouse; and as the board of guardians was then sitting for the admission of applicants, a most painful and heart-rending scene presented itself; poor wretches in the last stage of famine imploring to be received into the house; women who had six or seven children begging that even two or three of them might be taken in, as their husbands were earning but 8d per day; which, at the present high price of provisions, was totally inadequate to feed them. Some of these children were worn to skeletons, their features sharpened with hunger, and their limbs wasted almost to the bone. From a number of painful cases, the following may be selected. A widow with two children, who for a week had subsisted on one meal of cabbage each day; these were admitted into the poorhouse, but in so reduced a state that a guardian observed to the master of the house that the youngest child would trouble them but a very short time. Another woman with two children, and near her confinement again, whose husband had left her a month before to seek for work, stated that they had lived for the whole of this week upon two quarts of meal and two heads of cabbage. Famine was written in the faces of this woman and her children. In reply to a question from William Forster [the English Quaker], the guardians expressed their opinion that these statements were true. Of course, among so many applicants as there were in attendance (one hundred and ten), a great number were necessarily refused admittance, as there were but thirty vacancies in the house. The guardians appeared to exercise great discrimination and impartiality in the selection of the most destitute objects; but some of those who were rejected were so far spent, that it is doubtful if they would all reach their homes alive, as several of them had to walk five or six Irish miles.

(*Transactions of the Central Relief Committee of the Society of Friends ... 1846 and 1847*, 1852, p. 145-6.)

Report by James Hack Tuke.

The worst [workhouse] which I visited was that of Carrick-upon-Shannon. It was in a miserable state, and the doors were closed against further admissions, and although built for seven hundred, had but two hundred and eighty inmates. The gates were besieged by seventy or eighty wretched beings, who in vain implored for admission. Numbers of them were in various stages of fever, which was terribly prevalent in the neighbourhood, and the fever sheds overcrowded. Two months before my visit, the doors of the poor-house were opened and the inmates expelled, entailing upon them most dire misery. Stern necessity has, in a considerable degree, overcome the strong prejudices of the poor people to enter these houses, and they are now generally full.

Nearly two-thirds of the inmates of the union houses of Connaught are, as may be expected, children, many of them orphans. The neglected condition of the children in the union houses is a subject which often struck me as deserving serious attention. In many unions, owing to their bankrupt state, there are no books, and no means whatever for providing the necessary books and school requisites; and thus we may see hundreds of children wholly idle and unemployed, where a few pounds expense would enable them to be taught.

In the nineteen houses of Connaught there are about six-thousand children, and although in some there are really first-rate schools, the majority are quite insufficiently supplied with books or teachers, and several entirely without books. Three of the five unions of Mayo, containing eleven hundred and fifty children (of whom three hundred and fifty are orphans), are thus circumstanced. As these unions are deeply in debt, we cannot feel surprised that the feeding of the inmates has absorbed all their attention; and unless private charity, or the National School Society supply this want, these children will be still left wholly uneducated; nor is school-learning the only part of the education of these unfortunate children required; industrial employment, especially in handicraft trades, might fit them for earning their bread when they leave the house, and employ them profitably whilst there.

(James Hack Tuke, *A visit to Connaught in the autumn of 1847*, 1848, p. 16-17.)

A later artist's impression of people seeking admission to an Irish workhouse during the Famine; possibly based on an English source. At least one Irish workhouse, Lisnaskea, Co. Fermanagh, had a form of 'Dutch' gable, as appears here; the gaslight over the gate is anachronistic for Ireland. (Robert Wilson, *The life and times of Queen Victoria*, London, 1887-88.)

7. Qualifying for outdoor relief

The numbers fed by the soup kitchens amounted to three million, and the authorities feared that if strict control was not exercised the numbers receiving outdoor relief under the Poor Law might reach a similar level. They were particularly concerned with excluding the able-bodied, and devised a mechanism known as 'the workhouse test', whereby applicants for outdoor relief had to prove that they were destitute by becoming resident in the workhouse. Once they had resided for a period, thereby showing that they were genuine paupers, they were usually turned out and put on outdoor relief, thus providing space for a new batch to undergo the test. The Poor Law Commissioners issued several directives on strategies for limiting the numbers on outdoor relief.

Circular from Poor Law Commissioners to boards of guardians.

Poor Law Commission Office, Dublin, 26 August 1847.

The Poor Law Commissioners propose to offer a few suggestions in reference to those unions in which the guardians are convinced that it will become necessary for them, unless they adopt precautionary measures, to grant outdoor relief to able-bodied men during the approaching autumn. When the operations under the Temporary Relief Act [the soup kitchen act] are terminated on the 12th September, the Poor Law rates throughout the whole of Ireland will be liable for the relief of a mass of apparent destitution, which, in some districts, may prove wholly unmanageable unless the guardians have definite ideas of the precise evils which are most to be dreaded, and of the best way in which those evils can be counteracted or mitigated. The Commissioners deem it right, therefore, to make generally known the views which they themselves entertain on this important subject.

The Commissioners think that the evil which is most to be guarded against is the necessity of granting outdoor relief to able-bodied men; and that the main point for the guardians to keep steadily in view is to make their workhouse as extensively available as possible for the relief of this class. On the difficulty of preventing abuses in granting outdoor relief to able-bodied men, the Commissioners do not intend to dilate...

Very extensive experience has proved that relief may be granted to able-bodied men in a well-regulated workhouse without entailing the certainty of any very serious evils. Speaking generally, such relief combines the two important advantages: 1, that those who are really destitute will accept it ; and 2, that those who are not really destitute will not accept it.

The effect of a workhouse in bringing to light imposition has been manifested in a remarkable manner within the last fortnight in North Dublin Union. During the week ended Saturday, the 14th instant, there were above 20,000 persons on the relief lists of the North City electoral division; and as the operations under the Temporary Relief Act terminated in North Dublin Union on the 15th instant, the guardians on the 16th instant had to deal, for the first time, with the apparent necessity of having to provide relief for above 20,000 persons. On the morning of that day, however, owing to previous arrangements, they had room in the workhouse of their union for 400 individuals, and by offering workhouse relief to applicants ... the guardians were enabled in the course of six days, to reduce the number on the relief lists to nearly 3,000 persons. This tends to show that those who are not really destitute will not accept relief in a workhouse.

(*First annual report of the Commissioners for Administering the Laws for the Relief of the Poor in Ireland*, p. 63; P.P. 1847-48 (963) XXXIII.)

Report of Capt. Arthur Kennedy, Poor Law Inspector, Kilrush, Co. Clare, 24 February 1848.

I have from the commencement taken the relieving officers under my own especial protection and guidance, and I rejoice to say that I could discover no single case of abuse or relief administered to other than the absolutely and undoubtedly destitute. Had I left the relieving officers without this continuous support and guidance, the union would have been swamped ere now, as all who received relief last year (45,000) naturally expected its continuance, and still continue to importune and besiege the relieving officers. In the course of this scrutiny, I found many aged parents abandoned by their children who could well support them. All such cases were ordered to the workhouse that proper measures might be taken. I found widows with but one child, and women deserted by their husbands, the majority gone to America last year and intending to send for their families this year, together with a very few single women with illegitimate children. I ordered all of the latter class who were under fifty years of age into the workhouse.

The repugnance to enter the workhouse is beyond credence, and I am satisfied that the outdoor relief list might be reduced one-third by testing them. It would, however, be neither politic nor humane to adopt this course at present, as those on the list are beyond suspicion destitute, and there is an utter absence of any employment or mode of earning. A very few are employed at all, and the majority of that number for their food only; the current wages (where such are given) being 4d per day! I have not failed on every occasion to impress upon the ratepayers that they are only increasing their burdens by this short-sighted policy, thereby pauperizing a greater number, and insufficiency of food bringing them under the infirm class (and, consequently, a permanent charge) in their earlier years.

The destitution and suffering are on the increase, but not so rapidly as I anticipated. The law is, however, administered liberally; all who can legally claim (and some who cannot) outdoor relief, receive it, and admission to the workhouse is never refused. My great object is to obviate the necessity for outdoor relief to the able-bodied, I am so deeply impressed with its ruinous tendency upon such a population as this. The great difficulty and danger here is in relieving a people who are not disposed to help themselves, and the landlord and tenant class set them this culpable example of doing nothing.

(Papers relating to proceedings for the relief of the distress and the state of the workhouses in Ireland, p. 796-7; P.P. 1847-48 (955) LVI.)

The workhouse, Clifden, Co. Galway. (*The Illustrated London News*, 5 Jan. 1850.)

8. *The nature of outdoor relief*

*T*hroughout the Famine, official policy was that relief should be provided through the medium of food rather than money. The policy of the Poor Law Commissioners was that food should be provided cooked, usually either as soup or stirabout. But as even the sick and starving had to travel long distances to the workhouse a number of times a week to collect the food, most unions eventually issued the food uncooked. The procedure was that the relieving officers adjudicated on applicants for outdoor relief and issued ration cards to those eligible. Rations were doled out at the workhouse or at shops under contract to the board of guardians.

Extract from list of unions providing outdoor relief, 2 May 1849.

Ballinrobe
Uncooked yellow Indian meal. During last week a small portion of rye and Egyptian meal used, the supply of Indian meal being deficient.

Bantry
Full order recently issued: Indian meal will be issued uncooked, there being neither funds nor facilities for cooking.

Callan
In food not cooked.

Cashel
Uncooked Indian meal; and now partly rice to parties affected with dysentery or diarrhoea. Vice-guardians obliged to abandon for a time a contemplated arrangement for giving cooked food, owing to the difficulty of obtaining sufficient rates, as cooked food would be attended with more expense than raw meal.

Castlerea
No outdoor relief to able-bodied men yet given; when given, uncooked Indian meal to be used.

Clonmel
Raw meal on account of difficulties which have rendered it impracticable to give cooked food.

Dingle
Raw meal at present, but arrangements in progress for giving cooked food generally.

Ennistymon
Uncooked Indian meal.

Galway
Uncooked Indian meal.

Gort
Uncooked Indian meal.

Kanturk
Uncooked Indian meal.

Kilmallock
Uncooked Indian meal.

Kilrush
Cooked food; namely, rye and barley bread, to the extent of about 5,000 pounds weight weekly. The remainder in Kilrush union given in rations of rye, barley and Indian meal.

Listowel
Cooked food given in eleven electoral divisions. In six electoral divisions of Listowel union, uncooked Indian meal; in four divisions, no outdoor relief to able-bodied men.

Scariff
Biscuit furnished by commissariat as part of the grants-in-aid; and uncooked Indian meal.

Westport
Indian meal or rye meal.

(*Minutes of evidence before select committee on the operation of the Irish Poor Law*, p. 944-5; P.P. 1849 (507) XVI.)

Westport UNION.

STATE of the WORKHOUSE for the Week ending Saturday, the 8th day of July 1848.

Number of Inmates for which accommodation is provided:—
Workhouse, 1000
Temporary Buildings, —
Additional Workhouse, —
Permanent Fever Hospital, —
Fever Sheds, 30
Total, 1030

	Aged and Infirm		Able-bodied		Boys.	Girls.	Children under 2 years.	Born		Total.
	Males.	Fem.	Males.	Fem.				Males.	Fem.	
Remaining on previous Saturday, as per last Return,	8	7	368	301	167	115	38	—	—	1004
Admitted during the Week,	1	0	39	24	9	10	1	—	—	84
TOTAL,	9	7	407	325	176	125	39	—	—	1088
Discharged during the Week,	—	—	2	3	6	—	—	—	—	11
Died,	—	—	3	1	2	—	—	—	—	6
Total Discharged and Dead,	—	—	5	4	8	—	—	—	—	17
REMAINING ON THE ABOVE DATE,	9	7	402	321	168	125	39	—	—	1071

RETURN OF SICK AND LUNATICS.

Number in Hospital on the above date.	No. of Lunatics and Idiots in Workhouse on the above date.
In Workhouse Hospital, In Fever Hospital } 117	In separate Wards, In Wards with other Inmates }
Total, 117	Total, —

OBSERVATIONS.

RETURN of DESTITUTE PERSONS relieved out of the Workhouse, as by Relief Lists, for the last Week ended Saturday, the first day of July authenticated and laid before the Board of Guardians at this Meeting.

RELIEF DISTRICT.	Destitute Persons relieved out of the Workhouse under 10 Vict. c.31, s.1.		Destitute Persons relieved out of the Workhouse, but not comprised in Sec. 1.		Total relieved out of the Workhouse.	
	Number of cases relieved.	Number of Persons, including Applicant and Family, dependent on him or her.	Number of cases relieved.	Number of Persons, including Applicant and Family, dependent on him or her.	Cases.	Persons.
No. I.	375	1229	1350	3780	1725	5009
No. II.	482	1247	1312	3551	1794	4798
No. III.	142	357	727	1719	869	2076
No. IV.	401	1277	737	2544	1138	3821
No. V.	392	1155	1064	2750	1456	3905
No. VI.	303	752	582	1732	885	2484
No. VII.	207	430	488	1040	695	1470
No. VIII.	424	1611	1479	3131	1903	4742
No. IX.	296	1043	596	1846	892	2889
Car. forward	3022	9101	8335	22093	11357	31194

RELIEF DISTRICT.	Destitute Persons relieved out of the Workhouse under 10 Vict. c.31, s.1.		Destitute Persons relieved out of the Workhouse, but not comprised in Sec. 1.		Total relieved out of the Workhouse.	
	Number of cases relieved.	Number of Persons, including Applicant and Family, dependent on him or her.	Number of cases relieved.	Number of Persons, including Applicant and Family, dependent on him or not.	Cases.	Persons.
Bt. forward	3022	9101	8335	22093	11357	31194
No. X.	156	540	314	845	470	1385
No. XI.						
No. XII.						
No. XIII.						
No. XIV.						
No. XV.						
No. XVI.						
No. XVII.						
TOTAL,	3178	9641	8649	22938	11827	32579

COPY of MINUTES of Proceedings of the Board of Guardians, at a Meeting held on the 12th day of July 1848

PRESENT: In the Chair, William Robert Pecky Esq.

Other Guardians: Francis Hogreve Esq.

Poor Law Inspector Richd. M. Lynch Esq.

(A page from the minute book of the board of guardians of the Westport, Co. Mayo union. NLI Ms 12,609.)

VIII

FEVER AND DISEASE

The high levels of mortality during the Famine were not so much due to starvation as to the diseases which it fostered. The reason for a traditional association of famine and disease in Ireland was that a number of potentially fatal diseases, including typhus fever, relapsing fever and bacillary dysentery, all caused by micro-organisms, were endemic in the population; famine created the conditions in which they became active and attained epidemic proportions.

Typhus and relapsing fever are transmitted by the human body louse. Bacillary dysentery is spread by flies, fingers or infected food. As the Famine took hold, conditions were ideal for the spread of infectious diseases, because sanitation and standards of personal hygiene deteriorated, and louse infestation became common. Moreover, the diseases were easily transmitted as people were brought into close proximity in queues for meal or soup, on the public works, and in the workhouses.

The physical condition of the poor naturally deteriorated as the famine intensified. People were undernourished and many were afflicted with stomach disorders due to eating diseased potatoes or under-cooked Indian meal. They no longer received their habitually high intake of vitamin C from potatoes; resistance to infection was diminished, and many developed scurvy due to the deficiency. In addition, when people contracted disease, they were less resilient, and the resulting mortality was much greater than normal.

In the winter of 1846, outbreaks of typhus, relapsing fever and bacillary dysentery ('the bloody flux') assumed epidemic proportions in many areas. They were especially severe in the congested districts of the west and south-west, but the prevailing conditions facilitated the spread of the disease throughout the country. With the prevalence of eviction and emigration, there was considerable dislocation and movement of people, as individuals and entire families travelled into the towns and cities in search of food, work, or the emigrant ship. These people, unwittingly, carried disease into hitherto unaffected areas.

From their knowledge of previous famines in Ireland, the authorities were aware of the risk of major epidemics, but the country was ill-equipped to deal with an outbreak. At the beginning of the Famine, the total provision amounted to 28 fever hospitals, some basic facilities in about half the workhouses, and 500 out-patient dispensaries. In March 1846, Peel's administration established the Central Board of Health, which was given responsibility for providing additional facilities. When an epidemic failed to materialise in the following months, the Central Board was allowed to lapse. By the end of the year, however, fever and dysentery were prevalent in many areas, but it was only in February 1847, when many workhouses were overcrowded with fever patients, that the gravity of the situation was acknowledged and the Central Board of Health was reconstituted.

In April, the existing fever legislation was extended; the Central Board was given special funding to co-ordinate measures to deal with the epidemic. It extended the existing hospital facilities, provided temporary fever hospitals, and erected wooden sheds and army tents to accommodate patients. It also promoted better standards of hygiene and ventilation in the hospitals and, where feasible, greater separation of patients. In the area of prevention, it advocated the fumigation and white-washing of infected dwellings and the removal of manure heaps from the streets of towns and cities.

The epidemics peaked in most areas around the summer of 1847; the Famine, however, continued in some areas for a further four or five years; while it continued, the attendant diseases remained locally active with greater or lesser intensity. In the three years from mid-1847 to mid-1850, over half a million people were treated in fever hospitals and more than 50,000 died. But the majority of those afflicted with serious disease were never hospitalised and are not recorded. It has, however, been estimated that the majority of the million Famine casualties died of one or other, or sometimes a combination, of the many diseases then prevalent.

1. *A contemporary view of the Famine diseases*

During the Famine, the most prevalent fevers were typhus and relapsing fever. The former was characterised by delirium, a spotted rash and a darkening of the skin, from which it became known as fiabhras dubh *(black fever). Relapsing fever involved severe gastric and liver problems, often resulting in jaundice, whence the term* fiabhras buidhe *(yellow fever). An account of the Famine diseases in the light of contemporary medical knowledge is provided by William Wilde, a distinguished Dublin eye specialist (and father of Oscar Wilde). As medical commissioner for the 1851 census, he was responsible for assembling data relating to health and mortality. In the published report, he outlined the processes underlying the statistics.*

Report on Famine diseases by William Wilde.

Concurrent with the foregoing state of famine and the disruption of the social condition of the people, pestilence came upon the nation in the following order: fever, scurvy, diarrhoea and dysentery, cholera, influenza, and ophthalmia. Respecting the mooted question of famine and fever being cause and effect, we have evidence from the foregoing examination of the social and medical history of Ireland that while fever may spread epidemically, without being either preceded or accompanied by famine, but as simply the result of a peculiar epidemic constitution, of which the memorable period dating from 1814 is an example, yet, it is scarcely possible to lessen the physical strength of a people by withholding their customary amount of food, or to alter suddenly the chemical constituents of that people's usual source of sustenance, without rendering them liable to epidemic disease; while it is without the range of all probability that depression of mind, amounting to the despair consequent upon parents witnessing the lingering starvation of their offspring, or children observing the haggard looks and wasted forms of their parents and near relatives, could occur without producing fatal effects on the human frame. Furthermore, it is an established fact, that we cannot congregate together human beings in crowded masses, whether in camp or in huts, in barracks or workhouses, in overcrowded cities, or even upon public works, without pestilence of one kind or another being generated... Lastly, there must be immediate and total separation of the sick from the healthy, the living from the dead.

Fever, the great element of destruction for hundreds of years, which has not ceased to exist among us as the chief endemial or leaguer [prevalent and endemic] sickness of Ireland – either as the *tamh* or *teidhm* [plague] of very ancient times, or the *teascha* [fevers] of medieval ages – lurking in holes and corners of the island, but ever ready like an evil spirit to break out upon the slightest provocation, and which, it is said, appertains to its inhabitants even when under a different degree of latitude, had already, as may be seen by the foregoing entries, begun slowly and insidiously to increase in the number of cases and the malignancy of its type, so far back as the year 1840; thus marking by its epidemic advent the origin of that pestilential period to which we have already adverted, and of which the potato disease and the epizootics [diseases in animals] formed but constituents...

We need therefore only remark here that the type of the epidemic in several respects resembled those forms of fever which had prevailed in Ireland during previous periods of scarcity and distress, and that its most marked phenomena were excessive prostration; the great tendency to relapse, so as to resemble an inter-mittent; the general prevalence of petechiae (known popularly as the symptoms of 'spotted fever'); and the minute and generally diffused character of these spots so as to resemble some of the eruptive fevers; the occasional enlargement of the spleen; and the unusual tendency to excessive fluidity in the blood, as shown by the purpuric spots which prevailed in a great number of instances; and also by its combinations with scurvy and dysentery. To these peculiarities might be added the symptoms of the yellow tinge of the skin, such as had been already observed in previous epidemics, and which serves to link those great Irish pestilences with the diseases of other latitudes in the present era, and with the great yellow pestilences, which devastated Ireland, in common with the British Isles, in the sixth and seventh centuries.

Finally, we may remark, that the Irish typhus of the period was of a highly contagious nature, and was carried by those who fled in dismay from the famine and the pestilence to the sister kingdom – where it spread rapidly throughout Glasgow, Liverpool, Birmingham, Manchester and other towns and districts to which the Irish emigrants flocked. It was also carried on board the emigrant vessels, in which the crews and passengers were in several instances decimated by it, even before they reached the destined ports; while at Quebec and New York it spread its pestilential influence among those sufferers, who, wasted by previous destitution in Ireland, and the hardships and privations endured during the time they were cooped up between the decks of a closely-packed plague ship, became, even when allowed to breathe the pure air of the shore, ready victims for its fury.

Not only was fever the chief and most direct element of destruction during the Famine period, but the cause also of greatest panic amongst the people, and of extreme horror to the stranger and the eye-witness; for during the highest pressure of the disease, in the summer of 1847, and before accommodation for patients approached anything like the necessity of the time, most mournful and piteous scenes were presented in the vicinity of fever hospitals and workhouses in Dublin, Cork, Waterford, Galway, and other large towns. There, day after day, numbers of people, wasted by famine and consumed by fever, could be seen lying on the footpaths and roads waiting for the chance of admission; and when they were fortunate enough to be received, their places were soon filled by other victims of suffering and disease.

(*Census of Ireland for the year 1851*, part V,1, p. 246-7; P.P. 1856 (2087-1) XXIX.)

A contemporary lithograph drawn by A.S.G. Stopford. (NLI P&D.)

2. The risk of infection

The extract below is from a circular from the Poor Law Commissioners to boards of guardians designed to frighten them into providing better facilities for fever patients. The point that mortality was higher among upper-class patients was valid: fevers were endemic among the poor who had consequently developed a degree of immunity. In the 1840s, the nature of fevers was not fully understood; it was well known that they were infectious or contagious, but the human louse had not been identified as the carrier. Nevertheless, the measures advocated in the notice, 'Advice to prevent fever...' were sensible; where adopted, they inhibited the spread of disease.

Circular from the Poor Law Commissioners to boards of guardians.

The Commissioners have to add that mere motives of self-interest, without regard to higher considerations, render it advisable to make ample provision for the separation and cure of fever patients. Although fever may commence its ravages amongst the poorer classes, it scarcely ever fails, ultimately, to visit the rich; and it is to be observed that the mortality amongst rich persons affected with fever in Ireland is nearly ten times as great as amongst the poor under similar circum-stances. Indeed, melancholy instances will readily be called to mind by guardians, of highly-valuable members of society amongst the upper classes, whose career of usefulness has been cut short by fever during the present year. Now, it cannot be doubted that in the majority of cases the individuals adverted to caught fever from infection diffused by the poor. Hence, expenses incurred for the cure of destitute fever patients may be regarded to a certain extent as a kind of life insurance to the rich who are in health.

(*First annual report of the Commissioners for the Relief of the Poor in Ireland*, p. 99; P.P. 1847-48 (963) XXXIII.)

Lismore Fever Hospital, by Robert Armstrong, 1842. The fever hospitals were supported partly from the rates and partly from subscriptions raised locally. They were too small to cater for major epidemics. (NLI 1956 TX.)

(EIGHTH EDITION.)

Advice to prevent Fever, and other Infectiou Diseases amongst the Poor.

☞ ROSCREA DISPENSARY—*Open until ELEVEN O'CLOCK. on the Mornings of MON-DAYS, THURSDAYS and SATURDAYS, where the following Advice is supplied to the* Public, free of expense, *and where early and timely Medical Assistance should be applied for by* t he Poor.

" Admit pure air, 'twill aid your health :
In that you know, consists *your* wealth,
When *Fever* lurks, delay not cure,
But haste, some Medicine to procure."
MARTIN DOYLE.

No. 1.—Let your doors and windows be kept open in the day ; if you have not a window in the back part of your house, make one ; have them so hung as to be easily opened ; have a chimney with a good draught, so as to encourage a free current of air through your house.

No 2 Remove dung and putrid matter of every kind, from before, and from behind your houses, *as the vapour and smell proceeding from them (called "Malaria") has been found by Physicians to generate infectious Fever.*

No 3.—Scrape your floors with a spade and sweep them every day ; also the yards before and behind your houses as often as you can ; keep your hair cut short and comb it every day ; wash your hands and face ; keep your clothes, furniture, and utensils sweet and clean.

No. 4 —Dont, by any means, indulge in the use of spiritous or other fermented liquors, as intemperance in their use will to a certainty, render you more susceptible of contagion.

No. 5.—Potatoes, and other vegetables badly cooked, or half-boiled, as is a prevailing custom amongst the poor, are most unwholesome food.

No 6 —Lying on beds placed on the ground is very injurious to the health. Every family is recommended to be provided with bed-steads, be they ever so homely.

No 7.—Attention should be paid to have the bowels kept daily open, and if necessary, some *gentle* aperient medicine should be occasionally made use of for this purpose.

No. 8.—Dont go into any house where a person is sick, or has been ill of Fever ; dont attend the wake of any person who has died of fever ; if you do you will be infected yourself, and will communicate fever to your family.

No 9.—*Dont let Strolling Beggars enter your houses as they frequently carry infection from one house to another.*

No. 10.—Whitewash your walls inside and outside, with lime slacked in the house ; and while it continues hot and bubbling ; let this be done once a month while fever is prevalent.

No. 11.—If fever attacks your family ; as soon as the calamity is removed by recovery, or by death, employ the above means as soon as possible ; burn the staaw of the beds ; put all the clothes of the house into cold water, or into a strong solution of chloride of lime, one ounce to a quart of water, wring them out and wash them in hot water, soap and pot-ashes ; let every box, drawer, chest, &c. &c. be emptied and washed, and let the floor under the patient's bed be strewed with lime fresh slacked and hot. Let no person upon recovery go into a neighbour's house, nor into any public place of worship for *fourteen days.*

No. 12 —Heads of Families are strongly recommended to have a printed copy of this Advice pasted up in their houses, and to enforce a strict observance of its instructions.

No. 13—The Gentry are advised only to give employment to such persons as carefully attend to the rules therein contained.

No. 14.—A strict adherence to this plan constitutes the *sole* means for removing the principle cause which generates Typhus Fever in Ireland, viz :—*The fetid smell (called "Malaria") exhaled from animal and vegetable substances in a state of putrid fermentation.*

No. 15.—It is reasonable to hope, that every other cause will be eradicated by comfortable clothing, wholesome food, and good lodgings, which comforts, can only be obtained, through the medium of constant employment given to the poor.

No. 16.—REMEMBER ! ! !—That Cleanliness and good air will improve your health and strength, will check disease, and UNDER GOD will preserve you from all the variety of wretchedness and misery occasioned by INFECTIOUS FEVER,

WM. KINGSLEY, Physician to the Fever-Hospital and Dispensary Roscrea, &c.

☞ To be had by the Gentry for the use of their Tenantry, at P. C. EGGERS', Printer, Roscrea, at 4s. 2d. per 100.

3. Fever and the workhouses

The Central Board of Health had difficulty in forcing the boards of guardians to provide special accommodation for people suffering from fever, mainly because of the expense involved at a time when many unions were bankrupt. Eventually, in April 1847, when several workhouses were grossly overcrowded with fever patients, the government transferred the responsibility for providing additional accommodation to the relief committees. The combined efforts of the Central Board, the relief committees and the boards of guardians ultimately resulted in a substantial increase in accommodation for fever patients, mainly by means of temporary hospitals in rented buildings and specially constructed wooden sheds.

Report by Doctor Devlin, Medical Officer, Ballina workhouse.

The medical officer begs leave most earnestly to impress on the board of guardians the necessity of immediately providing increased accommodation for the sick poor now in the house, nearly five hundred of whom are at present under medical treatment and are located in the different parts of the house; that he is fearfully alive to the danger that must inevitably ensue, unless the guardians decidedly and at once erect buildings sufficiently capacious to meet the emergency. The medical officer is also desirous of impressing on the guardians the very great danger of admitting more paupers than the house was built to accommodate, as by so doing, from the overcrowded state of the wards and defective ventilation, the diseases which are now prevailing will become highly contagious (if not already so), and must assuredly assume a much more malignant and fatal type.

He hopes that the board of guardians, without reference to any miserable or mistaken economy, but looking solely to the health and cleanliness of the house and the well-being and comfort of the sick, will appoint a responsible and efficient staff of nurses, as the present arrangement is totally inadequate to meet the wants of the establishment. I need not advert to the impossibility of having justice done the sick poor without proper nurse-tending. It is self-evident, and I dare say it must appear strange even to the guardians, that in this large, overcrowded house, with so many on the sick list, we have not had one paid or responsible nurse.

The medical officer entreats that the board of guardians will take immediate steps to procure the increased accommodation required for at least 1,000 persons, not to be admitted but of those already in the house; and as regards the sick in fever and dysentery, he is of the opinion that unless the buildings be forthwith erected or other accommodation procured, the house will become a charnel or pest house, and no man's life, in it or connected with it, will be for the moment secure.

He further hopes the board at their sitting this day will not separate before ensuring to those in hospital a regular supply of drink, such as rice-water sweetened, in the absence of milk, and such nutriment as he may from time to time think necessary.

Workhouse Infirmary, Ballina, 22 February 1847.

(Extract from the minutes of the Ballina, Co. Mayo board of guardians, 20 Feb. 1847; NLI Ms 12,202.)

PLAN AND SECTIONS OF TEMPORARY FEVER WARDS

OF ECONOMICAL CONSTRUCTION
FOR **50** PATIENTS.
PREPARED FOR THE CENTRAL BOARD OF HEALTH IRELAND.

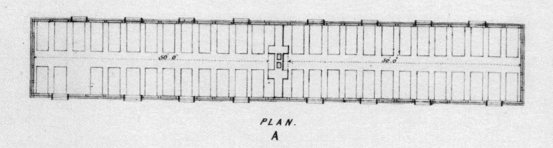

PLAN.
A

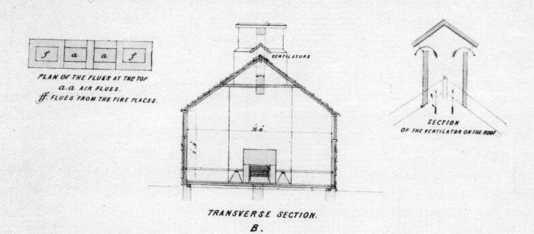

PLAN OF THE FLUES AT THE TOP
a.a AIR FLUES.
ff. FLUES FROM THE FIRE PLACES.

TRANSVERSE SECTION.
B.

SECTION
OF THE VENTILATOR ON THE ROOF

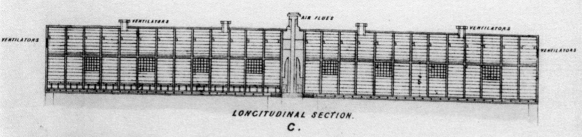

LONGITUDINAL SECTION.
C.

Size of Scantling.

Side Studs for nailing the upright boards to, 3×3 and 3.ft from Centre to Centre.
Heads and Sills to be 3×3.
Rafters to be 3×2. One over each upright Stud. Cross ties to be 3×1. Ridge 6×1¼.
Floor, Boards inch thick on joist 4×2 and 13 inches apart. Doors inch thick.
Contractors to include fastnings, grates, locks, and every thing necessary to render
the building complete. See report accompanying Plans dated March. 5 .47.

Geo. Wilkinson, Archt.
March, 1847.

Plans for fever sheds and beds.
(*Report of the Commissioners of Health, Ireland, on the epidemics of 1846-50*; P.P. 1852-53 (1562) XLI.)

4. James Mahony's Famine illustrations

The Cork artist, James Mahony, ARHA (1810-79), worked intermittently as an illustrator with The Illustrated London News *from 1845. In February 1847, he was commissioned to provide an illustrated report on conditions in west Cork where the fever epidemic was raging. His report was serialised and a dozen of his illustrations were featured. Mahony had a unique role in bringing the plight of the Famine victims to the notice of the British public; his emotive sketches were instrumental in eliciting an extremely generous response to the appeal by the British Relief Association in the early part of 1847. The* Illustrated London News *also published a number of later Famine illustrations by Mahony.*

Extracts from *The Illustrated London News,* 13 and 20 February 1847.

Uncoffin'd, unshrouded, his bleak corpse they bore,
From the spot where he died on the cabin's wet floor,
To a hole which they dug in the garden close by;
Thus a brother hath died – thus a Christian must lie!

'Twas a horrible end and a harrowing tale,
To chill the strong heart – to strike revelry pale,
No disease o'er this victim could mastery claim,
'Twas Famine alone mark'd his skeleton frame!

The bones of his grandsire and father too, rest
In the old abbey-yard, by the holy rites blest;
Their last hours were sooth'd by affection's fond cares,
Their last sighs were breath'd midst their friends
    tearful prayers!

Unshriven, untended, this man pass'd away,
Ere Time streak'd one hair of his dark locks with grey,
His requiem the wild wind, and [River] Ilen's hoarse roar,
As its swollen waves dash on the rock-girded shore.
    (C.C.T.)

The accounts from the Irish provincial papers continue to detail the unmitigated sufferings of the starving peasantry. Indeed, they are stated to be on the increase, notwithstanding the very great exertion of public bodies and individuals to assuage their pressure.

With the object of ascertaining the accuracy of the frightful statements received from the west, and of placing them in unexaggerated fidelity before our readers, a few days since, we commissioned our artist, Mr James Mahony of Cork, to visit a seat of extreme suffering, viz, Skibbereen and its vicinity; and we now submit to our readers the graphic results of his journey, accompanied by such descriptive notes as he was enabled to collect whilst sketching the fearful incidents and desolate localities; premising merely, that our artist must already have been somewhat familiar with such scenes of suffering in his own locality, Cork, so that he cannot be supposed to have taken an extreme view of the greater misery at Skibbereen.

'Funeral at Shepperton Lakes'.

'Woman begging at Clonakilty'.

After leaving Clonakilty, each step that we took westward brought fresh evidence of the truth of the reports of the misery, as we either met a funeral or a coffin at every hundred yards, until we approached the picturesque country of the Shepperton Lakes. Here, the distress became more striking, from the decrease of numbers at the funerals, none having more than eight or ten attendants, and many only two or three. We first proceeded to Bridgetown... and there I saw the dying, the living, and the dead, lying indiscriminately upon the same floor, without anything between them and the cold earth, save a few miserable rags upon them. To point to any particular house as a proof of this would be a waste of time, as all were in the same state; and, not a single house out of 500 could boast of being free from death and fever, though several could be pointed out with the dead lying close to the living for the space of three or four, even six days, without any effort being made to remove the bodies to a last resting place'.

'I started from Cork, by the mail (says our informant), for Skibbereen, and saw little until we came to Clonakilty, where the coach stopped for breakfast; and here, for the first time, the horrors of the poverty became visible, in the vast number of famished poor who flocked around the coach to beg alms. Amongst them was a woman carrying in her arms the corpse of a fine child, and making the most distressing appeal to the passengers for aid to enable her to purchase a coffin and bury her dear little baby. This horrible spectacle induced me to make some inquiry about her, when I learned from the people of the hotel that each day brings dozens of such applicants into the town.

A specimen of the in-door horrors of Scull [Schull] may be seen in the annexed sketch of the hut of a poor man named Mullins who lay dying in a corner upon a heap of straw supplied by the relief committee, whilst his three wretched children crouched over a few embers of turf, as if to raise the last remaining spark of life. This poor man, it appears, had buried his wife some five days previously, and was, in all probability, on the eve of joining her, when he was found out by the untiring efforts of the vicar, who, for a few short days, saved him from that which no kindness could ultimately avert. Our artist assures us that the dimensions of the hut do not exceed ten feet square; adding that, to make the sketch, he was compelled to stand up to his ankles in the dirt and filth upon the floor.

'Mullins' hut at Scull'. The visitor was the Rev. Dr Robert Traill, the local vicar, who succumbed to fever shortly after.

5. The incidence of fever

The incidence of fever correlated with that of famine and distress, and the epidemic was most severe in the west, the south-west and south Ulster. However, some areas where the Famine had little impact suffered serious outbreaks. For instance, Dublin City, which was overcrowded with refugees awaiting shipment to Liverpool, had a major epidemic; it peaked in June 1847 and did not subside until the following February. Diseases other than fever were also active. The condition mentioned on the next page by William Bennett, an English Quaker, 'in which the limbs and then the body swell...and...burst', was hunger oedema, known as 'famine dropsy'. It was not infectious and was caused by starvation.

Report in *The Freeman's Journal,* **27 July 1847.**

We have the best authority for stating that in one parish in this city there are no less than 1,000 patients ill of fever. The new cases in the same locality average thirty daily. This melancholy state of things is to be attributed principally to two causes: want of hospital accommodation and the use of unwholesome food... While fever patients pine, writhe, and perish, among the close, pestilential atmosphere of crowded lanes and alleys, spreading the disease, and dragging all who come in contact with them down to share their untimely graves, Cork Street Hospital is closed, though there is said to be still within its walls unoccupied accommodation. But the most melancholy feature of this sad state of things yields in power of appalling when compared with the heartless cruelty of meting out to the poor food from the bare sight of which one shrinks in horror.

Two specimens of this life-destroying charity-bread has been sent to our office. The test sample came to us from where it was being distributed, the relief depot, Bride Street; and we purpose to send it for inspection to the office of the Relief Commissioners. It is a kind of bread, black, mouldy, and of most noisome smell. It was made by the cook appointed under the Relief Commissioners. Two hundred loaves of this poisonous stuff were, we are informed, distributed for rations on the occasion the specimen sent to us was doled out! Need we be surprised to learn that fever is spreading when such predisposing causes, in the use of unwholesome food, exist? Need we wonder that fever, coming forth from the dens of

A lithograph drawn by A. MacLure. (Lord Dufferin and the Hon. G. F. Boyle, *Narrative of a Journey from Oxford to Skibbereen...*, *1847*). The two student-authors distributed £50 collected at Oxford University.

squalid misery where it usually lurks, assails, 'as a giant refreshed from wine', the higher classes; and, like the destroying angel, slays a victim in almost every house, when those higher classes tamely look on the deeds that are being done in the case of the poor? It should seem to be a wise ordination of providence that, when the higher classes permit famine to slay the poor, pestilence arises from that slaughter and slays the higher classes in turn.

Report by William Bennett on conditions in Co. Mayo.

Belmullet, Co. Mayo, 16th of third-month, 1847.
We now proceeded to visit the district beyond the town, within the Mullet. The cabins cluster the roadsides, and are scattered over the face of the bog, in the usual Irish manner where the country is thickly inhabited. Several were pointed out as 'freeholders'; that is, such as had come wandering over the land, and squatted down on any unoccupied spot, owing no fealty and paying no rent.

We spent the whole morning in visiting these hovels indiscriminately, or swayed by the representations and entreaties of the dense retinue of wretched creatures, continually augmenting, which gathered round and followed us from place to place, avoiding only such as were known to be badly infected with fever, which was sometimes sufficiently perceptible from without by the almost intolerable stench...

The scenes of human misery and degradation we witnessed still haunt my imagination with the vividness and power of some horrid and tyrannous delusion rather than the features of a sober reality. We entered a cabin. Stretched in one dark corner, scarcely visible from the smoke and rags that covered them, were three children huddled together, lying there because they were too weak to rise, pale and ghastly; their little limbs, on removing a portion of the filthy covering, perfectly emaciated, eyes sunk, voice gone, and evidently in the last stage of actual starvation. Crouched over the turf embers was another form, wild and all but naked, scarcely human in appearance. It stirred not, nor noticed us. On some

straw, soddened upon the ground, moaning piteously, was a shrivelled old woman, imploring us to give her something, baring her limbs partly, to show how the skin hung loose from the bones, as soon as she attracted our attention. Above her, on something like a ledge, was a young woman, with sunken cheeks, a mother, I have no doubt, who scarcely raised her eyes in answer to our enquiries, but pressed her hand upon her forehead, with a look of unutterable anguish and despair.

Many cases were widows whose husbands had recently been taken off by the fever, and thus their only pittance, obtained from the public works, was entirely cut off. In many, the husbands or sons were prostrate under that horrid disease, the results of long-continued famine and low living, in which first the limbs, and then the body, swell most frightfully and finally burst. We entered upwards of fifty of these tenements. The scene was invariably the same, differing in little but the number of the sufferers or of the groups occupying the several corners within. The whole number was often not to be distinguished, until, the eye having adapted itself to the darkness, they were pointed out, or were heard, or some filthy bundle of rags and straw was perceived to move.

Perhaps the poor children presented the most piteous and heart-rending spectacle. Many were too weak to stand, their little limbs attenuated, except where the frightful swellings had taken the place of previous emaciation. Every infantile expression had entirely departed; and, in some, reason and intelligence had evidently flown. Many were remnants of families, crowded together in one cabin, orphaned little relatives, taken in by the equally destitute, and even strangers; for these poor people are kind to one another to the end. In one cabin was a sister, just dying, lying by the side of her little brother, just dead. I have worse than this to relate, but it is useless to multiply details, and they are in fact unfit. They did but rarely complain. When we enquired what was the matter, the answer was alike in all: 'Tha shein ukrosh', 'indeed the hunger' [*tá sinn ocrach*, we are hungry].

(*Transactions... of the Society of Friends, 1852*, p. 162-4.)

6. *Cholera*

In addition to diseases which were due to famine, an epidemic of Asiatic cholera broke out in December 1848. It spread from the Continent to Britain; the first significant outbreak in Ireland was in Belfast. By January 1849 it had spread to many parts of the country; mortality was especially heavy in towns and cities. The Poor Law unions were responsible for the care and treatment of patients, but many were in financial difficulties and could not afford the expense of proper preventive or remedial measures. As a consequence, the epidemic was particularly severe in the distressed unions of the west. It peaked in April and had run its course by July; mortality probably exceeded 20,000.

Notice issued by the Central Board of Health.

The patient to be put into warm blankets, and [to be given] a vomit of two teaspoonfuls of powdered mustard in a teacup of warm water, or a tablespoonful of common salt in a pint of warm water. Dry heat of all sorts to be applied; the cramped limbs to be hand-rubbed, a little flour interposed to prevent excoriation. Then half a glass of whiskey with some powdered ginger; to be repeated often whilst coldness continues at intervals of an hour. A few grains of sal volatile in a little water may be given, when the patient is much reduced, and he may occasionally get a little tepid water. A pint of blood may be taken from a full young person within the first half hour, whilst moderate heat continues. After full vomiting by mustard, a pill to be taken every third hour of five grains of calomel and one of opium. Every fourth hour, a teaspoonful of ether and twenty drops of laudanum; heat to be applied as before. In every case, a poultice of equal parts of stale breadcrumbs and mustard powder, converted into a soft mass by vinegar and spread on linen, should be applied to the stomach.

(NLI Proclamations Collection.)

Extract from *The Freeman's Journal*, 8 May 1849.
[At the time, newspapers copied from each other.]

Cholera

Tuam: It gives us much pleasure to state that although several rumours are afloat, yet no decided case of cholera has up to the present appeared in this town.

Ballinasloe: In Ballinasloe and Ballinrobe, it is still raging to a great extent and the deaths are very numerous.

Loughrea: In Loughrea, some few cases had appeared, chiefly among the inmates of the workhouse. Three cases have appeared in Headford, one of which has been fatal, but the others have recovered.

Dunmore: We have heard it reported that cholera has appeared among a few of the poor people in the neighbourhood of Dunmore, but not to any extent. (*Tuam Herald.*)

Galway: The total number of cases, including those of the workhouse, since eleven o'clock yesterday (Friday) amounted only to fourteen, and the deaths, nine. This fatal disease may therefore be said to have almost disappeared from this locality – we hope permanently. (*Galway Vindicator.*)

Cork: From the cholera reports today, it appears that the disease is declining. (*Southern Reporter.*)

CHOLERA MAP

● Towns of 2,000 inhabitants and upwards visited by Cholera between 1848-50

○ Towns not visited by Cholera

N

0   50 miles

0   80 km

(*Report of the Commissioners of Health, Ireland, on the epidemics of 1846-50*; P.P. 1852-53 (1562) XLI; redrawn by Brian MacDonald.)

7. Famine burials

Funerals in the elaborate traditional manner were not feasible in the circumstances of the time. In addition, special graveyards had to be provided in many areas. The archives of the Department of Irish Folklore at University College Dublin are a major source of information on Famine burials. In particular, they include the responses to a questionnaire circulated by the Irish Folklore Commission for the centenary of the Famine in 1945; four extracts are reproduced here. The oral tradition harmonises fairly closely with contemporary sources, and often has a quality of immediacy which other accounts lack. Sometimes, however, it suggests an evasive reticence. This may reflect an element of guilt in survivors of the Famine; for instance, farmers or shopkeepers may have felt that they should have done more to help out their destitute neighbours.

Boherbue, Co. Cork

South of Boherbue there is a famous Famine graveyard at Sceac (Scagh). It is in Derrinagree parish and is marked in the old Ordnance [Survey] map... A road led from Boherbue to it. It was only a narrow pathway and was called 'Bothairín na gCorp' [the little road of the corpses]... About forty years ago an Australian called to see the place. He was fairly old and said his father, an emigrant, often worked conveying the Famine victims to Scagh graveyard. His father had the large box and it was used again and again carrying the corpses. They were often buried together in one hole. Scagh graveyard has not been used since the Famine days and is very neglected.

(Seán MacCárthaigh; Main Collection, Ms 1068, p. 254-5.)

Croom, Co. Limerick

The deaths in my native place were many and horrible. The poor famine-stricken people were found by the wayside, emaciated corpses, partly green from eating docks and nettles, and partly blue from the cholera and dysentery. They were buried where they were found by opening the fence and shifting the poor corpse into the gap formed. The ditch* (raised fence) was then built over the body and some stones set into the breastwork of the fence to mark the grave. The memory in later years of a Famine burial having been made at a certain point produced a superstitious fear in the minds of the people; a fear which had its origin, I think, in the horrible dread of contagion which filled the survivors in an area where death mowed a wide swathe. I know two places pointed out to me by my mother nearly half a century ago where such burials took place.

(Daithí Ó Ceanntabhail; Main Collection, Ms 1068, p. 50-51.)

[* The terms 'ditch' and 'dike' were often transposed in Ireland.]

Coalisland, Co. Tyrone

Basket coffins are known to have been made locally. Local people knew the art of basketry from having to work extensively at turf. Deaths occurred from disease rather than from starvation, and owing to the long distance to the graveyard and the weakness of the survivors, it is known that some were buried in fields near the dwellings. Such burial places were marked by a tree (or a sapling which grew into a tree). Corpses in many cases were wheeled to the graveyard... Where there were several deaths in one house, the bodies were rolled in sacking and buried without coffin of any kind.

(James Donnelly; Main Collection, Ms 1069, p. 8.)

Castlerea, Co. Roscommon

When a person was near death, he or she was removed from other parts of the workhouse to a large room at the gable end of the workhouse (the gable nearest the town of Castlerea). This room was called 'the black room', and the gable, 'the black gable', for in this room the sick person was allowed to die; sometimes there were up to seven persons in this room. From the window in this room there were a few boards slanting down to the earth, and beneath was a huge grave or pit. When a death occurred, the corpse was allowed to slide down the boards into the pit beneath, and lime was put over the corpse, along the boards and over the gable. This caused the wall to get black and gave the name 'the black gable'.

(Johnny Callaghan; Main Collection, Ms 1069, p. 255.)

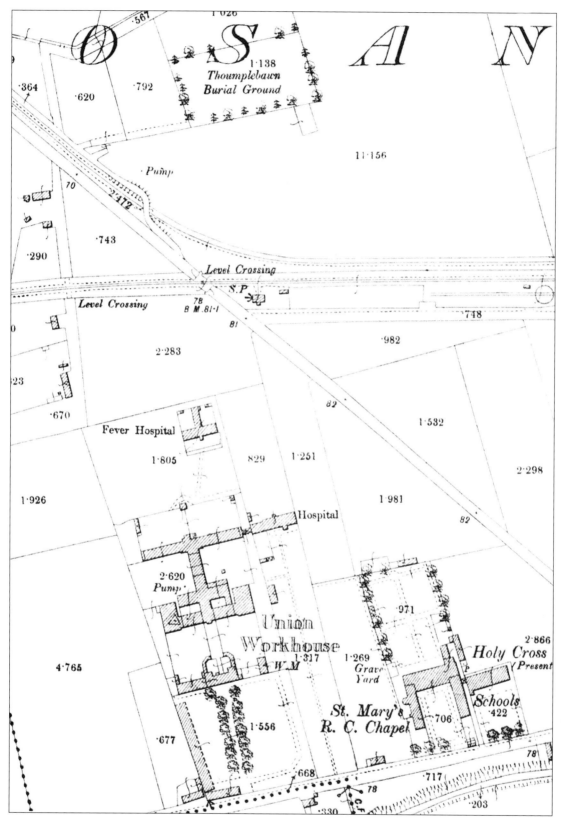

The Famine graveyard, Teampaillín Bán [the little white graveyard], to the north of the fever hospital at Listowel, Co. Kerry. The corpses were taken from the hospital and workhouse along a road on the left of the map. The graveyard has been restored as a memorial to the Famine dead. The map also shows a convent graveyard in the foreground and features from a later period, including railway lines. (Ordnance Survey, 1897, 1/2500, sheet x,12.)

IX

CHARITY

In Ireland, there was a long tradition of hospitality, alms and informal charity, whereby the destitute were maintained by relatives, friends and neighbours. There were also various charitable groups and organisations, and during the Famine these supplemented the relief provided by the state. From their experience of previous famines, the authorities were well aware of the potential contribution of organised charity, and throughout the Famine the state agencies co-operated with the various charitable organisations.

The first impetus for a co-ordinated approach to charitable relief came from the state Relief Commission established in November 1845. It advocated the formation of local relief committees to collect subscriptions and administer relief. The commitment and effectiveness of the committees varied considerably, but in general they had an important role in stimulating the charitable response at local level and channelling it into positive action. Apart from the relief committees, one of the first voluntary organisations in the field was the Mansion House Committee, which had provided relief during a food shortage in 1831; it was re-established in October 1845 under the chairmanship of Lord Cloncurry. On its revival, its first initiative was to organise a survey to assess the probable extent of the shortages arising from the failure of the potato crop. Another organisation also active in 1831, the Irish Relief Association, was revived in September 1846. It was followed in December by the General Central Relief Committee; between them, the two organisations raised over £100,000.

While members of all religious denominations were concerned at the distress and many of their leaders organised relief measures, the Quakers made an outstanding contribution. They had a long tradition of philanthropic work and were involved in relief in a number of previous crises, including the great famine of 1740-41. They were particularly effective at fund-raising, especially as they had close links with Quaker communities overseas. Moreover, they were internationally well-regarded and were used as a conduit for relief by groups in many parts of the world. Many of the activists came from the business community and were concerned that their efforts should be of a developmental nature and directed at eliminating the root causes of distress. In particular, they aimed at promoting personal and community initiative and self-reliance in the distressed areas.

The other main charitable organisation was the British Relief Association established in January 1847. The committee included prominent businessmen and it succeeded in attracting contributions from all levels of society, from Queen Victoria downwards. It also acted as a channel for donations from various parts of the Empire. It collected a total of £470,000, which in terms of today's money would be at least twenty million pounds. In his book, *The Irish crisis* (1848), Trevelyan noted that the famine of 1740-41 attracted little notice outside of Ireland (see above, p.19). The situation from 1846 onwards was markedly different, mainly due to press publicity. The appalling conditions in Ireland were reported in considerable detail in newspapers in Britain, the United States and other countries. There was a spontaneous reaction which resulted in the formation of relief committees in many towns and cities, and substantial sums were raised throughout the world. Notable contributions were received from Antigua, Bombay, Calcutta, Florence, Grahamstown (South Africa), Hobart (Tasmania), Hong Kong, Jamaica, Munich, Nova Scotia, Indian tribes in Canada, and the Choctow Indians in the United States.

An important factor in the response from abroad was that by the 1840s there was a substantial Irish diaspora, especially in Britain, the United States and Canada. Its contribution was effected largely through the medium of Irish activists on relief committees, and by Irish groups and organisations. Even more substantial was the amount remitted by way of private donation from the Irish abroad to their stricken families back home in Ireland.

1. An outline of Famine relief

In 1852, the Quakers published a review of their activities in a publication, Transactions, *which includes an outline of the work of the principal relief organisations; sections are included on the following pages. In addition to the organisations involved in relief, consideration should also be given to the thousands of individuals around the world who supported them with their contributions. Tribute should also be paid to the many thousands, perhaps millions, in Ireland who, in one way or another, assisted their neighbours in distress. In his book,* The last conquest of Ireland (perhaps), *John Mitchel generously acknowledged the role of the clergy and some landlords in providing relief.*

John Mitchel on the contribution of clergy and landlords.

In the meantime, the famine and the fever raged; many landlords regained possession without so much as an ejectment, because the tenants died of hunger; and the county coroners, before the end of this year, were beginning to strike work – they were so often called to sit upon famine-slain corpses. The verdict, 'death by starvation', became so familiar that the county newspapers sometimes omitted to record it; and travellers were often appalled when they came upon some lonely village by the western coast, with the people all skeletons upon their own hearths.

Irish landlords, sir, are not all monsters of cruelty. Thousands of them, indeed, kept far away from the scene, collected their rents through agents and bailiffs, and spent them in England or in Paris. But the resident landlords and their families did, in many cases, devote themselves to the task of saving their poor people alive. Many remitted their rents, or half their rents; and ladies kept their servants busy and their kitchens smoking with continual preparation of food for the poor. Local committees soon purchased all the corn in the government depots (at market price, however), and distributed it gratuitously. Clergymen, both Protestant and Catholic, I am glad to testify, generally did their duty; except those absentee clergymen, bishops and wealthy rectors who usually reside in England, their services being not needed in the places from whence they draw their wealth. But many a poor rector and his curate shared their crust with their suffering neighbours; and priests, after going round all day administering Extreme Unction to whole villages at once, all dying of mere starvation, often themselves went supperless to bed.

(John Mitchel, *The last conquest of Ireland (perhaps)*, 1861, p.30-33.)

'Irish beggar-woman and children'. (*The Lady's Newspaper*, 15 Jan. 1848, courtesy of BL.)

Review of Famine relief organisations.

In the summer of 1846, the potatoes looked remarkably well and there appeared every prospect of an abundant harvest, when it pleased an over-ruling providence that almost the whole crop should be destroyed in one week. The failure of the potato was not the only loss. The wheat was barely an average crop, and the barley and oats were deficient. The money value of the loss in potatoes and oats was computed by the government to amount to sixteen millions sterling. The announcement of this dreadful calamity did not at first produce the alarm which might have been expected. The idea of millions being reduced to starvation was too great to be quickly realised. Many believed that the accounts of the failure were exaggerated, while others who knew that the crop was lost persuaded themselves that the consequences would not be so very serious. It was not long before all such doubts and hopes were dispelled. The accounts which came in from every part of the country gave full proof of the awful calamity of impending famine.

A deep sympathy was aroused, and great anxiety prevailed to do something to relieve the rapidly increasing distress. As far back as the beginning of 1846, nearly £14,000 had been subscribed at Calcutta, when the intelligence of the partial failure had reached India. The distribution of this sum, under the name of the Indian Relief Fund, commenced on the 24th of fourth-month, 1846, and continued during the remainder of the year. The earliest association formed in consequence of the failure of 1846 was the Irish Relief Association, whose meetings were held at Upper Sackville Street. This society, whose exertions in the famine of 1831 have been already noticed, was reorganised on the 2nd of ninth-month, 1846. The subscriptions received by them exceeded £42,000. The General Central Relief Committee, over which the Marquis of Kildare presided, was formed on the 29th of twelfth-month. The contributions placed under their care amounted to upwards of £83,000, including a grant of £20,000 made to them by the British Relief Association.

In the distressed districts, government offered to double the local subscriptions, and although many of the gentry, and others who could afford to do so, had liberally subscribed in the spring of 1846 to relieve the distress which then existed, they again responded with much liberality to the appeal made in the autumn of the same year. It is impossible to estimate the sacrifices, and even privations, to which many of every class in Ireland cheerfully submitted in their efforts to relieve the distress which surrounded them. In England, when the extent of the calamity was ascertained, a great and general sympathy was excited. The British Association for the Relief of the Extreme Distress in Ireland and Scotland was formed in first-month, 1847.* The total amount of subscriptions received by them exceeded £470,000. Ladies also formed associations in different parts of Great Britain, some for supplying clothing, and some for promoting industrial occupations amongst the female peasantry.

Before any committee was formed, as well as for a long time after, a large amount of private contributions was poured into every part of the country, chiefly through the agency of the clergy of the Established Church. It is not our province to record the noble self-denial shown in individual cases, or to narrate the unwearied exertions of the different associations in collecting subscriptions and distributing relief; yet we cannot avoid this passing allusion to these exertions, whilst relating our own part in the transactions of that eventful period, and rendering an account of the execution of the trust confided to us.

(*Transactions of the Central Relief Committee of the Society of Friends in 1846 and 1847*, Dublin, 1852, p.30-33.)

*Potato crops were also damaged by blight in Scotland, where there was considerable distress, especially in the Highlands.

2. The Society of Friends

The relief provided by the Quakers had a total value of almost £200,000. Much of it consisted of shipments of food from the United States. Grants of food and money totalling approximately £150,000 were dispensed; each of the thirty-two counties got grants. Co. Meath got the smallest amount (£232); the main beneficiaries were Cork (£35,000), Galway (£16,000), Kerry (£14,000), Mayo (£13,000), Clare (£9,000), and Donegal (£8,000). In addition, about £38,000 was devoted to special schemes, including free clothing, the improvement of fisheries, the promotion of spade cultivation, and the establishment of a model farm and agricultural school at Colmanstown, Co. Galway.

DISBURSEMENTS.

	£	s.	d.		£	s.	d.
Grants in money and food for gratuitous distribution ...					151,114	1	0
Expenditure for the encouragement of the Fisheries	5,365	1	1				
Less repayments received	480	3	9				
					4,884	17	4
Amount paid for clothing distributed ...	7,772	6	2				
Less repayments received	1,756	18	9				
					6,015	7	5
Cost of green crop seeds distributed in 1848					6,271	14	2
Expense of land cultivation by spade labour in the County of Mayo in 1848 ...	7,469	7	9				
Less amount of sales of produce ...	1,756	2	2				
					5,713	5	7
Grants for cultivation by spade labour					275	0	0
Grants to the Farm Committee of the Society of Friends, for the establishment of a Model Farm and Agricultural School at Colmanstown, County of Galway					13,500	0	0
Insurance, brokerage, storage, &c. on provisions from America					2,574	14	9
Cost of manufacturing biscuit from American donations of flour, and of grinding oats					426	4	4
Grant to Belfast Ladies' Industrial Association for Connaught					500	0	0
Grant to Ladies' Industrial Society, for normal lace school, Wentworth-place, Dublin					100	0	0
Sundry expenses of Central Relief Committee and its auxiliaries at Cork, Limerick, Waterford and Clonmel :—							
Rent, office furniture, &c.	304	7	2				
Postage and carriage of parcels ...	249	4	10				
Printing, stationery, and advertising, including the cost of printing this report	1,095	2	8				
Travelling expenses of deputations to various parts of Ireland ...	647	8	11				
Salaries of assistant-secretary, book-keepers, clerks, &c.	1,836	18	4				
Petty charges	53	1	10				
					4,186	3	9
Balance remaining unappropriated					2,765	7	1
					£198,326	15	5

(*Transactions of the Central Relief Committee of the Society of Friends*, 1852, appendix.)

Central Relief Committee of the Society of Friends

Richard Allen
Joseph Allen
Edward Alexander
Edward Barrington
Richard Barrington
Joseph Bewley, *Secretary & Treasurer*
Samuel Bewley
Thomas Bewley

William Doyle
Joshua Harvey, M.D.
William Hogg
William Malone
Thomas Pim
James Pim, Jun.
Jonathan Pim, *Secretary*
William Harvey Pim

Thomas Pim, Jun., *Treasurer*
James Perry, *Treasurer*
Henry Perry
William Robinson
Henry Russell
Thomas H. Todhunter
William Todhunter
Adam Woods.

Corresponding Members

William J. Barcroft, Redford, Moy
Jonathan Pike, Beechgrove, Dungannon
Thomas C. Wakefield, Moyallen, Gilford
James N. Richardson, Lisburn
Thomas Hancock, Lisburn
John Pim, Jun., Belfast
Thomas Clibborn, Hall, Moate
Marcus Goodbody, Clara
Thomas Thacker Pim, Mountmellick
Richard Dowd, Brusna Mills, Roscrea
James Forbes, Christianstown, Kildare
Joseph Haughton, Ferns
Joseph Malcomson, Mayfield, Portlaw
Benjamin Grubb, Clonmel
John Abell, Limerick
William Woods, Limerick
Abraham Beale, Cork
Ebenezer Pike, Cork
Thomas Harvey, Youghal
Joshua W. Strangman, Waterford
Thomas White Jacob, Waterford.

Auxiliary Committees

Cork

Abraham Beale
Ebenezer Pike
William Harvey
Thomas Wright
Joseph Harvey
Joshua Beale
Thomas Harvey, Youghal
Abraham Fisher, Youghal.

Waterford

Richard Allen
Joshua William Strangman
Thomas W. Jacob
Joseph S. Richardson
Thomas Robinson White
George White
James Walpole
Samuel White
Thomas H. Strangman.

Clonmel

Barclay Clibborn
Joseph Clibborn
Robert Davis
William Davis
Thomas J. Grubb
Joseph Grubb
Benjamin Grubb
John Hughes
Thomas Hughes
Samuel Fayle
Joshua Malcomson
John T. Pim.

Limerick

James Alexander
John Abell
William Alexander
Thomas Fitt
Isaac W. Unthank
James Harvey
Samuel Alexander
William Woods.

(*Transactions* …, appendix.)

3. *The British Relief Association*

The British Association for the Relief of the Extreme Distress in Ireland and Scotland was formed on 1 January 1847. Its chairman was Thomas Baring, M.P., and the secretary was Stephen Spring-Rice, son of Lord Monteagle. There was an extremely generous response from a very wide spectrum of groups, organisations, corporate bodies and private individuals. Queen Victoria initially donated £1,000; following a sharp remonstrance by Spring-Rice, the sum was doubled. It was popularly believed in Ireland, however, that she gave only five pounds. Individuals who made substantial donations included Benjamin Disraeli, W.E. Gladstone, Sir Robert Peel, Lord John Russell, Charles Trevelyan and Charles Wood.

BRITISH RELIEF ASSOCIATION.

Committee.

THOMAS BARING, ESQ. M.P.
HENRY BARNEWALL, ESQ.
CHARLES JAMES BEVAN, ESQ.
SIR GEORGE CARROLL, ALDERMAN.
THE LORD ROBERT CLINTON.
J. J. CUMMINS, ESQ.
RAIKES CURRIE, ESQ. M.P.
RIGHT HON. THE EARL OF DALHOUSIE.
T. FARMER, ESQ.
SAMUEL GURNEY, ESQ.
ROBERT HANBURY, ESQ.
THOMSON HANKEY, JUN. ESQ.
M. J. HIGGINS, ESQ.
THE HON. ARTHUR KINNAIRD.
HENRY KINGSCOTE, ESQ.
THE RIGHT REV. THE LORD BISHOP OF LONDON.
SAMUEL JONES LOYD, ESQ.
W. G. PRESCOTT, ESQ.
THE BARON L. DE ROTHSCHILD, M.P.
DAVID SALOMONS, ESQ. ALDERMAN.
ABEL SMITH, ESQ.
G. R. SMITH, ESQ.

Auditors.

SIR JAMES WEIR HOGG, BART. M.P.
J. B. HEATH, ESQ.

Honorary Secretaries.

THE HON. S. E. SPRING RICE.
FRANCIS CARLETON, ESQ. (*deceased.*)
E. CANE, ESQ.

Extract from list of subscribers.

Her Most Gracious Majesty The Queen,	£2,000
H.R.H. Prince Albert	500
His Imperial Majesty The Sultan	1,000
[of Turkey – the Ottoman Empire]	
Her Majesty The Queen Dowager, equally	1,000
His Majesty The King of Hanover,	
as Duke of Cumberland and Chancellor of	
the University of Dublin	1,000
H.R.H. The Duchess of Kent	300
H.R.H. The Duke of Cambridge	300
H.R.H. The Duchess of Gloucester	200
H.R.H. The Duchess of Cambridge	100
H.R.H. The Princess Sophia, deceased	100
H.G. The Archbishop of Canterbury, deceased	300
The Lord Chancellor	300
H.G. The Archbishop of York, deceased	100
H.G. The Archbishop of York,	
2nd donation	100

(*British Association for the Relief of the Distress … Report*, London, 1849.)

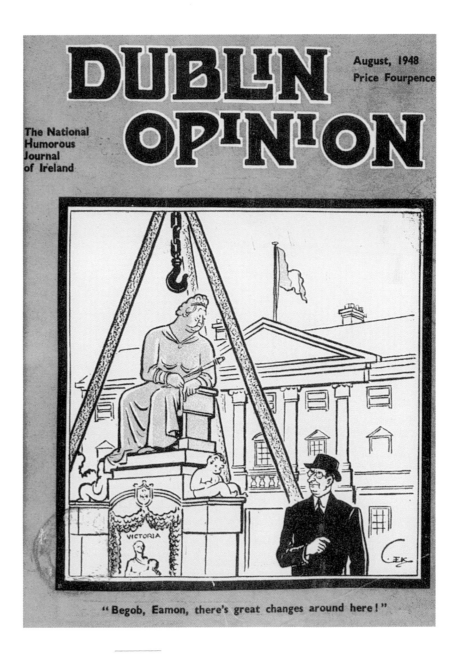

The cartoonist CEK (Charles E. Kelly) stages an exchange between Queen Victoria and Éamon de Valera outside Leinster House, the Irish Oireachtas (parliament) building, as her statue was removed. A Teachta Dála (member of parliament) is reputed to have waved farewell with a five-pound note.

4. The operations of the British Relief Association

The aim of the British Relief Association was the relief of the 'very numerous class of sufferers…who are beyond the reach of the government'. It worked closely, however, with the authorities, and put its supplies at the disposal of the Relief Commission, which arranged for their distribution by the commissariat and relief committees. Considerable assistance was given to distressed Poor Law unions. Of the £470,000 raised, one-sixth was devoted to distress caused by failures of the potato crop in Scotland. The Association had a number of agents in the field, the most notable of whom was a Polish nobleman, Count Strzelecki, who was responsible for counties Donegal, Sligo and Mayo.

(A page from the minute book of the Finance Committee of the British Relief Association; NLI Ms 5218.)

Extract from letter of Count Strzelecki to Stephen Spring-Rice.

Agency of the British Relief Association in Ireland, Reynold's Hotel, Dublin, 5 October 1847.

To the Honourable Stephen Spring-Rice.

The project of clothing of the convalescent seems to be of difficult execution; for few unions have a proper organisation of hospitals, and in those most afflicted with fever there is hardly a provision made to shelter the sick and thus no authentic source for obtaining a list or information of convalescents nor means for distributing to them the bounty. The Society of Friends had their ends totally defeated in that respect and with all their efforts could not prevent most of their clothes from finding way into pawnbroker shops. Should the Committee, however, direct their benevolent intention towards the clothing of schoolboys and girls rather than the convalescent, they would secure not only all practical security to their grants, but would confer undoubted benefits upon a good many of districts in which the schools are not attended, as much from the utter nakedness of children as also from their want of bread, and which they must daily procure by begging. I have written two official letters to you upon this subject and I am anxious that you should put forth a plan of setting aside a sum not only for the clothing of schools of both sexes by the clothes made in Ireland and out of Irish stuff, but also for procuring to them one meal per day of rye bread made and baked on the spot, and by which, in addition to instruction, the children would acquire early habits of a higher standard of food and clothing so necessary to them, and so influential upon the future prospects of the Irish peasantry.

Believe me most faithfully yours, de Strzelecki.

(NLI Ms 13,397(1), Monteagle Papers.)

Despatch from the Governor of Canada.

To the Right Honourable Earl Grey [Colonial Secretary].

My Lord,

I have the honour to state for your honour's information that very large subscriptions for the relief of Irish and Scotch distress have been made in this province. I have no means of ascertaining with accuracy the amount which has been raised, but I am disposed to think, from enquiries which I have made, that it does not fall short of £20,000. To this fund, the inhabitants of all creeds and origins have liberally contributed. It will be gratifying to your lordship to learn that several of the Indian tribes have expressed a desire to share in relieving the wants of their suffering white brethren. The sum subscribed by them already exceeds £175.

Elgin and Kincardine [James Bruce, 8th Earl of Elgin and 12th Earl of Kincardine],
Government House, Montreal, 28 May 1847.

(*Copies of despatches addressed to the Secretary of State from the governors of Her Majesty's colonial possessions relating to the money voted...for the relief...in Ireland and Scotland*, p. 7; P.P. 1847 (853) LIII.)

5. The role of the British press

The press in Britain had an influential role in creating public awareness of the crisis in Ireland. It was initially sympathetic, as evidenced, for instance, by the reports in The Illustrated London News. *British coverage, however, was coloured by traditional anti-Irish prejudice and by political and practical considerations; its general tenor was that the Irish were a backward race and lived on an inferior food – the potato; they were ungrateful and disloyal; Ireland was a drain on British resources; Britain was being flooded with Irish paupers.* The Times *and the satirical magazine* Punch, *in particular, reinforced traditional animosities, and alienated the sympathies of the British upper and middle classes.*

Extracts from a letter to *The Times*, 4 January 1847.

No doubt it bears an invidious aspect, and is a course open to obvious and shallow taunts, for anyone to dissuade, as you have, in my opinion most rightly, dissuaded your readers from the indulgence of a blind and thoughtless charity in contributing through a subscription list to the relief of the Irish poor. This has been the usual resource in all previous emergencies of the kind; and with what result? Why, the money went to pay the rents of landlords, who themselves refused to contribute a farthing to save their own tenantry from starving; nay, it actually purchased in Liverpool and Bristol the corn grown by those tenants, and sent it back to feed the very men who had raised, but had been forced to sell it, to satisfy the pressing demands of their landlord or his agent! And this is precisely what will again take place when any money is subscribed here. Even at this moment, the Liverpool papers record daily arrivals of oats from Ireland in that port, coming from districts where people are starving, and sent over here on account of the landowners...

It is true that with the corn they send over their poor too! But we have to pay for the former and feed the latter. The anticipated invasion of Irish pauperism has commenced. 15,000 have already within the last three months landed in Liverpool, and block up her thoroughfares with masses of misery, which, by our law, must be and is relieved. And the cry is, 'still they come'! How should it be otherwise? On this side of the Channel the law insures them against starvation. On the other, they are allowed to starve, and must starve unrelieved! According to Mr Chadwick, the usual annual immigration is from 300,000 to 400,000. This year we expect it to be doubled.

HEIGHT OF IMPUDENCE.

'Irishman to John Bull: "Spare a trifle yer Honour, for a poor Irishman to buy a bit of – – a Blunderbuss with" '.

(*Punch*, 12 Dec. 1846.)

An *Illustrated London News* editorial.

London, Saturday, 16 January 1847.
The advocacy of so holy a cause as that of 'feeding the hungry, and clothing the naked' is a delightful task, and one of the very few sacred pleasures that fall to the lot of the journalist in his toilsome routine of professional occupation. It is, therefore, with the purest satisfaction that we direct attention to the glorious progress which the good work of subscription, in aid of the starving famishing poor of Ireland, is making, in the hope that the truly Christian example which has already been set by the benevolent and charitable, in the very highest as well as the middle ranks of society, may, when pointed out for imitation, be speedily and extensively followed, and produce the good fruit which is to be expected in a land so proverbial for promptly affording succour to the wretched in distress as England justly is…

We have not done our duty by Ireland. We have undertaken to manage its affairs, and see the result. How different to that which our exertions have produced in our own happy England? Ireland is in such an abject state of perpetual impoverishment, that the failure for a single season of the crop of one inferior description of esculent [food], the potato, the total loss of which scarcely creates the most temporary inconvenience in England, prostrates and paralyses wretched Ireland, and dooms her most hapless people to all the unspeakable horrors of famine and pestilence; and that, too, despite her natural resources and fertility of soil being confessedly of the very highest order.

It is a truth, then – a sad and humiliating truth – that, for much of poor Ireland's calamitous visitation at the present time, England – great, wealthy, powerful England – 'whose merchants are princes' and whose children are called 'the honourable of the earth', is to a great extent accountable. But, while faithful to our mission, we do not hesitate to proclaim in the ears of our countrymen this truth, all bitter and unpleasant though it be, in the firm belief that the opportunity of amelioration will not be thrown away. We are, at the same time, convinced that the magnanimity which enables them to hear with calmness a just reproach will inspire them with a generous spirit of ardour in the cause of charity, which shall not be the less efficacious from its being sustained by a sentiment of duty.

THE ENGLISH LABOURER'S BURDEN;

OR, THE IRISH OLD MAN OF THE MOUNTAIN.

[See *Sinbad the Sailor.*

Loans to combat distress in the west of Ireland were regarded as unacceptable burdens on England's respectable poor. (*Punch,* 24 Feb. 1849.)

6. Relief from the United States

In addition to substantial sums sent home privately by the Irish in the United States during the Famine, organised aid from that source amounted to a million pounds. Much of it came from Irish groups, but significant donations were also received from towns and cities which had little or no Irish presence. The city of Albany in New York State had a 10% Irish population in 1830; by 1855 it had risen to 30%. A relief committee was established there in February 1847. It adopted a very professional approach to fund-raising, and hired collectors for each ward in the city at a fee of ten dollars each.

Extract from a list of donations from New York State.

Hopewell, Ontario County: 25 barrels corn, 2 barrels wheat, 4 bushels barley; the whole valued there at $71.21.

By Charles J. Folger of Geneva, Treasurer: 27 barrels corn-meal.

15 barrels *ditto* from Phelps, Ontario County (shipped May 4th).

From Carlisle, Schoharie County: articles of new and second-hand clothing valued at $81.23.

From Hamilton: 54 barrels corn, 2 boxes clothing.

From Lebanon: 23 barrels corn, 2 boxes clothing.

From Lodi, Seneca County, by John De Mott, Augustus Woodworth and Peter Himood, Committee: 38 barrels of corn, clothing etc., valued there at $107.96 for Ireland and Scotland.

By William Seaver, Committee, from Batavia: 45 barrels superfine flour.

From Oakfield, 13 barrels *ditto*; from Darien 5 barrels *ditto*; the whole valued there at $409.50.

By Lorenzo Golding, Correspondence Secretary, of French Creek, Chautauqua County Irish Relief Society: 2 barrels corn, 1 barrel wheat, 1 box corn.

From Lakeville, Livingston County, by L.F. Olmsted: 30 barrels flour, 1 box clothing.

From G. Robinson and S.D. Kittle of Ames, Montgomery County: 1 box clothing valued at $7.30. From Norwich, by Oliver Jennison: 16 barrels corn, 1 barrel pork valued at $56.50.

From Portage, Allegany County, by Horace Hunt, L. Smith and O.J. Messenger: Corn for Ireland and Scotland, 15 barrels flour, 22 barrels corn, 1 barrel peas, 1 box cloth, clothing etc., valued there at $177.

From New Berlin, Chenango County, by A.C. Welsh, Samuel White, Samuel Medbury, Dr D Loomis, H.O. Moss: corn: 14 barrels rye, 29 corn, 1 beans, being remainder of 76 barrels contributed; valued with freight at $165. (Notify Gen. A.C. Welsh of receipt).

From Little Falls, by Zenas C. Priest: 28 barrels corn-meal, contributed by individuals employed on the Western Division of the Utica & Schenectady Railroad.

From Annesville, by R. Bacon, Committee Secretary: a further contribution of 21 sacks corn.

From Sterling, by Rev. William L. Roberts, Curry T. Green, D.B. Smith, J.P. Hunter, John McCrea, James Green, James Lester, and William Kevill: 60 bags corn, 3½ barrels rye flour, 3½ bushels beans, valued there at $163.50. (W.K. wishes information of disposition of donation.)

(McKinney Library, Albany Institute of History and Art.)

Letter from Albany Relief Committee to Messrs Jonathan Pim and Joseph Bewley.

As the Central Committee of the State of New York, we are now making, through the agency of the committee in New York City, shipments of food for the sufferers in Ireland. We commit it to the care of the ever-active benevolence of the Central Committee of the Society of Friends in Dublin, confident that it will be distributed by them without regard to any claims or influence, except those of humanity and prudence. At the particular request, however, of many contributors, we have offered the control of the distribution of 2,000 barrels of corn-meal, in equal parts, to the joint order of the Roman Catholic archbishop, and the Reformed Catholic archbishop or bishop, of the several cities of Dublin, Armagh, Cashel and Tuam, if they shall think their direction will facilitate distribution to points not otherwise reached, or relieve the committee of which you are the secretaries from some of its arduous and responsible duties.

These 2,000 barrels are the equally mingled contributions of the Roman Catholic and Protestant citizens of the city of Albany, and you will please deliver or forward according to any such joint orders as shall await the arrival of the meal; and if none are given, you will please distribute without delay those 2,000 barrels with the residue as you may deem expedient. The contributions in money and grain etc. already received by us, and which we are sending as rapidly as possible, amount to about $24,000; and much more is awaiting the opening of our canal navigation, ready to be forwarded to us and to Ireland and Scotland.

On behalf of the other members of our committee, Messrs Delavan, Olcott, Dexter, Norton, and myself, with great respect, I am your obedient servant, Charles M. Jenkins, Chairman of Central Irish Relief Committee, Albany, New York, 28 April 1847.

(McKinney Library, Albany Institute of History and Art.)

The United States frigate *Macedonian*, one of a number of naval vessels which brought relief to Ireland. (*The Illustrated London News*, 7 August 1847.)

X

EVICTIONS

The victims of famine usually endure starvation, malnutrition and disease. In the case of the Irish Famine of the 1840s, however, many of the victims were afflicted with the additional trauma of eviction from their homes and subsequent homelessness. It was not a coincidental circumstance, but rather an integral and almost inevitable feature of the dynamic set in motion by the failure of the potato crop over a prolonged period.

Even before the Famine, the spectre of eviction was always on the horizon for smallholders, cottiers and landless labourers. Unlike the large farmers who leased their lands for a fixed term of at least twenty-one years, the people at the lower levels were often either tenants-at-will or rented their property on a year-to-year basis. They rented from a landlord, middleman or farmer; provided they paid the rent punctually and caused no trouble, they were allowed to remain indefinitely. Landlords were generally concerned at the prevalence of subletting, the sub-division of holdings into unviable units, and the consequent congestion and poverty. Provided the overall rental was satisfactory, however, they were generally complacent and allowed the situation to continue. In the decades before the Famine, only a minority of landlords resorted to wholesale eviction as a means of consolidating smallholdings into viable farms.

For many landlords, however, the position changed drastically in 1846, with the second failure of the potato crop. As smallholders, cottiers and the landless were rendered destitute and unable to pay their rents, the landlords' incomes contracted. Then, at the very time when they had to adapt to reduced incomes, landlords found that their expenses were escalating. While they accepted that most of the state loans advanced for relief schemes would ultimately have to be repaid from the Poor Law rates for which they were largely liable, the situation became acute in the summer of 1847. Thereafter, relief was to be provided by the Poor Law system alone and was to be financed from current rates.

The main beneficiaries of the Poor Law system, in the workhouse or on outdoor relief, were those with rateable valuations of £4 or less, whose rates were paid by the landlords. In effect, not only were the landlords obliged to forego their rents, but they were being forced to maintain their defaulting tenants. The burden on landlords was especially severe in the congested areas, where rentals were most reduced and the numbers requiring maintenance were greatest. In the circumstances, it was almost inevitable that many landlords resorted to eviction as a means of removing their difficulties.

In many areas, landlords carried out wholesale evictions of tenants-at-will and smallholders whose leases had expired. The holdings were then consolidated into viable farms; these were usually let to people with sufficient capital and initiative to develop the property, pay rent to the landlord, and rates to support the workhouse.

In reforming their estates, the landlords were acting in accordance with the advice tendered by British governments and economists in the decades before the Famine. But while reform was undoubtedly necessary in the long term, its implementation by a process of mass eviction in a period of famine and widespread destitution was, by any standards, inhumane. Nevertheless, it had the full support of the law and, by default, of the Liberal government and, indeed, the parliament of the day. The government took no action of any consequence to stop or regulate evictions, nor to care for the dispossessed, other than to direct them to the workhouses, which in many cases were already dangerously overcrowded.

The government did, however, put pressure on landlords whose estates were in financial difficulty. Legislation was enacted in 1848 and 1849 to facilitate the sale of encumbered estates. The new proprietors, in some instances, contributed to reform of the landed estate system, but they did little for the plight of destitute tenants in the latter years of the Famine; indeed, they proved as ready as their predecessors to evade their moral and legal obligations by means of mass eviction.

1. Benevolent landlords

In bad years, a minority of landlords traditionally assisted their tenants by reducing rents or allowing them to go into arrears. Apart from humanitarian considerations, they believed that it was good business practice and ultimately in the best interests of their estates. The estate of James Du Pre (Alexander), 3rd Earl of Caledon, amounted to 30,000 acres in counties Armagh and Tyrone. The Slator estate was relatively small; it survived the Famine, but was sold in the Encumbered Estates Court in 1864.

NOTICE.

THE TENANTS on the Estates of the Right Hon. the EARL OF CALEDON, in the Counties of ARMAGH and TYRONE, are requested to take Notice, that my Office will open for the Receipt of His Lordship's Rents, *due on the 1st of May last, on Monday, the 4th day of January next,* when it is hoped the following arrangement will be observed :—

COUNTY OF ARMAGH.

Robert Watson & Hugh Morrow's division, - 1st Week.

COUNTY OF TYRONE.

Timothy Marshall & Hugh Scott's division, - 2d Week.
Jeremiah Marshall & Jas. Lindsay's, division, 3d Week.

In consequence of the failure of the POTATO CROP, I am instructed by His Lordship to make the following early communication to his Tenantry, and to express to them (particularly those holding *Small Farms*) the sincere sympathy he feels for the loss they have sustained, and his willingness to mitigate their distress.

LORD CALEDON, after mature consideration, has approved of the following Scale of Reduction in the Rents of the current Year, viz. :—

All Tenants Residing on their Farms, and holding them either by Lease, or at Will, and paying Mr. BRASSINGTON'S Valuation,—

Under 5 Statute Acres of Arable Land, a Reduction of	50 per Cent.
Above 5 and not exceeding 10 Acres, - - -	40 per Cent.
Above 10 and not exceeding 15 Acres, - - -	25 per Cent.
Above 15 and not exceeding 25 Acres, - - -	15 per Cent.
Above 25 and not exceeding 35 Acres, - - -	10 per Cent.

It is considered that any Tenant holding more than 35 Acres, at a fair Rent, is compensated for the loss of his Potato Crop by the present high price of Grain, and other articles of Produce.

With Tenants holding under old Leases, dated prior to 1816, the following Scale will be observed, viz :—

Under 5 Statute Acres of Arable Land, a Reduction of	30 per Cent.
Above 5 and not exceeding 10 Acres, - - -	20 per Cent.
Above 10 and not exceeding 15 Acres, - - -	15 per Cent.
Above 15 and not exceeding 25 Acres, - - -	10 per Cent.

The above Scale LORD CALEDON believes to be equitable and just, but in addition to the Reduction of Rents, his Lordship desires me to say, that he hopes to find Remunerative Employment, as he has hitherto done, for every Man residing on his property, who may be placed in a condition to require it.

** LORD CALEDON has also instructed me to give COALS as usual to the Labouring Classes at a Reduced Price, and arrangements are made to distribute MEAL to them also at a moderate rate.

☞ For myself, I trust the Tenantry will respond to his LORDSHIP's kindly feeling towards them, by punctual Payment of their Rents, without which, it is impossible for a considerate Landlord to meet the heavy responsibilities placed upon him at the present time.

HENRY L. PRENTICE, Agent.

CALEDON OFFICE, *14th October,* 1846.   ARMAGH :—PRINTED BY J. McWATTERS.

(NLI Proclamations Collection.)

TO MY TENANTRY
IN THE
COUNTIES of CAVAN & LONGFORD

In consequence of the Distress prevailing in this Country, from the loss sustained by the Failure of the Potato Crop, I have come to the resolution of making a REDUCTION on the Half-year's Rent now payable as follows :—

£

Tenants	paying	5 yearly and under,	....	30 per Cent.
Do.	Do.	10	and Do.,	....	20 per Cent.
Do.	Do.	15	and Do.,	....	15 per Cent.
Do.	Do.	20	and Do.,	....	10 per Cent.
Do.	Do.	25	and Do.,	....	5 per Cent.

All Tenants paying more than £25 yearly, are expected to pay their Rents in Full.

All Tenants wishing to avail themselves of this abatement, must have their Rents paid on or before the 25th December.

This abatement does not extend to any Freehold Leases granted in and previous to the year 1830.

To all Tenants now owing Two Years' Rent and upwards, I hereby offer a clear receipt, (and Five Pounds over and beyond the same), who shall deliver up peaceable possession to my Agent, on or before the First day of MAY ; and those of my Tenantry who are defaulters, and do not avail themselves of these advantages, will not consider me bound to them after this offer.

All Tenants paying up Arrears shall be allowed Thirty-three per Cent., or one-third on the amount paid.

H. B. W. SLATOR.

White-Hill, 17th November, 1846.

(NLI Proclamations Collection.)

Caledon, Co. Armagh. (F.O. Morris, *A series of picturesque views of seats of the noblemen and gentlemen of Great Britain and Ireland ...*, London, 1866-80, vol. IV.)

2. The legality of eviction

The contract between landlord and tenant was usually formalised in a lease, which specified the property, the duration of the letting, and the rent. In the event of dispute, either party could appeal to a court of law. The most common scenario, however, was that the landlord took proceedings to eject the tenant on the grounds of non-payment of rent, or because the lease had expired and was not being renewed. In such cases, he had to show cause in court and obtain a civil decree; this entitled him to the protection of police and military when effecting the eviction. The system was outlined in uncompromising terms by John Mitchel. While his book, The last conquest, *promoted an extreme nationalist agenda, its section on the history of eviction had considerable validity.*

An outline of eviction law by John Mitchel.

As a condition of Catholic emancipation, the 'forty-shilling franchise' had been abolished, so that the privilege of voting for members of parliament should be taken away from the great mass of the Catholic peasantry. This low franchise had theretofore induced landlords (for the sake of securing political power) to subdivide farms and create voters. The franchise abolished, there was no longer any political use for the people; and it happened about the same time that new theories of farming became fashionable. 'High farming' was the word. There was to be more grazing, more green-cropping; there were to be larger farms; and more labour was to be done by horses and by steam. But consolidation of many small farms into one large one could not be effected without clearing off the 'surplus population'; and then, as there would be fewer mouths to be fed, so there would be more produce for export to England. The clearance system, then, had begun in 1829, and had proceeded with great activity ever since; and as the tenants were almost all tenants-at-will, there was no difficulty in this, except the expense.

The code of cheap ejectment was therefore improved for the use of Irish landlords. As the laws of England and Ireland are extremely different, both in regard to franchise and land-tenure, and as the ejectment laws were invented exclusively for Ireland, to clear off the 'surplus population', I shall give a short account of them.

There had been an act of George III (1815) providing that in all cases of holdings, the rent of which was under £20 (this included the whole class of small farms), the assistant barrister at sessions (the county judge) could make a decree at the cost of a few shillings to eject any man from house and farm. Two years after, the proceedings in ejectment were still further simplified and facilitated by an act making the sole evidence of a landlord or his agent sufficient testimony to ascertain the amount of rent due. By another act of the first year of George IV [1820], it was declared that the provisions of the cheap ejectment act 'had been found highly beneficial' (that is to say, thousands of farms had been cleared off), 'and it was desirable that same should be extended'. Thereupon, it was enacted that the power of summary ejectment at quarter-sessions should apply to all holdings at less than £50 rent; and by the same statute the cost of procuring ejectment was still farther reduced. In the reigns of George IV and Victoria, other acts were made for the same purpose, so that the cost and trouble of laying waste a townland and levelling all its houses had come to be very trifling. You will admit that there is cheap justice in Ireland, at least for some people.

In many parts of the island, extermination of the people had been sweeping. At every quarter-sessions in every county, there were always many ejectments; and I have seen them signed by assistant barristers by hundreds in one sheaf. They were then placed in the hands of bailiffs and police, and [they] came down upon some devoted [selected] townland with more terrible destruction than an enemy's sword and torch. Whole neighbourhoods were often thrown out upon the highways in winter, and the homeless creatures lived for a while upon the charity of neighbours; but this was dangerous, for the neighbours were often themselves ejected for harbouring them. Some landlords contracted with emigration companies to carry them to America 'for a lump sum'... Others did not care what became of them; and hundreds and thousands perished every year of mere hardship.

Now, sir, I hardly expect you to believe all this. You will think that the prejudice of the narrator exaggerates somewhat. But there are in these United States this moment at least one million of persons, each of whom knows the truth of every word I have written, and could add to my general statement circumstances of horror and atrocity that might make you tremble with rage as you read.

It is but fair to tell, that sometimes an ejecting landlord or agent was shot by desperate houseless men. What wonder? There were not half enough of them shot. If the people had not been too gentle, forgiving and submissive, their island could never have become a horror and scandal to the earth.

(John Mitchel, *The last conquest of Ireland* (*perhaps*), Dublin, 1861, p.92-4.)

'The ejectment'. (*The Illustrated London News*, 16 Dec. 1848.)

3. The process of eviction

The English Quaker philanthropist, James Hack Tuke, gives a good account of the procedure followed in one of the thousands of evictions carried out during the Famine. In this instance, the landlord or middleman was non-resident, and the text illustrates the fact that absentees had even less sense of community with their tenants, or sympathy for their plight, than was the case with resident landlords. The concession of forgiving arrears of rent in return for peaceable surrender of their homes and holdings was purely nominal, and was of no consequence to destitute tenants in depressed areas such as Erris in Co. Mayo. The gulf between landlord and tenant is pointed up in the reference to a dinner party on an evening when a large number of starving tenants were rendered homeless.

'The day after the ejectment'. (*The Illustrated London News*, 15 Dec. 1848.)

———

James Hack Tuke on evictions.

Although so much has already been said about evictions, I can hardly omit to mention one instance which occurred very shortly before my visit, and which presents a striking instance of the cruelty connected with that system of extermination which many Irish landlords think themselves justified in adopting. The extreme western portion of Erris is a narrow promontory called the 'Inner Mullet'. Upon this wretched promontory, a proprietor named Walsh, residing in another part of the country, has an estate from which he was desirous of ejecting a number of tenants by the usual summary process of unroofing and eviction. As no less than 140 families were to be turned out and cast forth to beg or perish, for the poorhouse was fifty miles distant and could not have contained them, it was natural to expect some resistance from persons with such prospects.

The landlord, therefore, summons the sheriff to his assistance – the stipendiary magistrate is requested to call out the police; but a maddened tenantry may overcome a handful of police. Fifty soldiers, therefore, headed by the commanding officer of the district, are added to the force. It is thought the 'kindest' way to prevent bloodshed, by showing a superior power. Arrived at the scene of action, the troops are stationed in reserve behind a hill, and the landlord and sheriff, protected by forty policemen, proceeded to announce their errand. The tenants are commanded to quit – they are told that their landlord forgives all arrears, on condition of their quietly giving up possession of their hovels and holdings, and leaving their crops should they have any. But the poor tenants, knowing the consequence of this, remonstrate – entreat, at least for time – but all in vain; the decree has passed.

The policemen are commanded to do their duty. Reluctantly indeed they proceed, armed with bayonet and muskets, to throw out the miserable furniture: dirty time-worn stools and bed-frame, if any, ragged cover-lid [coverlet], iron pot; all must be cast out, and the very roof of the hovel itself thrown down. But, the tenants make some show of resistance – for these hovels have been built by themselves or their forefathers who have resided in them for generations past – seem inclined to dispute with the bayonets of the police, for they know truly that, when their hovels are demolished, the nearest ditch must be their dwelling, and that thus exposed death could not fail to be the lot of some of their wives and little ones. But the signal is given to the soldiers, and, overawed by the unexpected sight, the tenants are compelled to submit, and in despair and dismay to see the ruthless work proceed.

Six or seven hundred persons were here evicted; young and old, mother and babe were alike cast forth, without shelter and without the means of subsistence! A favoured few were allowed to remain, on condition that in six months they would voluntarily depart. 'A fountain of ink (as one of them has said) would not write half our misfortunes'; and I feel that it is utterly beyond my power to describe the full misery of this and similar scenes. At a dinner party that evening, the landlord, as I was told by one of the party, boasted that this was the first time he had seen the estate or visited the tenants. Truly, their first impression of landlordism was not likely to be a very favourable one!

(James Hack Tuke, *A visit to Connaught in the autumn of 1847; a letter addressed to the Central Relief Committee of the Society of Friends,* Dublin, 1847, p. 24-26.)

4. West Clare and Kilrush union

Relative to its population, Clare was the county which suffered most from evictions, especially in the latter years of the Famine. In the period 1849-54, almost one in ten of the population was rendered homeless. Kilrush union was particularly notorious and several landlords were involved; when a few prominent landlords in an area gave the lead in resorting to eviction, others found it easier to follow their example. Most of those evicted were tenants-at-will who had no legal protection. In addition, the 'Gregory clause', which excluded those with more than a quarter of an acre from Poor Law relief, had already forced many of them to relinquish their holdings; the landlords then took advantage of their change in status to evict them from their cabins.

List of evictions, and the persons expelled from their houses, on the lands of Moveen, the property of James Westropp, Esq. – May 15, 1849.

						MOYARTA ELECTORAL DIVISION				
No.	House of Families	No. in Family	Males	Females	Quantity of Land	Yearly Rent			Cause of Eviction	Title	Observations
						£	s	d			
1	Margaret Keane, widow	7	3	4	10 acres	10	0	0	Non-payment	At will	
2	Kate Houlehan . . .	6	2	4	3 ,,	3	0	0	,,	,,	
3	Lawrence Galvin . . .	3	2	1	Cabin		. .		. .	,,	Work-rent
4	James Meany	6	3	3	1 acre	1	0	0	Non-payment	,,	
5	Felix Meany	6	4	2	Cabin		. .		. .	,,	Work-rent
6	Michael Scanlon . . .	5	3	2	½ acre	0	10	0	Non-payment	,,	
7	Pat Galvin	6	3	2	Cabin		. .		. .	,,	Work-rent
8	Martin Downs	3	2	1	2 acres	2	0	0	Non-payment	,,	
9	Mary Scanlon, widow	5	2	3	2 ,,	2	0	0	,,	,,	
10	Joan Flahive, widow .	3	. .	3	Cabin		. .		. .	,,	Work-rent
11	Catherine Houlihan .	2	. .	2	,,		. .		. .	,,	,,
12	John Meany	4	2	2	,,		. .		. .	,,	,,
13	Pat Meany (Pat) . . .	7	4	3	4½ acres	3	7	0	Non payment	,,	
14	Mary Delohery, widow	4	1	3	Cabin		. .		. .	,,	Work-rent
15	Mary O'Brien, widow	4	2	2	,,		. .		. .	,,	,,
16	Mary Meany (Hourigan)	3	1	2	,,		. .		. .	,,	,,
17	Pat Meany (James) . .	4	2	2	,,		. .		. .	,,	,,
18	Hugh Flaherty	8	4	4	,,		. .		. .	,,	,,
19	Laurence Walsh . . .	6	4	2	,,		. .		. .	,,	Work rent. This man gave up his land before.
20	John Mullany	6	5	1	10½ acres	7	19	6	Non payment	,,	
21	John Lynch (Daniel) .	6	3	3	10½ ,,	7	17	6	,,	,,	
22	Denis McMahon . . .	6	4	2	10½ ,,	7	17	6	,,	,,	
23	Margaret Lynch . . .	1	. .	1	Cabin		. .		. .	,,	Work-rent
24	John Lynch	8	4	4	10 acres	7	10	0	Non-payment	,,	
25	Daniel Lynch	7	6	1	12 acres	9	0	0	,,	,,	
26	John Lynch (Martin) .	8	5	3	11 ,,	9	3	0	,,	,,	
27	Pat Gorman	7	3	4	11 ,,	8	5	0	,,	,,	
28	Joe Gorman	5	3	3	11 ,,	8	5	0	,,	,,	
29	Darley Mullanny . . .	5	2	3	Cabin		. .		. .	,,	Work-rent
30	Mary Donnell, widow	5	3	2	23 acres	16	10	0	Non-payment	,,	
31	Margaret Cahill . . .	2	. .	2	Cabin		. .		. .	,,	Work-rent
32	Michael Houghrahan .	6	3	3	,,		. .		. .	,,	,,
		164	85	79							

(Reports and returns relating to evictions in the Kilrush union, p.56; P.P. 1849 (1089) XLIX.)

Report by Capt. Arthur Kennedy on evictions in the Kilrush union.

7 May 1849.

I find that my constant and untiring exertions make but little impression upon the mass of fearful suffering. As soon as one horde of houseless, and all but naked, paupers are dead or provided for in the workhouse, another wholesale eviction doubles the number, who, in their turn, pass through the same ordeal of wandering from house to house, or burrowing in bogs or behind ditches, till broken down by privation and exposure to the elements, they seek the workhouse or die by the roadside. The state of some districts of the union during the last fourteen days baffles description; 16 houses, containing 21 families, have been levelled in one small village in Killard division, and a vast number in the rural parts of it. As cabins become fewer, lodgings, however miserable, become more difficult to obtain. And the helpless and houseless creatures thus turned out of the only home they ever knew, betake themselves to the nearest bog or ditch, with their little all, and thus huddled together, disease soon decimates them.

Notwithstanding that fearful and (I believe) unparalleled numbers have been unhoused in this union within the year (probably 15,000), it seems hardly credible that 1,200 more have had their dwellings levelled within a fortnight. I have a list of 760 completed and of above 400 in preparation. It appears to me almost impossible to successfully meet such a state of things; and the prevailing epidemic [cholera], or the dread of it, aggravates the evil. None of this houseless class can now find admittance save into some overcrowded cabin, whose inmates seldom survive a month. I have shown Dr Phelan some of these miserable nests of pestilence, which I am at a loss to describe.

Five families, numbering 20 souls, are not unfrequently found in a cabin consisting of one small apartment. At Doonbeg, a few days since, I found three families, numbering 16 persons, one of whom had cholera, and three in a hopeless stage of dysentery. The cabin they occupied consisted of one wretched apartment about twelve feet square. It was one of the few refuges for the evicted, and they were unable to reckon how many had been carried out of it from time to time to the grave.

(*Reports and returns relating to evictions in the Kilrush union*, p.46; P.P. 1849 (1089) XLIX.)

The village of Moveen, three miles south-west of Kilkee. (*The Illustrated London News*, 22 Dec. 1849.)

5. The landlords' position

The English philanthropist, Rev. Sidney Godolphin Osborne, contributed a remarkable series of letters on the social issues of the day to The Times, over the period 1844-88. In 1849, he visited the west of Ireland, and published a number of letters on local conditions. The letters are fair and objective; in the extract given here, he outlines the difficult situation of many landlords under the Poor Law regime. While eviction in time of famine was especially cruel, many landlords adopted that course only as a last resort. Osborne published the letters and additional material in Gleanings in the west of Ireland (London, 1850), a useful source on the later period of the Famine.

Extract from a letter by S.G. Osborne.

The working of the Irish Poor Law.

I have waded through this gloomy retrospect that I might bring you to see the causes which have begotten eviction. I have no hesitation in asserting that no account yet given in England has conveyed to the English public any just idea of the number of houses which have, within these two years past, been razed to the ground, or allowed to remain roofless. I have travelled successive days' journeys, and seen the whole country, on both sides of the road, with far the greater proportion of houses unroofed. I have seen what appeared to be whole villages in this condition. I will not single out particular proprietors as carrying on this system; it seems in the west the one general pervading system. It is not denied that it is so. It is to me a fearful sight for many reasons – a painful sight; and yet I have learned to admit that it is to a great degree a natural, inevitable result of the war now carrying on in the west of Ireland between fast-fading property and increasing pauperism.

Proprietors have seen every test fail by which it was hoped to diminish the amount of claimants on the rates. The poorhouses are overflowing; in many unions out-relief at an enormous expense barely supports its recipients in the possession of a life fast declining under the small amount of food they receive for the work exacted from them; owners have seen no choice but to use every weapon they possess to clear their estates, or to allow all profit from them to be wholly absorbed by the rate collector. Not only does the cabin house a man whose land from necessity is often untilled – a man who can pay no rent, but a man with a family who must be sustained in his unprofitable condition, more or less, at the cost of the proprietor. The rates of all holders under £4 – a numerous class – are wholly paid by the owner of the soil; he is also forced to allow to other higher classes of tenants a poundage on the rent they pay him, according to the Poor Law rate they have paid.

A case will also not unfrequently occur, in which the owner has to pay for each poor rate more than the entire holdings pay to him: the real tenant has erected other habitations beside his own; at the Poor Law valuation, they altogether are rated to a sum more than equal to the rent the landlord has to receive; being all under £4 in value he has to pay for them all. Again, an occupier gets into arrears with the rate collector and absconds, leaving his occupation bare of everything that will pay rent or rate; the landlord not only has to lose his rent, but is in the end saddled with arrears of rate due from a tenant who for years past may have paid him nil.

Under what is called the 'Gregory clause' relief cannot be granted to a man in occupation of more than a quarter of an acre; if he surrenders all his holding but the said quarter of an acre, it is not in law a good surrender; he may claim back the land from the owner; nay, I am told, go on it and take away the crops the owner may have put upon it. Since the potato failure three years since, thousands of occupiers have been unable to pay rent, are in arrear of rates, are daily merging into the pauper class; how, sir, if the Irish landholders had been themselves the most frugal of men, if they were a race wholly unencumbered, could they, would they, be expected not to rid themselves of such a tenantry, entailing on them such indefinite liability – productive to them of no return?

I do not deny the cruel hardship on the ejected families, but it appears to me the result of the sad option of their remaining [is] to swallow up all the little means remaining to the proprietary of affording employment or occupation for any. It is but fair to say that hundreds of these roofless houses have been voluntarily surrendered; many thousands of the late occupants have had passages paid for them to America, and have taken them as a boon. I could tell tales, which would rival those of Captain Kennedy, of horrors connected with this unhousing of a people – I turn, however, from the sad task; when a country is diseased to the very heart of its social life, as the west of Ireland is, it answers no good purpose to expose sores, however disgusting, which one feels to be only, after all, a sure accompaniment of the general ailment.

(*The Times,* 5 July 1849; reprinted in *The Freeman's Journal,* 6 July 1849.)

'Driving cattle for rent between Oughterard and Galway'. Landlords were entitled to distrain stock or crops in lieu of rent arrears; in cases of eviction, assets were also sometimes seized. (*The Illustrated London News,* 29 Dec. 1849.)

6. *The government's attitude to evictions*

The laws governing relations between landlord and tenant afforded scant protection to tenants. Some particularly callous evictions, including those on the Blake estate in Co. Galway, were raised in the House of Commons. Government ministers, however, claimed that the state had no role in such cases, but suggested that if landlords acted illegally, it was up to the tenants to take civil action in the courts. While the Prime Minister, Lord John Russell, was concerned at the situation, his 1848 bill designed to eliminate some of the more inhumane features of evictions was so watered down by the landlord-dominated House of Lords as to be purely cosmetic. These extracts from the debate on the Blake evictions include contributions from an English radical M.P., the Attorney-General, and a former Prime Minister.

'Scalpeen', from the Irish *scailp*, shelter; here, a hut has been erected by an evicted tenant within the walls of his tumbled house. (*The Illustrated London News*, 15 Dec. 1849.)

Extracts from a parliamentary debate.

Forcible Ejectments (Ireland).

On the question that the House do resolve itself into a Committee of Supply, Mr Poulett Scrope [M.P. for Stroud] rose to move an humble Address to Her Majesty, that she will be graciously pleased to direct an indictment to be preferred by Her Majesty's law officers against the parties concerned in the illegal destruction of several houses, and the forcible ejectment of their inmates, which took place within the union of Galway, on or about New Year's day last, and which appears to have occasioned the deaths of several of the unfortunate beings so ill-treated, by the evidence taken on oath before Major McKie, Poor Law inspector of the union, by order of the Poor Law Commissioners...

The Attorney-General [Sir John Jervis] thought that he could relieve the honourable gentleman from the difficulty in which he was placed. He had asked whether an indictment was to be preferred by the law officers of the Crown against the parties concerned in the illegal destruction of several houses in Galway, as appeared by the evidence taken before Major McKie, the Poor Law inspector of the union of Galway. There was no doubt of the law upon the subject. If a landlord gave a notice to quit to a tenant after the period of his tenancy had expired, such landlord had a perfect right to enter the premises, provided he did so peaceably. If he entered by force he might be indicted for such forcible entry; and if a riot was occasioned, the party might be indicted for a riot. If, on the other hand, the entry was made before the notice to quit had expired, and before the term for which the tenant held his lease had ended, the tenant was entitled to a civil remedy. Of the law there was no doubt whatever. He apprehended that it was not usual in this country, certainly not in Ireland, to make any amount of private wrong the subject of a public indictment.

Sir Robert Peel: I can easily believe that the honourable and learned gentleman, the Attorney-General, is perfectly correct in stating that, according to the existing law, the government cannot interfere in this matter; but if that be so, it is the more incumbent upon us, when cases of this kind are brought under the notice of the House, where the law affords no remedy, and where the government are powerless, to exercise at any rate the moral power which we possess, by marking our indignation against such occurrences. Major McKie, in his report to the Poor Law Commissioners, stated:

'It would appear from the evidence recorded that the forcible ejectments were illegal; that previous notices had not been served; and that the ejectments were perpetrated under circumstances of great cruelty. The time chosen was, for the greater part, nightfall on the eve of the New Year. The occupiers were forced out of their houses with their helpless children, and left exposed to the cold on a bleak western shore in a stormy winter's night; that some of the children were sick; that the parents implored that they might not be exposed and their houses left till the morning; that their prayers for mercy were vain; and that many of them have since died. I have visited the ruins of these huts (not at any great distance from Mr Blake's residence); I found that many of these unfortunate people were still living within the ruins of those huts, endeavouring to shelter themselves under a few sticks and sods, all in the most wretched state of destitution; many were so weak that they could scarcely stand when giving their evidence. The site of these ruins is a rocky wild spot, fit for nothing but a sheepwalk'.

That these ejectments were illegal is expressly stated in the report of this gentleman to the Commissioners. I know, however, that the law is powerless in procuring redress in such cases; but I know also that the mere statement of the facts in the House of Commons, accompanied with the expression of such feelings as can alone be excited when such facts are narrated to us, will not be without its influence; and I must say that we owe an obligation to the honourable gentleman (Mr Scrope) for bringing forward this motion; for not having permitted this ponderous volume to rest in oblivion; and for having invited us, by our comments, to mark our sense of the proceedings referred to.

(*Hansard*, House of Commons, 24 March 1848, 1006-10.)

7. Encumbered estates

Legislation enacted in 1848 and 1849 facilitated the sale of bankrupt estates through the agency of the Encumbered Estates Court. The procedure was that the owner or a creditor petitioned the court to undertake the sale of the estate. The government's hope that the failed landlords would be replaced by practical entrepreneurs from Britain who would reform the Irish rural economy was not realised. The majority of purchasers came from the ranks of the Irish landed gentry. After the Famine, however, there was a general improvement in the standard of estate management. A nationalist perspective on the government's solution to the problem of encumbered estates is provided by A.M. Sullivan (editor of The Nation *for the period 1858-77).*

A.M. Sullivan on the Encumbered Estates Act.

Towards the close of 1847, or early in 1848, it became noised about in Ireland that the government contemplated a scheme for removing the debt-loaded landlord class in Ireland. The necessity for some such step, its usefulness, its national importance, none could deny, and none more freely admitted than the Irish proprietors themselves. Without touching on the broader and deeper question of the abstract utility of facilitating the transfer of land and its sale in small parcels, there were in Ireland peculiar reasons why such a project must be beneficial. A large section of the landlord class were little better than nominal proprietors. A mountain-load of mortgages or a network of [family] settlements rendered them powerless to attempt or carry out any of the numerous reforms and improvements which a really free and independent owner might arrange with his tenantry.

Many an Irish gentleman, with a nominal rent-roll of thousands or tens of thousands a year, possessed in reality to his own use scarcely so many hundreds. To not a few of the class, the hollowness and unreality of their position had become intolerable. The lord of some ancient mansion or ivied castle, with estates that reached in miles on either hand, often envied the humble merchant of £500 a year, who had no state to maintain, no retinue to support, no false position in society to uphold. With men so circumstanced, indulgence to their tenantry was almost impossible, and the temptation to cupidity, to rack-renting, and to extortion was strong and ever pressing. It was true statesmanship to afford a cure for evils so serious and so complicated.

The Irish Encumbered Estates Act, regarded in this sense, was one of the greatest legislative boons ever conferred on Ireland. In its actual results, good and evil, hurt and service, cause for satisfaction and cause for regret are considerably mingled. In some very important particulars, the expectations and designs of its promoters have been disappointed and contradicted. But when every allowance has been made, there still is to be said that a great and incalculable gain has been achieved, though at somewhat of painful price.

The measure, excellent in itself, was proposed and presented to Ireland at such a time and under such circumstances as to give it a decidedly sinister aspect. To no man, to no class of men, can a sentence of abolition or extinction be welcome at any time. 'Life is sweet'. But when men feel that special advantage is taken of a special misfortune in order to encompass their destruction, for no matter how great a public good – if they are 'struck when down' – they regard the proceeding with a peculiar bitterness. Thus felt many an Irish landlord the proposal of the Encumbered Estates Act. It came upon him, he would say, when he needed rather indulgence, consideration, and aid. It caught him in a moment of helplessness and exhaustion. Whatever chance he might have of retrieving his position at any other time, he had none now. Landed property was a drug in the market. On many estates, no rents had been paid during the Famine. On some, the poor rates had reached twenty shillings in the pound of yearly valuation. To challenge Irish landlords at such a moment with the stern ultimatum of 'pay or quit' was naked destruction. To visit upon them at the close of the Famine the penalty for inherited

After years of famine, land prices were seriously depressed. Among those forced to sell below the real value was Lord Gort, who carried out no evictions during the Famine. (Encumbered Estates Court Rentals.)

indebtedness and embarrassment was, in many cases, sacrificing the innocent for the sins of their forefathers – sacrificing them under circumstances of peculiar hardship and injustice. In fine, the Encumbered Estates Act ought to have been passed long years before – in some period of tranquillity and comparative plenty. Enacted when it was, it could but wear an aspect of harshness or hostility; could accomplish its unquestionably useful aims only at the cost of excessive sacrifice and suffering. What were those aims? ...

The comments and glossary of some English newspapers seemed to supply an answer to this very natural interrogatory, but it was one not calculated to recommend the bill in Ireland. We were told to read between the lines of the government measure a plan for the more sure effectuation of the new plantation.

Not alone were the Irish tenantry to be replaced by English and Lowland-Scotch 'colonists', but the Irish landlords also were to be cleared off, an English proprietary being established in their stead. 'English capital' was at long last to flow into Ireland in the purchase of these estates. The dream of Elizabeth and James and Charles was to be accomplished in the reign of Victoria. The island was to be peopled by a new race; was to be anglicised 'from the centre to the sea'. In truth, between evictions and emigration on the one hand, and the working of the Encumbered Estates Court on the other, so it seemed that it would be. 'In a few years more', said the London *Times*, 'a Celtic Irishman will be as rare in Connemara as is the Red Indian on the shores of Manhattan'.

(A.M. Sullivan, *The story of Ireland*, Dublin, 1870, p. 281-6.)

XI

EMIGRATION

On the eve of the Famine, emigration was already an established feature of Irish life, and the numbers were steadily increasing. The most common destinations were Britain, the United States, Canada and Australia. The level of emigration reflected local economic trends; north Connacht, south Ulster and the midlands had relatively high levels, due to the erosion of domestic spinning and weaving with the advance of the industrial revolution.

Considering that three million were living at subsistence level, the incidence of emigration was not especially great. Part of the explanation was that the very poor did not have the resources in terms of skills, education or finance to make emigration a feasible option. Moreover, in congested districts, communities were close-knit, there were strong ties of family and kinship, and people were prepared to endure privation at home rather than face the uncertainty of life in a foreign land for which they were ill-equipped.

This negative attitude to emigration changed utterly with the Famine. In the first half of 1846, there was a marked increase in numbers. This early Famine emigration was induced by fear of a depression rather than a ruinous and life-threatening famine. That autumn, however, with the second failure of the potato crop, very substantial numbers regarded emigration as their most practical option. Although trans-Atlantic emigration was normally confined to the spring and summer, such was the urgency to avoid the prospect of a hungry winter in Ireland that many thousands risked the hazards of an autumn or winter crossing. By 1847, as the starvation and its attendant diseases intensified, the sense of urgency took on an aspect of hysteria. Between 1845 and 1851 the numbers amounted to 1.2 million; by 1855 another .9 million had departed, giving a total of 2.1 million for the period 1845-55.

Travel was expensive, and finance generally determined the destination. While the cheapest fare to Britain was less than five shillings, it constituted the average weekly wage on the state relief works. The fare to Canada was at least fifty shillings, and that to the United States seventy shillings. It was thus prohibitively expensive for those at subsistence level, and the numbers who emigrated from the congested districts were less than might be expected. Those without resources were trapped, unless assisted by remittances from relatives already established abroad. Such family bridges largely account for the relatively high levels of emigration from regions such as north Connacht and south Ulster, from which significant numbers had previously gone abroad. Large numbers of destitute did, however, manage to emigrate, at least to Britain. Some availed of emigration schemes funded by landlords as a means of clearing their estates. In addition, some Poor Law unions and various charities funded the emigration of individuals and families for whom it would otherwise have been impossible.

As with other features of the Famine, emigration had its own dynamic; it was a spontaneous popular movement, and the government had minimal involvement. The government had long approved of emigration as a means of reducing the population, and considered the feasibility of state schemes to promote emigration to the colonies. The colonies, however, were unwilling to be flooded with unskilled Irish paupers, and the cost was considered prohibitive. Moreover, as emigration was already proceeding at a level approaching a quarter of a million a year, state assistance was considered unnecessary. The government's only contribution was in improving certain health and safety aspects of emigration by belatedly amending the shipping legislation.

The Famine emigrants were mainly young men and women between the ages of twenty and thirty-five, but there were also entire families. The majority were unskilled and Catholic; 25% were Irish-speaking. In most cases, they eventually found a better life. In the first years of the Famine, when people were at risk from hunger and disease, public opinion in Ireland regarded emigration as a welcome relief for those able to undertake it. Attitudes soon changed, however, especially among nationalists; ever since, large-scale emigration has been considered as an evil which should be totally unnecessary in a country as fertile as Ireland.

1. *Preparing to emigrate*

Anotable feature of emigration was that it involved considerable expense. The emigrant had to take into account the costs arising from suitable clothing, transport to the point of embarkation, provisions for the voyage, the passage, the onward journey to a suitable destination, and maintenance for a period prior to employment. For many, all that was considered essential was the fare for the crossing; they walked to the port, took little or no provisions, were unable to proceed beyond the point of landing, and there depended on charity until they found employment. Prospective emigrants sometimes solicited the clergy or the landlord for assistance. The letter reproduced in facsimile is from a tenant, Hugh Bohey to Richard Beere, agent for the O'Hara estate at Annaghmore, Co. Sligo.

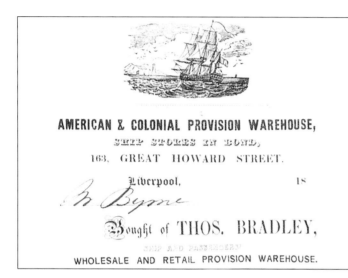

A receipt from an outfitter used by Irish emigrants travelling via Liverpool. (NLI Ms 10,753.)

'Irish emigrants leaving home – the priest's blessing'. (*The Illustrated London News*, 10 May 1851.)

Hon.ed Sir,

the petition of Hugh Bohey of Carrewgavenan humbly shoeth that he is a man that has ten in Family and the Support of them will Soon Destroy him, these awful times, Unless he Gets Sending Some of them to america, he Can at least Spare three of them and will Send them to america if your honour Gives any reasonable Afsistance – by do doing the will here after Send petitioner Some Relief, that will Enable him to pay your honour the Rent as usual – if you do not afsist me we will in a Short time be Very Desolate – and all become Paupers – by your honours Complience petitioner is in duty bound and will pray ————

May the 28th 1847   *Hugh Bohey ————*

Honoured Sir,
The petition of Hugh Bohey of Carrewgavenan humbly shoeth that he is a man that has ten in family, and the support of them will soon destroy him, these awful times, unless he gets sending some of them to America. He can at least spare three of them and will send them to America, if your honour gives any reasonable assistance. By so doing the[y] will hereafter send petitioner some relief, that will enable him to pay your honour the rent as usual. If you do not assist me we will in a short time be very desolate – and all become paupers. By your honours complience petitioner is in duty bound and will pray.
Hugh Bohey. May the 28th, 1847.

(NLI Ms 20,370; O'Hara Papers.)

'The Cove [Cobh] of Cork, now Queenstown', 1842 – the port from which many emigrants sailed. (NLI 220TA.)

2. Well-to-do emigrants

The newspapers and other sources suggest that throughout the Famine a large percentage of emigrants were not the destitute but people with resources. They included tradesmen with savings, business people with capital, and some farmers. The majority of those from the farming class were the adult children. Previously, they would have remained on to inherit the farm, marry into a farm, or rent a farm. But the prospects were now uncertain, and landlords were less accommodating than in the relatively good times before the Famine. Moreover, with the unprecedented numbers on relief, the Poor Law rates were a considerable drain on farm incomes in many areas.

FOR NEW YORK.

TO SAIL ON THE 26TH AUGUST.

THE First Class Packet Ship "HIGH-LAND MARY," 800 Tons—CHARLES PAYNE, Commander.

This magnificent Ship will be comfortably fitted up for the accommodation of passengers, who will be supplied with Water, Fuel, Medicine, and Provisions, according to Act of Parliament.

For Passage, Apply to

THOMAS H. PUNCH,

(1758)   13, Merchant's Quay, Cork.

(*The Cork Southern Reporter*, Aug. 1848.)

Report on emigration by William Wilde.

According to the report of the Census Commissioners for 1841, the annual average emigration between 1831 and 1841 was 40,346, and from the 30th June in the latter year to the end of 1845 it averaged 61,242 per annum. Such, however, was the effect of the potato blight, and the warning voice of the pestilence, that the number rose to 105,955 in 1846, after which the emigration seemed to partake of the nature of an epidemic, and in 1847 the numbers who left the country more than doubled those who departed in the previous year. Owing to a slight mitigation of the potato blight, and a consequent improvement in the harvest of 1847, there was an arrest of the exodus in the beginning of 1848, when the numbers who emigrated only amounted to 178,159; but in the following year they again rose to 214,435. In 1850, the amount of emigration was 209,054. The emigration reached its highest point in 1851, when the numbers amounted to 249,721, after which they gradually decreased to 150,222 in 1854.

Yet, even in 1855, long after the extreme poor, the panic-stricken, and the destitute, had passed to other countries, or had found a refuge in the workhouses, or a rest in the grave, the remarkable spectacle of whole families – usually well-dressed, intelligent-looking people of all ages and sexes, the mere infant as well as the extremely aged – might be observed passing through the metropolis on the way to the emigrant vessel. Not the least peculiar feature in the extensive emigration of this period was the amount of money transmitted to their friends in Ireland by those who had already gone away; remittances which rose from the sum of £460,000 in 1848, to £1,404,000 in 1852, and, according to the reports of the Emigration Commissioners, amounted in contributions, either in the form of prepaid passages or of money sent home by the Irish emigrants, from 1848 to 1854, both inclusive, to as much as £7,520,000 – remittances 'which afford so honourable a testimony of the self-denial and affectionate disposition of the Irish'.

(*Census of Ireland for the year 1851*, part V,1, p. 243 (P.P. 1856 (2087-1) XXIX.)

Reports in *The Freeman's Journal*, 1 April 1846.

There are thirteen large vessels advertised to sail from this port next month for British North America, and the passenger berths in a dozen are nearly all engaged! The freight of trans-Atlantic emigrants will exceed 2,000 persons from Limerick this spring.

(*Limerick Chronicle.*)

The tide of emigration has already set in at this port. Early in the season as it now is, numbers of persons intending to quit old Ireland to seek the means of existence denied them, in the backwoods of America, or, perhaps, in the disputed territory of Oregon, have left this city per the steamers to take shipping at Liverpool. Others are determined to take shipping at this port, and our quays are crowded with respectable-looking persons of both sexes dressed in the garb of emigrants. They appear entirely to belong to the class of farmers who are termed respectable, and none of the lower classes of the peasantry seem to be among them. There are more than an ordinary number of emigrant ships at our quays.

(*Waterford Freeman.*)

The tide of emigration from this port has fairly set in for the season. Already over twelve vessels are about to take their departure from our port, all of them having their full complement of passengers, for various places on the shores of the New World. It is remarkable that the persons who are now going to seek a home far away from the green land of their birth, appear to belong to the better and more comfortable class of peasantry. We, or indeed the oldest inhabitants, do not remember on our quays such a number of people preparing to embark. There will be at least 2,000 persons taken out in the course of this and the next month to America.

(*Galway Mercury.*)

'The causes of emigration in Ireland'.
(*The Lady's Newspaper*, 13 Jan. 1849; courtesy of BL.)

3. Britain

In the minds of most Irish emigrants, America was the preferred destination. Mainly due to financial restraints, however, about 300,000 settled in Britain. Many headed inland from the ports, and eventually found employment in industrial cities such as Birmingham, Manchester or Glasgow. Considerable numbers failed to find employment; they became a burden on the local ratepayers and aroused considerable hostility in some areas. Liverpool had a particular problem as, in addition to paupers, a large population of near-destitute Irish spent considerable periods waiting for the onward passage to America. As a result of local agitation, relatively small numbers were returned to Ireland.

(*The Freeman's Journal*, Nov. 1849.)

(*The Nation*, May 1846.)

'Departure of the *Nimrod* and *Athlone* steamers [from Cork] with emigrants on board for Liverpool'. (*The Illustrated London News,* 10 May 1851.)

Irish emigrants embarking for America at Waterloo Docks, Liverpool. (*The Illustrated London News*, 6 July 1850.)

Editorial from *The Liverpool Mail*, 30 Jan. 1847.

We think the parish authorities have evinced a proper degree of forebearance in allowing the innumerable swarms of Irish beggars to infest the streets of Liverpool so long. But there is a limit to everything, and we have reason to know that, unless the present hired invaders be returned to Dublin or Waterford, their numbers will be daily increased. It is a fact that would disgrace any country but Ireland, that subscriptions are raised by persons who call themselves the gentry of Dublin and other places to pay the passage of these vagrants to Liverpool. Instead of having the pride or the honesty to maintain their own poor, as the poorest parish in England does, they export them in ship-loads to prey upon the humanity of this country. This conduct is not only indecent, it is criminal and ought to be punished. Dublin is a magnificent city, they tell us, full of magnificent buildings, full of lawyers and priests; it has a university full of students, a court and a castle, splendid levees and balls, dashing and money-spending soldiers, distilleries and breweries, and wine and spirit stores without number. Is it not a magnificent city? Where is there a shopkeeper or a tradesman who does not keep a horse or a jaunting car, if not a box in the country? In short, there are more saddle horses and car horses in the Irish metropolis than in all Lancashire.

And yet the gentry and other wealthy inhabitants of this magnificent city have the meanness to subscribe their shillings to transmit their own famishing poor to beg in England. And it is the women, too, chiefly, and young children they send, in one of the most inclement winters ever known. We have reason for believing that many of the most importunate of these women have borrowed children with them whom they pass off as their own.

We have no desire to send the hungry woman, or even the female impostor, empty away. Nor have we any wish to stay the impulses of genuine charity. But we deny that there is any charity in the case so long as the gentry over the water can live in the style they have done and are doing at this very hour, and while there is so much prosperity in the large seaport towns of Ireland, and while such an abundance of corn and all sorts of provisions is being poured into that country from the supplies, and at the expense, of this. Give these beggars, we therefore say, a loaf of bread and send them home.   (Courtesy of BL.)

4. Estate emigration schemes

A number of landlords financed emigration schemes to clear their estates and to ease the burden of paupers on the rates. They included Major Denis Mahon of Strokestown Park, Co. Roscommon. In 1847, he paid £4,000 for the emigration of one thousand tenants to Canada. Almost a quarter died on the voyage; the survivors were sick or in a distressed condition on arrival. Mahon was murdered later that year, but the crime was not directly related to the emigration. An extract from his agent's ledger is here reproduced. Another notable scheme was that organised by William Steuart Trench, agent for Lord Lansdowne's impoverished estate at Kenmare, Co. Kerry. Again, considerable hardship resulted, and the reality was infinitely more grim than Trench's account suggests.

Dr. Major Denis Mahon (Emigration Acct.)	£	s	d
Brought forward £	237	6	10
Winny Brennan (Cloonrane) Gratuity in lieu of passage to America	1	0	0
Biddy Carly on Surrendering — do —	1	0	0
Mary Dogherty — do — — do —	1	10	0
John Ross Mahon's Expenses to & from Liverpool	6	12	8
J & W Robinson for Passage to Quebec of 467 Statute Adults at £3.2.6. each	1,459	7	6
—Do— for Extra Stores supplied	233	8	9
Provisions during Stay in Liverpool	11	0	6
J Curley for Passage to New York	4	15	0
Heywood Son & Co for Exchange on £1550 lodged in London	1	18	9
Steam Packet Co for Freight of Emigrants Luggage to Liverpool	9	0	0
Mrs Carley (Coachmans Wife) Gratuity on going to America	2	0	0
J & W Robinson — on account of passage of Tenants — balance paid by themselves	8	0	0
Do. do do	8	0	0
Widow Bryan O'Hara in lieu of Passage to America	1	0	0
James Feeney (old turf cutter) to buy Clothes on going to America	1	0	0
Terce McDermott (Tully) on Surrendering in lieu of passage to America	1	0	0
Bridget Hagan (Cordrummon) — ditto —	1	0	0
William Coffey (Mullavetrin) — ditto —	1	0	0
Rose Byrne for holding & Crop — ditto —	4	0	0
John Maguire Old and unable to go to America	1	0	0

(NLI Ms 10,138, Pakenham Mahon Papers.)

Trench's account of the Kenmare emigration.

The broad sketch of the plan I laid before him [Lord Lansdowne, November 1850] was as follows: I showed him by the poorhouse returns that the number of paupers off his estate and receiving relief in the workhouse amounted to about 3,000; that I was wholly unable to undertake the employment of these people in their present condition on reproductive works; and that if left in the workhouse, the smallest amount they could possibly cost would be £5 per head per annum, and thus that the poor rates must necessarily amount for some years to come to £15,000 per annum, unless these people died or left – and the latter was not probable. I stated also that hitherto the people had been kept alive in the workhouse by grants from the rates-in-aid and other public money, but that this could not always go on; that the valuation of his estate in that district scarcely reached £10,000 per annum; and thus, that the rates necessary to be raised in future off the estate to support this number of people, would amount to at least thirty shillings in the pound. I explained further to him, that under these circumstances, inasmuch as the poor rates were a charge prior to the rent, it would be impossible for his lordship to expect any rent whatever out of his estate for many years to come.

The remedy I proposed was as follows: that he should forthwith offer free emigration to every man, woman and child now in the poorhouse or receiving relief and chargeable to his estate; that I had been in communication with an emigration agent, who had offered to contract to take them to whatever port in America each pleased, at a reasonable rate per head; that even supposing they all accepted this offer, the total, together with a small sum per head for outfit and a few shillings on landing, would not exceed from £13,000 to £14,000, a sum less than it would cost to support them in the workhouse for a single year; that in the one case he would not only free his estate of this mass of pauperism which had been allowed to accumulate upon it, but would put the people themselves in a far better way of earning their bread hereafter; whereas by feeding and retaining them where they were, they must remain as a millstone around the neck of his estate, and prevent its rise for many years to come; and I plainly proved that it would be cheaper to him, and better for them, to pay for their emigration at once than to continue to support them at home.

His lordship discussed the matter very fully, and with that kindness, good sense, and liberality which characterised all his acts; and on my leaving Bowood [Lansdowne's English seat] he gave me an order for £8,000 wherewith to commence the system of emigration, with a full understanding that more should be forthcoming if required.

I shall not readily forget the scenes that occurred in Kenmare when I returned and announced that I was prepared at Lord Lansdowne's expense to send to America every one now in the poorhouse who was chargeable to his lordship's estate, and who desired to go; leaving each to select what port in America he pleased – whether Boston, New York, New Orleans, or Quebec.

The announcement at first was scarcely credited; it was considered by the paupers to be too good news to be true. But when it began to be believed and appreciated, a rush was made to get away at once...

A cry was now raised that I was exterminating the people. But the people know that those who now cried loudest had given them no help when in the extremity of their distress, and they rushed from the country like a panic-stricken throng, each only fearing that the funds at my disposal might fail before he and his family could get their passage.

(William Steuart Trench, *Realities of Irish life*, London, 1868, p. 122-5.)

5. The Atlantic crossing

Trans-Atlantic passenger liners were too expensive for most Famine emigrants. The vast majority sailed as steerage passengers in cargo vessels which shipped timber or corn on the return journey. Facilities were minimal and conditions were appalling. In the winter of 1846 and throughout 1847, mortality rates from fever, dysentery, malnutrition and hardship were extremely high. To draw attention to the situation, Stephen de Vere, brother of Aubrey de Vere and a nephew of Lord Monteagle, undertook a voyage to Canada as a steerage passenger in the spring of 1847, an unprecedented course for somebody of his class. His subsequent report embarrassed the government into amending the legislation governing the trans-Atlantic passenger trade.

FOR QUEBEC,
To Sail on or about the 10th of APRIL instant,
Wind and Weather permitting,
The splendid Fast Sailing, Copper-fastened First-class
BRIG,
Mary and Harriett,
Burthen per Register 322 Tons,
JOHN SHAXSON, COMMANDER,

THIS fine Vessel is now in Port, and will positively Sail about the above-mentioned period. Emigrants should lose no time in securing their Berths, a great many having been already engaged.

The MARY and HARRIETT has fine height between Decks, is commanded by a Master well acquainted in the Trade, and is admirably adapted for the conveyance of Passengers. She will be fitted up in a manner to ensure comfort and accommodation, and abundantly supplied with Fuel and Water, together with Flour and Oatmeal, agreeable to Act of Parliament.

Application to the Captain on Board, or to
JOHN SIDLEY,
Ship and Emigration Agent, Henry Street, Limerick, or to any of the undermentioned :—
George Taylor, Kilrush ; Joseph J. Brommell, Gas Works, Nenagh ; M'Namara and Son, Ennis.
March 24.

A typical advertisement of the period. (*The Limerick Chronicle*, March 1847.)

Stephen de Vere's report.

London, Canada West, November 30, 1847.

The fearful state of disease and debility in which the Irish emigrants have reached Canada must undoubtedly be attributed in a great degree to the destitution and consequent sickness prevailing in Ireland; but has been much aggravated by the neglect of cleanliness, ventilation, and a generally good state of social economy during the passage, and has been afterwards increased and disseminated throughout the whole country by the mal-arrangements of the government system of emigrant relief. Having myself submitted to the privations of a steerage passage in an emigrant ship for nearly two months, in order to make myself acquainted with the condition of the emigrant from the beginning, I can state from experience that the present regulations for ensuring health and comparative comfort to passengers are wholly insufficient, and that they are not, and cannot be enforced, notwithstanding the great zeal and high abilities of the government agents.

Before the emigrant has been a week at sea, he is an altered man. How can it be otherwise? Hundreds of poor people, men, women, and children, of all ages from the drivelling idiot of ninety to the babe just born; huddled together, without light, without air, wallowing in filth, and breathing a fetid atmosphere, sick in body, dispirited in heart; the fevered patients lying between the sound, in sleeping places so narrow as almost to deny them the power of indulging, by a change of position, the natural restlessness of the diseased; by their agonized ravings disturbing those around and pre-disposing them, through the effects of the imagination, to imbibe the contagion; living without food or medicine except as administered by the hand of casual charity; dying without the voice of spiritual consolation, and buried in the deep without the rites of the Church.

The food is generally ill-selected, and seldom sufficiently cooked, in consequence of the insufficiency and bad construction of the cooking places. The supply of water, hardly enough for cooking and drinking, does not allow washing. In many ships, the filthy beds, teeming with all abominations, are never required to be brought on deck and aired; the narrow space between the sleeping berths and the piles of boxes is never washed or scraped, but breathes up a damp and fetid stench until the day before arrival at quarantine, when all hands are required to 'scrub up', and put on a fair face for the doctor and government inspector. No moral restraint is attempted; the voice of prayer is never heard; drunkenness, with its consequent train of ruffianly debasement is not discouraged, because it is profitable to the captain who traffics in the grog.

In the ship which brought me out from London last April, the passengers were found in provisions by the owners, according to a contract and a furnished scale of dietary. The meat was of the worst quality. The supply of water shipped on board was abundant, but the quantity served out to the passengers was so scanty that they were frequently obliged to throw overboard their salt provisions and rice (a most important article of their food), because they had not water enough both for the necessary cooking, and the satisfying of their raging thirst afterwards.

No cleanliness was enforced; the beds never aired; the master during the whole voyage never entered the steerage and would listen to no complaints; the dietary contracted for was, with some exceptions, nominally supplied, though at irregular periods; but false measures were used (in which the water and several articles of dry food were served), the gallon measure containing but three quarts, which fact I proved in Quebec, and had the captain fined for; once or twice a week, ardent spirits were sold indiscriminately to the passengers, producing scenes of unchecked blackguardism beyond description; and lights were prohibited, because the ship, with her open fire grates upon deck, with lucifer matches and lighted pipes used secretly in the sleeping berths, was freighted with government powder for the garrison of Quebec.

The case of this ship was not one of peculiar misconduct; on the contrary, I have the strongest reason to know from information which I have received from very many emigrants well-known to me who came over this year in different vessels, that this ship was better regulated and more comfortable than many that reached Canada.

(*Papers relative to emigration to the British provinces in North America*, p. 13-14; P.P. 1847-48 (932) XLVII.)

The scene between decks on an emigrant ship. (*The Illustrated London News*, 6 July 1850.)

6. Canada

Immigrants to Canada entered by way of quarantine stations on Partridge Island, for New Brunswick, and Grosse Isle, mainly for Quebec. In 1847, the inspection and accommodation facilities were inadequate for the unprecedented numbers suffering from malnutrition, fever and dysentery. The crisis was particularly acute on Grosse Isle. The accommodation soon became seriously overcrowded; the sick had to remain on board ship for weeks in appalling conditions, and mortality levels were extremely high. Eventually, the authorities were forced to abandon all attempts at quarantine and allow the immigrants to proceed unchecked. As a result, many towns and cities experienced serious fever epidemics, notably St John, Quebec and Montreal.

Extract from report on Grosse Isle.

Two days after the arrival of these vessels, four more came in, viz, the barque *John Francis*, ship *Agnes*, from Cork, and barques *George* and *Royalist*, from Liverpool. These four vessels had lost on the passage, which had been short, 112 of their passengers, and had more than double that number lying ill with fever and dysentery. Having no room in our crowded hospitals to accommodate this number, I resolved at once to convert the sheds used for healthy passengers into hospitals, by which additional accommodation was at once obtained for 600. On the 30th of the month [May], four large hospital marquees were pitched and fitted with 64 beds each, and a large number of bell-tents were also fitted with beds, and that evening 400 more sick were landed, increasing our number to 1,200. But there still remained 35 vessels in quarantine, having on board 12,175 souls, and great numbers of these were falling ill and dying daily.

It was with much difficulty that people could be found to make coffins, dig graves, and bury the dead. As already observed, all our regular hospital servants were either ill or exhausted by fatigue. Dr Benson, the gentleman engaged to assist, took fever and died after a short illness. On the 1st of June, I received the aid of two other medical assistants, in addition to Drs Jaques and McGrath; and the superintendent of the 'Board of Works was employed to erect new hospitals and to build cook-houses for the passengers' sheds used as temporary hospitals, and now crowded in every part.

All the remedial means that may be adopted, however, will not prevent the occurrence of sickness and death to a fearful extent on shipboard so long as fever and destitution prevail in Ireland as it now does. Some one of the many passengers is sure to embark either just recovering from fever, with foul clothes and bedding, or with the seeds of the disease latent in his system, which the change of life and the discomforts of a sea voyage rapidly develop in so favourable a locale as the hold of a vessel.

G. M. Douglas, M.D., Medical Superintendent. Quebec, 27 December 1847.

(Papers relative to emigration to the British provinces in North America, p. 5-9; P.P. 1847-48 (985) XLVII.)

Partridge Island, by A. J. Hill, in *L'Opinion Publique,* 26 Jan. 1871; in 1847, 2,000 of the 16,000 Irish immigrants died. (National Archives of Canada, C30790.)

Petition to Queen Victoria.

Most Gracious Sovereign,

We, your Majesty's loyal subjects, the Mayor, Aldermen and citizens of the city of Montreal, most humbly represent:

That wholesale immigration, composed of men with capital, or of men able and willing to labour, will always be acceptable and beneficial to your Majesty's faithful Canadian subjects; and that immigrants of either class cannot fail to acquire every necessary, most of the comforts, and many of the luxuries of life; but that paupers unused to labour, mendicants with large families, averse from every industrious pursuit, whole cargoes of human beings in a state of destitution and in every stage of disease, must prove as they have already proved, a grievous burthen to the resident colonial population.

That thousands of men, women and children of this description have this season arrived, and are daily arriving; that the mortality among them is appalling, and that a pestilence is seriously apprehended. That your petitioners have learned with equal surprise and pain that some Irish landlords, among whom is said to be one of your Majesty's ministers [Lord Palmerston, who had an estate in Co. Sligo], have resorted to the expedient of transporting the refuse population of their estates to Canada...

That the taxpayers of Canada, though heavily burthened, will continue to meet the demands of the resident poor, who have natural claims on their charity; and that they cannot resort to the measure lately adopted not only upon this continent by the seaboard cities of the United States, but in Liverpool, rigorously to exclude the shiploads of famishing beings arriving in search of food and shelter ... that the means of your petitioners are exhausted, that frightful suffering and great mortality prevail, that famine and pestilence may ensue, and that the emergency is one admitting of no delay...

John E. Mills, Mayor [he died of fever shortly after],
J.P. Sexton, City Clerk.
City Hall, Montreal, 23 June 1847.

(*Papers relative to emigration to the British provinces in North America*, p. 8; P.P. 1847-48 (50) XLVII.)

'The Famished', a representation of Grosse Isle by John Falter, 1974. (© 3M, Saint Paul, Minnesota. All rights reserved. Reproduced with permission.)

7. The United States

The favoured destination of emigrants to the New World was the United States. Although 80% were from a rural background, possibly only 6% settled on the land or engaged in agriculture. The majority found employment in the cities as unskilled labour, and worked in heavy industry, mining, and in railroad and canal construction. They were slow to assimilate and, as in Ireland, lived in close communities. As their numbers were augmented by generations of new arrivals, they maintained their ethnic identity and much of their traditional culture, of which their religion – Catholic or Protestant – was a prominent feature. The letter reproduced on the next page is from a girl who took part in an emigration scheme for the Crown estate at Kingwilliamstown, near Kanturk, Co. Cork, in 1849.

Report from *The New York Tribune*, 9 January 1847.

The Irish Heart.

Jacob Harvey states in *The Courier* that he has taken the pains to call upon all the houses [banks] in this city who are in the daily practice of drawing small drafts on Ireland, and has received from them an accurate return of the amounts received for these small drafts for the entire year 1846, and also during the last sixty days. The result is so creditable to his own countrymen that he cannot avoid publishing it as an incentive to those who have as yet done nothing to go and do likewise.

(*The Londonderry Journal*, Jan. 1849.)

Total amount remitted by labouring Irish, male and female, during 1846 from New York, $808,000, of which there were in November and December $175,000. These remittances are sent to all parts of Ireland, and by every packet; and we may judge of the relief afforded to a very large number of poor families in a year when they are cut short of their usual food, the potato. It has required no public meetings, says Mr Harvey, no special addresses, to

(*The Belfast Newsletter*, April 1848.)

bring forth these remittances from the poor, nor do they look for any praise for what they have done. It is the natural instinct of the Irish peasant to share his mite – be it money or potatoes – with those poorer than himself; and he thinks he has but done a Christian duty, deserving of no special applause.

It is fitted to exalt our estimate of human nature to record such a proof of the self-sacrifice and severe self-denial through which alone such a sum as is here stated, $808,000, could in one year be remitted from their savings by the Irish at labour and at service in and around this city. Of what other people in the world under like circumstances can such a fact be truly stated?

(Courtesy of BL.)

'The Irish exodus' – a late and sentimentalised representation. (A.M. Sullivan, *The story of Ireland*, Dublin, 1867.)

Extract from an emigrant's letter.

[Spelling as in the manuscript.]

New York, 22 September 1850.

My dear father and mother, brothers and sisters,
I write these few lines to you hopeing that these few lines may find ye all in as good state of health as I am in at present, thank God. I received your welcome letter to me dated 22nd of May, which was a credit to me for the stile and elligence of its fluent language, but I must say rather flattering. My dear father, I must only say that this is a good place and a good country, for if one place does not suit a man he can go to another and can very easy please himself. But there is one thing that's ruining this place, especially the frontirs towns and cities where the flow of emmigration is most. The emmigrants has not money enough to take them to the interior of the country which oblidges them to remain here in York and the like places, for which reason I would advise no one to come to America that would not have some money after landing here that [would] enable them to go west in case they would get no work to do here; but any man or woman without a family are fools that would not venture and come to this plentyful country where no man or woman ever hungerd or ever will, and where they will not be seen naked.

But I can assure you there are dangers upon dangers attending comeing here; but, my friends, nothing venture, nothing have. Fortune will favour the brave.

Have courage and prepare yourself for the next time that that worthy man, Mr Boyen [Michael Boyan, agent for Crown lands at Kingwilliamstown], is sending out the next lot, and come you all together couragiously and bid adiu to that lovely place, the land of our birth; that place where the young and old joined together in one common union, both night and day engaged in innocent amusement. But alas, I am now told it's the gulf of miserary, oppression, degradetion and ruin of evry discription, which I am sorry to hear of, so doleful a history to be told of our dear country.

This, my dear father, induces me to remit to you in this letter 20 dollars, that is four pounds, thinking it might be some acquisition to you untill you might be clearing away from thet place all together; and the sooner the better, for beleive me I could not express how great would be my joy at seeing you all here together, where you would never want or be at a loss for a good breakfast and dinner. So prepare as soon as possible, for this will be my last remittince untill I see you all here. Bring with you as much tools as you can as it will cost you nothing to bring them [Sandy McCarthy was the estate carpenter]...

Margaret MCarthy.

(National Archives, Quit Rent Office, Corresp. King-williamstown; reproduced from Eilish Ellis, *State-aided emigration schemes from Crown estates in Ireland, c.1850 ; Analecta Hibernica*, No. 22, 1960.)

8. Australia

As the cost of a passage to Australia was £15 (four times that to the United States), the level of emigration was relatively low, both before and during the Famine. The continent needed immigrants, however, and the Australian authorities and the government organised a scheme to sponsor emigration from the United Kingdom. Over fourteen thousand Irish availed of the scheme. They included 4,175 orphan girls aged from fourteen to eighteen, from workhouses throughout the country. They were well treated and soon found employment. The Australian authorities, however, decided that it would be difficult to absorb additional unskilled girls and the scheme was discontinued.

'On board an Australian emigrant ship: emigrants on deck'. (*The Illustrated London News*, 20 Jan. 1849.)

EMIGRATION TO SOUTH AUSTRALIA.

FREE PASSAGE.

MESSRS. MARSHALL AND CO., of LONDON, are authorised by HER MAJESTY'S COLONIAL LAND AND EMIGRATION COMMISSIONERS, to grant a Free Passage to the above eminently healthy and prosperous Colony to Married Agricultural Labourers, Shepherds, Male and Female Domestic and Farm Servants, Bricklayers, Carpenters, Masons, Smiths, and Miners. The demand for Labour in South Australia is urgent, and is well remunerated in Wages, Provisions, Lodging, &c.

The first Ship will leave Plymouth on the 28th of May.

All particulars will be furnished on application personally, or if by letter (post-paid) to the undersigned Agents.

MR. SAMUEL ELLIS,
AND
MR. EDWARD PARNELL,
38, LOWER ORMOND QUAY, DUBLIN.

*** First Class Ships for Sydney, Port Philip, Cape of Good Hope, Quebec, and Montreal.

(*The Nation*, May 1846.)

Memorandum of the Commissioners of Colonial Lands and Emigration.

17 February 1848.

...But we should anticipate a more decided benefit from the adoption of this plan in respect of female orphans. Lord Grey [Colonial Secretary] is well aware of the necessity which exists for preserving the proportion of the sexes in any large emigration to a new country. Single men willing to emigrate are to be found in abundance. But we learn from the reiterated complaints of our selecting agents that the difficulty of procuring single females of an eligible character is one of the greatest embarrassments against which they have to struggle. It is said, however, that a large number of well-conducted young women are to be found among these orphans; the emigration of these persons will be of material service, by placing us at liberty to accept from other sources a corresponding number of young men whom we might otherwise have been compelled to reject. We have, therefore, drawn up a paper, which, with some modifications as Lord Grey may deem fit, might, we think, be transmitted to the Irish government, with a request that they would take the proper means for communicating it to the guardians of the different parishes [i.e. unions] from which emigrants may be expected. It is, we think, obvious that the character of this emigration, consisting entirely of young persons, will necessitate a closer moral and religious superintendence than has hitherto been thought expedient or even practicable in emigrant ships.

(*First annual report of the Commissioners for administering the Laws for Relief of the Poor in Ireland*, p. 151-2; P.P. 1847-48 (936) XXXIII.)

Return of orphan girls sent out from workhouses in Ireland, as emigrants to Australia.

Unions	Total Number	Unions	Total Number	Unions	Total Number	Unions	Total Number
Abbeyleix	28	Clogheen	33	Gorey	21	Mullingar	70
Antrim	31	Clogher	15	Gort	16	Naas	15
Ardee	22	Clones	29	Gortin	4	Navan	25
Armagh	57	Clonmel	59	Granard	24	Nenagh	85
Athlone	53	Coleraine	20	Kanturk	30	Newcastle[West]	56
Athy	37	Cookstown	33	Kells	26	New Ross	34
Ballina	87	Cootehill	15	Kenmare	25	Newry	35
Ballinasloe	53	Cork	61	Kilkeel	11	Newtownards,	7
Ballinrobe	25	Dingle	20	Kilkenny	59	Newtownlimavady	17
Ballycastle	6	Donegal	31	Killarney	35	Oldcastle	22
Ballymena	14	Downpatrick	23	Kilmallock	30	Omagh	19
Ballymoney	10	Dublin North	46	Kilrush	30	Parsonstown	65
Ballyshannon	20	Royal Hiber-		Kinsale	29	Rathdown	19
Balrothery	10	nian Military	24	Larne	19	Rathdrum	15
Baltinglass	16	School		Letterkenny	30	Rathkeale	60
Banbridge	36	Dublin South	56	Limerick	74	Roscrea	90
Bandon	20	Dublin Mendi-		Lisburn	12	Scariff	20
Belfast	64	city Institution	5	Lismore	37	Shillelagh	22
Boyle	51	Dundalk	7	Lisnaskea	44	Skibbereen	110
Callan	28	Dunfanaghy	7	Listowel	37	Sligo	68
Carlow	52	Dungannon	31	Londonderry	40	Strabane	29
Carrickmacross	38	Dungarvan	40	Longford	77	Stranorlar	8
Carrick-on-Shannon	60	Dunmanway	14	Loughrea	73	Thurles	30
Carrick-on-Suir	23	Dunshaughlin	16	Macroom	13	Tipperary	87
Cashel	70	Edenderry	18	Magherafelt	27	Trim	12
Castlebar	15	Ennis	40	Mallow	20	Tuam	57
Castleblaney	14	Enniscorthy	41	Midleton	26	Tullamore	53
Castlederg	6	Enniskillen	107	Milford	9	Waterford	48
Castlerea	20	Ennistymon	23	Mohill	45	Westport	10
Cavan	60	Fermoy	55	Monaghan	16	Wexford	61
Celbridge	8	Galway	47	Mountmellick	37	**Total**	**4,175**

(*Third annual report of the Commissioners for Administering the Laws for Relief of the Poor in Ireland*, 1850, p. 133-4; P.P. 1850(1243) XXVII.)

XII

AFTERMATH

Although conditions in the distressed areas had improved by the early 1850s, many features of the Famine continued as realities for several decades. Evictions were still widespread, emigration proceeded apace, and more than a million still lived at subsistence level. The potato blight caused considerable hardship from time to time, but people were now less dependent on potatoes, and failure of the crop never again had such disastrous consequences.

It has been estimated that a million people died as a direct result of the Famine, that is, about one in eight of the population. As is usually the case with famines, mortality was greatest among the very young and the very old. Also, while people from all social classes and in all regions of the country died from one or other of the diseases prevalent at the time, the vast majority of those who died were the poor in the distressed areas. The statistics indicate that the mortality was mainly rural and that the classes which suffered most were the labourers and the smallholders. Connacht had the highest level of mortality (one in four of the population), but the rural poor were vulnerable irrespective of geographical location; they accounted for most of the deaths even in counties with medium or low levels of excess mortality.

The loss from emigration was of even greater magnitude, and amounted to 1.2 million in the period 1845-51. It continued at a high level after the Famine, and claimed up to half of each rising generation for the remainder of the century; by 1910, it had accounted for five million. In the long run, emigration was undoubtedly the most significant feature of the Famine, as it provided the basis for the Irish diaspora, which today exceeds the population of Ireland by a factor of at least ten. In the United States alone, forty million people claim some Irish ancestry. There, the Irish have retained a considerable degree of ethnic identity, and constitute an important element in the cultural and political life of the country.

For many of the Irish abroad, the Famine had emotive political resonances. The attitude of the first generation of Famine exiles was shaped by nationalist revolutionaries, the most notable of whom was John Mitchel. He aimed to transform the passive hostility towards Britain into an active militancy by charging the British with genocide. Such perceptions of the British role in the Famine contributed to the evolution of the physical force movement among the Irish in the United States and to its sustenance in Ireland. In this century, the Irish in America made a significant financial contribution to the War of Independence, and their involvement in Irish affairs continues to the present day.

The charge of genocide on the part of the British government was unjustified. The government was parsimonious in providing resources, but it certainly did not want the Irish to starve. It was, however, paralysed by doctrinaire ideology and bureaucracy, and proved incapable of formulating and implementing pragmatic policies to manage a crisis which should have been well within the capacity of the then mighty British Empire. In terms of finance, the resources provided were inadequate. They amounted to about £7 million, as against £8 million provided from Irish sources, mainly Poor Law rates, and a further £7.5 million in remittances from emigrants. Moreover, in accordance with the policy of minimal state intervention, most of the £7 million was in the form of loans, but these were later cancelled to some extent. The state contribution seems minimal when contrasted with £20 million allocated a few years earlier to compensate West-Indian slave-owners for emancipation, or with almost £70 million invested in the futile Crimean War in the mid-1850s.

A century and a half later, governments and associations of governments are still inadequate in their response to famine and poverty. Just as we find it difficult to comprehend why a million Irish were not saved from starvation and death in the 1840s, so future generations will find it even more incomprehensible that, in this age of advanced technology, mass communication, sophisticated medicine, and unprecedented wealth, several million people are allowed to die of malnutrition every year, and that their passing provokes so little concern in the rest of humanity.

1. Population and excess mortality

The issue of excess mortality during the Famine is complex. The main indicators are the 1841 census (population 8,175,125) and the 1851 census (6,552,385), which indicate a decline in population of over 1.6 million. The population was, however, rising prior to the Famine, and was probably over 8.5 million in 1846; thereafter, the birth rate dropped due to famine conditions and emigration. On that basis, the loss in population was over two million. Of those, close to a million died and 1.2 million emigrated. The map reproduced on the next page shows the decline in population over the decade 1841-51. The decline was attributable to deaths, emigration and a falling birth rate.

Estimated average annual rates of excess mortality 1846-51 (per thousand).

County	rate	County	rate	County	rate
Mayo	58.4	Kerry	22.4	Wicklow	10.8
Sligo	52.1	Queen's	21.6	Donegal	10.7
Roscommon	49.5	Waterford	20.8	Limerick	10.0
Galway	46.1	Longford	20.2	Louth	8.2
Leitrim	42.9	Westmeath	20.0	Kildare	7.3
Cavan	42.7	King's	18.0	Down	6.7
Cork	32.0	Meath	15.8	Londonderry	5.7
Clare	31.5	Armagh	15.3	Carlow	2.7
Fermanagh	29.2	Tyrone	15.2	Wexford	1.7
Monaghan	28.6	Antrim	15.0	Dublin	– 2.1
Tipperary	23.8	Kilkenny	12.5		

(Joel Mokyr, *Why Ireland starved: a quantitative and analytical history of the Irish economy, 1800-1850*, London, George Allen & Unwin, 1983, p.267.)

'Funeral at Skibbereen'. (*The Illustrated London News*, 30 Jan. 1847.)

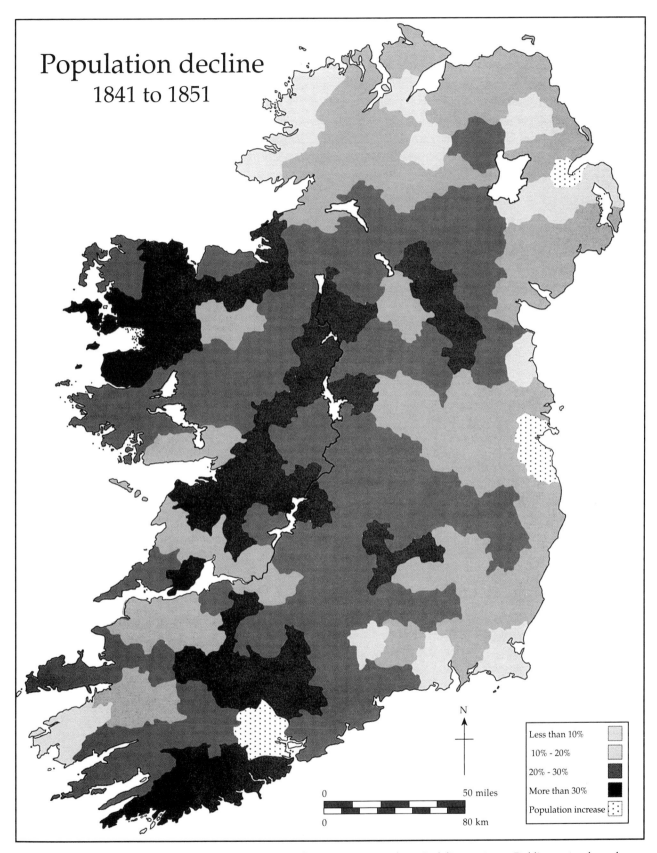

Population decline
1841 to 1851

N

Less than 10%	
10% - 20%	
20% - 30%	
More than 30%	
Population increase	

0   50 miles

0   80 km

(R. Dudley Edwards and T. Desmond Williams (editors), *The Great Famine: studies in Irish history, 1845-52*, Dublin, 1956; redrawn by Brian MacDonald.)

2. The political legacy

*F*ollowing the failure of the campaign for Repeal of the Union in 1843, nationalist politicians were in disarray, and failed to make any impact on government policy during the Famine. Eventually, the Repeal movement split, and the physical force element, Young Ireland, brought about an abortive insurrection in July 1848. The Rising was doomed to failure, but later it had a certain symbolic significance. A number of the Young Ireland leaders afterwards promoted the physical-force movement among the Irish in the United States. The most notable was John Mitchel, who used the Famine as a symbol of British oppression in Ireland. His emotive arguments had considerable impact both in the United States and in Ireland, and tended to politicise the Famine.*

Mitchel's assessment of the Famine.

This very dismal and humiliating narrative draws to a close. It is the story of an ancient nation stricken down by a war more ruthless and sanguinary than any seven years' war, or thirty years' war, that Europe ever saw. No sack of Magdeburg, or ravage of the Palatine, ever approached in horror and desolation to the slaughters done in Ireland by mere official red-tape and stationery, and the principles of political economy. A few statistics may fitly conclude this dreary subject.

The census of Ireland in 1841, gave a population of 8,175,125. At the usual rate of increase, there must have been, in 1846, when the Famine commenced, at least eight and a half million; at the same rate of increase, there ought to have been, in 1851 (according to the estimate of the Census Commissioners), 9,018,799. But in that year, after five seasons of artificial famine, there were found alive only 6,552,385 – a deficit of about two millions and a half. Now, what became of those two millions and a half?...

Now, that million and a half of men, women, and children, were carefully, prudently, and peacefully slain by the English government. They died of hunger in the midst of abundance, which their own hands created; and it is quite immaterial to distinguish those who perished in the agonies of famine itself from those who died of typhus fever, which in Ireland is always caused by famine.

Further, I have called it an artificial famine: that is to say, it was a famine which desolated a rich and fertile island that produced every year abundance and superabundance to sustain all her people and many more. The English, indeed, call that famine a dispensation of providence; and ascribe it entirely to the blight of the potatoes. But potatoes failed in like manner all over Europe, yet there was no famine save

John Mitchel in the dock. In May 1847, he was sentenced to fourteen years transportation for treason. In May 1853, he escaped from prison in Van Diemen's Land (Tasmania) to the United States. (NLI P&D.)

in Ireland. The British account of the matter, then, is first, a fraud – second, a blasphemy. The Almighty, indeed, sent the potato blight, but the English created the famine.

And lastly, I have shown you in the course of this narrative – that the depopulation of the country was not only encouraged by artificial means, namely, the Outdoor Relief Act, the Labour Rate Act [which put the cost of relief works on the rates], and the emigration schemes, but that extreme care and diligence were used to prevent relief coming to the doomed island from abroad; and that the benevolent contributions of Americans and other foreigners were turned aside from their destined objects – not, let us say, in order that none should be saved alive, but that no interference should be made with the principles of political economy...

The subjection of Ireland is now probably assured until some external shock shall break up that monstrous commercial firm, the British Empire; which, indeed, is a bankrupt firm, and trading on false credit, and embezzling the goods of others, or robbing on the highway, from pole to pole; but its doors are not yet shut, its cup of abominations is not yet running over. If you have read this narrative, however, you will never wonder hereafter when you hear an Irishman in America fervently curse the British Empire. So long as this hatred and horror shall last – so long as our island refuses to become, like Scotland, a contented province of her enemy, Ireland is not finally subdued. The passionate aspiration for Irish nationhood will outlive the British Empire.

(John Mitchel, *The last conquest of Ireland (perhaps)*, Dublin, 1861, p. 322-5.)

The only engagement of the 1848 Rising was at Ballingarry, Co. Tipperary, where a detachment of fifty armed police took refuge in the Widow McCormack's cottage. (*The Illustrated London News*, 12 Aug. 1848.)

3. The land

Many aspects of the Famine continued into the present century. Those living at subsistence level were still vulnerable, emigration continued, and in the 1880s and 1890s there was considerable distress and evictions were widespread. Nationalist politicians, however, in particular the agrarian radical Michael Davitt and the charismatic Charles Stewart Parnell, were determined that the clearances of the Famine period should not be repeated. They mounted effective resistance, and eventually achieved the complete reform of the land system, whereby the landlords were bought out and the tenants became freeholders. The reform provided greater harmony and stability in rural Ireland, and in the long run contributed to raising living standards for most classes.

DINNER IN THE EVICTED TENANT'S WARD,

Evicted tenants in the workhouse at New Ross, Co. Wexford. By the 1880s, nuns were alleviating the regime in some workhouses, as emphasised in this illustration from a nationalist newspaper. (*United Ireland,* 2 Oct. 1886.)

Emigrants embarking at an Irish port. (*L'Illustration*, Paris, 11 Nov. 1865.)

Men breaking stones and women carrying stones on relief works at An Cheathrú Rua (Carraroe), Co. Galway, 1898. (The Mansion House Committee, *Relief of distress in the west and south of Ireland, 1898*, [1898], p.11.)

4. The British view

In Britain, the general consensus was that the Famine was caused by divine providence, and that the government did all that was humanly possible to reduce its impact. These sentiments are expressed in The Spectre, the final stanza of which is here reproduced. Queen Victoria followed much the same line in a speech delivered during her visit to Ireland in August 1849: 'I gladly share with you the hope that the heavy visitation, with which providence has recently visited large numbers of my people in this country, is passing away. I have felt deeply for their sufferings, and it will be a source of heartfelt satisfaction to me if I am permitted to witness the future and lasting prosperity of this portion of the United Kingdom'.

STANZA IV.

Ne'er dream that thy sister fails fondly to love thee,

Ne'er think that in pride she would fain rise above thee,

Ne'er imagine, if Fate with its sorrows yet prove thee,

    There fails in her eye the soft tear:

Thine uplifting the pride of her statesmen would be,

With delight would her sons thy prosperity see,

And if sorrow yet hang o'er thy blighted roof-tree,

    They pray renew'd joy may be near.

Queen Victoria and Prince Albert passing the Rotunda Hospital, Dublin. (*The Illustrated London News*, 11 Aug. 1849.)

5. The Irish Famine and World Hunger

One hundred and fifty years after the Irish Famine, grinding poverty, chronic hunger, and periodic famine are realities for millions of people in many parts of the world. The President of Ireland, Mary Robinson, is playing a remarkable role in focusing attention, both in Ireland and abroad, on the situation in the developing world. In the following address, President Robinson considers the Irish experience of the 1840s, and relates it to that of the deprived and marginalised peoples of the world today.

The President of Ireland, Mary Robinson. (*The Irish Times.*)

... Although the agenda of this conference is very diverse, nevertheless, simply by its existence and by your presence here, you will, inescapably, have to address a single issue. It is the issue which underlies all contemporary discussions of famine, hunger and poverty. And it is the growing gap – not simply between rich and poor – but between the idea of hunger and the fact of it.

Let me give you, right away, an example of the fact of hunger and its companion circumstance, which is poverty. And let me put that against the idea of it. In 1993, we are informed, more than twelve million children under the age of five died in the developing world. This in itself is a terrible fact. What is almost as terrible is that figure could, according to the World Health Organisation report, have been cut to 350,000 – almost one thirty-fourth – if those children had the same access to health care and nutrition as the modern Irish child. Now how did the idea of hunger so fail the fact of it, that a vast waste of human life occurred in the midst of our knowledge, our understanding, and our resources, and yet was not prevented?

Hunger and poverty need to become realities. They became a reality to me when in Somalia I sat beside women whose children were dying – children whose mothers were dying. As a mother, I felt the sheer horror of that. But as the Head of State of a country which was once devastated by famine, I also felt the terrible and helpless irony that this could actually be happening again. And quite frankly I felt then, and I have never lost, a profound sense of anger and outrage and, indeed, self-accusation that we are all participants in that re-enactment...

And yet having begun like this, I want to make clear that I believe that ideas about hunger and poverty in themselves are both valuable and essential. It is only our capacity to relate the ideas to the reality that is in question. I am particularly aware of their value because this year has seen the start of the 150th anniversary of the Irish Famine. In this commemoration we are fortunate to see a real treasure of retrospect – from books of scholarship to schoolchildrens's drawings, to a renewed interest in folklore, to the establishment of the Famine Museum at Strokestown – which allows us to look back at an event which more than any other shaped us as a people. It defined our will to survive. It defined our sense of human vulnerability. It remains one of the strongest, most poignant links of memory and feeling that connects us to our diaspora. It involves us still in an act of remembrance which, increasingly, is neither tribal nor narrow...

Ironically, the economic migration on which the Irish embarked in their hundreds of thousands was not only a painful necessity, it represented a vital freedom, a second chance of survival. But would a people today, enduring the devastation of famine, and needing exactly that refuge from it, in the same places, under the same circumstances, be able to avail of it? The answer must be no. The door which was open for the Irish, through which they entered into the cities and circumstances of a new life – and I am not minimising the hardship of that entry – is now closed.

It is closed, I should say, in the West. It is closed in the very places which have the resources to make the entry through that door sustaining. But in much poorer places – where the cost of opening those doors is huge – they stand open. Why is it that the neighbours who are themselves hard-pressed, who have so little to give, give it more freely than those who have more and will not part with it? Is it simply that they retain that empathy that comes from recent experience? And, if so, we need to ask what it is that makes us lose that human empathy?

We need to reflect carefully on the purpose of commemorating an event such as the Famine. The terrible realities of our past hunger present themselves to us as nightmare images. The bailiff. The Famine wall. The eviction. The workhouse. And yet how willing are we to negotiate those past images into the facts of present-day hunger? How ready are we to realise that what happened to us may have shaped our national identity, but is not an experience confined to us as a people? How ready are we to see that the bailiff and the workhouse and the coffin ship have equally terrible equivalents in other countries for other peoples at this very moment?

For every lesson our children learn about the Famine relief of 1847, they should learn an equal one about the debt burden of 1995. For every piece of economic knowledge they gain about the crops exported from Ireland during the Famine years, let them come to understand the harsh realities of today's markets, which reinforce the poverty and helplessness of those who already experience hunger. As they learn with pride how we as a people clung to education, how we held on to poetry and story-telling in the midst of dire poverty, let them become acquainted with the declining literacy rates of the most vulnerable countries in our modern world.

I began by noting the gap between the idea of hunger and the reality of it. I recognise the difficulty of finding a language to close that gap. But if we are to account for the sheer horror of the disparity between twelve million children who died in one year and the few hundred thousand it could have been if the world's resources were better distributed, then we will need to send young people into the world who have been prepared, through the challenge of education on this topic, to close that gap between the idea of hunger and the fact of it. We need to help them to face the future with the understanding that famine is not something which can be understood only through history. It must be understood with every fibre of our moral being.

(Extracts from keynote address by President Mary Robinson at the International Conference on Hunger hosted by Glucksman Ireland House, New York University, May 1995).

A contemporary sketch of a survivor of the Irish Famine, Co. Galway, 1850 – a symbol of starving children, then and now. (NLI 2003TX.)

INDEX

(p= picture)